Praise for

Discipline with Love and Limits—
Completely Revised and Updated Edition

"As the mother of six, I have found this book an invaluable beacon along the challenging road of parenting. It has been the go-to resource to inform and validate my parenting decisions, while granting me the fortitude to stand strong when I needed it most! Thank you!"

> —Melissa Bernstein, Co-Founder and Chief Creative Officer,
> Melissa & Doug

"I love the easy-to-use format that parents can turn to again and again 'in the moment' to help children develop necessary skills for success. The tools in this beloved book change everyday struggles into teachable moments."

> —Wendy Webb, Mother, Grandmother and National Trainer,
> Parents as Teachers

"As a clueless first-time mom, it's so hard to balance my desire to give my child everything she wants with the need to raise a resilient, independent kid. This book shows the way!"

> —Jen Saxton, Founder & CEO of Tot Squad

"I believe that this book helps parents manage common, everyday behavioral issues efficiently and effectively. I confidently give this book to families, and they are so grateful for the support."

> —Stephen J. Lauer, PhD, MD, Associate Professor and Associate Chair,
> Pediatrics, The University of Kansas School of Medicine

"When I read this book's advice for the different behaviors, I felt like, 'Eureka! There IS a manual on how to parent!' I think every new parent should get a copy along with her newborn!"

—Mariana Ramírez, LMSW, Director, Juntos, Center for the
Advancing Latino Health

"This completely updated book is the answer you've been looking for to raise a resilient, caring, problem-solving child. It is packed with the latest research in a very readable format followed by tips that can be referenced for years to come."

—Laura Kaiser, Past Board Chair Communities in Schools
of Mid-America Inc.

"The discipline framework in this book really helps me talk with families about attachment, positive discipline, and the daily challenges of healthy parenting!"

—Kathryn Ellerbeck, MD, MPH, FAAP, Associate Professor of
Pediatrics; Developmental Pediatrician, Developmental and
Behavioral Sciences, The University of Kansas School of Medicine

"Even with ideal role models and a healthcare background, parenting has been my most difficult undertaking. Each child is challenging in unique ways. This book has been a healthy, reinforcing influence on my parenting practice, facilitating my guidance in ways that support my children to flourish."

—Kelli Kramer-Jackman, PhD, APRN, FNP, BC, RN-BC

"Parenting can be tough work! This book adds positive, constructive tools to any parent's toolbox."

—Christopher J. Mehus, PhD, LMFT, Research Faculty,
Institute for Translational Research in Children's Mental Health,
University of Minnesota

"I loved *Discipline with Love and Limits* when it first came out. This revised edition builds on its foundation of supporting all kinds of families with kindness and respect, which is at the heart of the thinking and writing that created this vital parent companion."

—Mark Weiss, Director of Education, Operation Respect

"A healthy, safe, and enduring attachment is a child's lifeline. The wisdom and science provided in this book guides parents and caregivers in the practice of calm, curious, empathic, and loving responses to any child in their care."

—Dennis Meier, PhD, Marriage and Family Therapist

"We know that toxic stress and Adverse Childhood Experiences (ACEs) have lifetime dangerous health consequences. So how do we help prevent or reverse their harmful effects? This book does just that. It's every parent and caregiver's essential supportive, protective, discipline handbook."

—Robin Shanberg Winner, Executive Director, Synergy Services, Inc.

"This expanded edition gives us tools in these very challenging times to help develop greater resilience in parents and children, and empower them to affirm the goodness and kindness that is within them to help guide us to a more respectful, peaceful, time."

—Peter Yarrow of Peter, Paul and Mary; President Emeritus and Co-founder, Operation Respect

"In a world where instant gratification is the norm and information on anything and everything is flooding our minds, it is great to have this resource in our toolbox to effectively parent children."

—Teresa Lovelady, MBA, MSW, President & CEO, HealthCore Clinic, Inc

"This book is as valuable as having a wise, caring family member by your side as you walk the path of parenting and caring for children."

—Laura Schmidt, Founder/Chief Positive Person, Notes to Self

Jerry L. Wyckoff, PhD and Barbara C. Unell

discipline

with Love and Limits

PRACTICAL SOLUTIONS TO
OVER 100 COMMON CHILDHOOD
BEHAVIOR PROBLEMS

Completely Revised and Updated

Da Capo
LIFE
LONG

Da Capo Press
Hachette Book Group
1290 Avenue of the Americas, New York, NY 10104
www.dacapopress.com
@DaCapoPress

Printed in the United States of America

First Edition: July 2019

Published by Da Capo Press, an imprint of Perseus Books, LLC, a subsidiary of Hachette Book Group, Inc. The Da Capo Press name and logo is a trademark of the Hachette Book Group.

The Hachette Speakers Bureau provides a wide range of authors for speaking events. To find out more, go to www.hachettespeakersbureau.com or call (866) 376-6591.

The publisher is not responsible for websites (or their content) that are not owned by the publisher.

Print book interior design by Amy Quinn

Library of Congress Cataloging-in-Publication Data

Names: Wyckoff, Jerry, 1935- author. | Unell, Barbara C., 1951- author.
Title: Discipline with love and limits : practical solutions to over 100
    common childhood behavior problems / Barbara C. Unell and Jerry Wyckoff.
Description: Revised edition. | New York, NY : Da Capo Press, [2019] |
    Includes bibliographical references and index. | Jerry Wyckoff is the
    first named author on the earlier edition.
Identifiers: LCCN 2019014515| ISBN 9780738285696 (pbk. : alk. paper) | ISBN
    9780738285702 (ebook : alk. paper)
Subjects: LCSH: Discipline of children. | Child rearing.
Classification: LCC HQ770.4 .W927 2019 | DDC 649/.1--dc23
LC record available at https://lccn.loc.gov/2019014515

ISBNs: 978-0-7382-8569-6 (paperback), 978-0-7382-8570-2 (ebook)

10 9 8 7 6 5 4 3 2 1

LSC-C

Contents

Our heritage and ideals, our codes and standards—the things we live by and teach our children—are preserved or diminished by how freely we exchange ideas and feelings.

—Walt Disney

When our children were little, we often heard said, "Time just flies by. Your kids will be grown in a blink of an eye. Treasure the time you have together!" We did—and still do.

We dedicate this book to our precious families: Robert, Millie, Amy, Justin, Leah, Noah, Allison, Armon, Christopher, Sasha, Alexander, Julian, Hieronymus, and Samira.

And to you the reader and your children and grandchildren.

Preface

Dear Reader,

What if you knew of prescriptions that you could give your children that would reduce their lifetime risk of mental and physical health problems, including obesity; depression; anxiety; suicide; substance abuse; attention and impulse control; sexual, physical, and psychological abuse; heart disease; diabetes; lung cancer; and more?

And what if these prescriptions could be given hundreds of times a day and could be FREE—no pharmacy needed? And on top of everything else that is good about them, what if they could be healthy for children of all ages *and* for you when you use them?

Well, we wrote this book to give you these very "prescriptions"—what we call "What to Dos" and "What Not to Dos"—with evidence-based outcomes. And now they are yours!

New research indicates that building the capabilities of adult caregivers can help strengthen the environment of relationships essential to children's lifelong learning, health, and behavior, according to the Center on the Developing Child at Harvard University. *Supportive, responsive relationships with caring adults as early in life as possible can mitigate stress so it does not become toxic and lowers the lifetime risk of learning health and behavior problems.*

This information is *the* game changer for everyone who supports parents in the most important job they will ever do—parenting. That's why we reshaped our best-selling book, *Discipline Without Shouting or Spanking*, into this book, which is twice the size, with four times the number of prescriptions—"What to Dos" and "What Not to Dos." We translated the research to help parents build supportive, responsive relationships with their children every day.

With unending gratitude to all the researchers, scientists, educators, parents, and children who taught us these lessons, we pass them along with immeasurable admiration and anticipation.

Looking forward,
Barbara and Jerry

Introduction

Why Is Parenting So Stressful?

Friendly and always in motion, almost three-year-old Jack and his happy-go-lucky sister, five-year-old Ellie, loved swim lessons at their community pool until one fateful day in July. On that particular day, Jack decided that he didn't want to get in the water. Or even near it.

Their veteran swimming teacher, Sally, coached all the kids to sit down poolside, get their goggles on, and jump in, just as she had for the past four lessons.

"No!" Jack screamed, throwing his goggles with all his strength away from him toward his mom, Sara, and Grandma Wendy, a longtime early childhood education professional, who both came to every lesson.

And then he proceeded to start crying . . . and crying . . . and crying. He broke into a major temper tantrum and ran away from the pool.

Sara and Wendy looked at each other in horror. *Usually Jack thinks swimming is fun! Why is he so mad?* Their hearts started pounding in their chests. They could feel a hot mixture of shock, embarrassment, worry, and panic.

■　■　■

Such is the crazy-making, stressful, everyday experience of parenting—a thousand times a day—feeling lost, embarrassed, and worried, and absolutely not knowing the right thing to do to get our child's behavior back on track. Sara and Wendy faced split-second questions: What do we do now? Will the coach do something, or is it our job to run after him? And then what? Do we make him go into the pool? Go home? And what about Ellie? Just leave her here? HELP!

Just writing this story made our own heart rates go up, as we remembered these times as parents ourselves. We empathized with the stress Sara and Wendy must have felt.

Yes, it is a fact of life that young children are in the prime physical, emotional, and independence-loving years of life—curious, inventive, eager to spread their wings with every breath they take. Likewise, when children are mad, sad, or frustrated, they are obstinate, inhibited, clingy, and demanding. Children discover every day that the world is challenging, exciting, and confusing, which makes teaching them sometimes like working with fertile ground and sometimes like gardening in rock!

Our children's chameleon-like personalities and inability to use adult logic sometimes make them tough customers for discipline. That includes setting limits and routines and teaching them to clean up their rooms, use good manners, and treat others kindly and with respect. Our children need these lessons and want them from infancy forward.

Why? Because when they learn what the rules are and how to follow routines, they feel more secure and know what to expect. That makes life more predictable and less stressful. And when children are not stressed, they are less likely to be anxious or depressed, or choose to abuse alcohol and drugs. Lower stress allows children to develop emotional strength, self-control, self-discipline, and the ability to tolerate frustration.

On the other hand, children who don't have rules and routines, and are allowed to do whatever they want, live by impulse and are not sure what to expect in the world and how to manage themselves. They are therefore more likely to have frequent tantrums, make unreasonable demands, use poor judgment, and be fearful because they are consistently under stress. They can't self-regulate and don't have executive functioning skills. In short, they don't know what to do because they have not developed the ability to do so. And when they go outside the house and into a world of rules and structure, they won't know what to do and how to respond because they have never had to follow rules or structure. This creates an even higher level of stress for them.

That's how meaningful these teachable moments of discipline are.

■ ■ ■

So how do we keep the stress of parenting in the "good stress" category—where it motivates us to respond in caring, supportive, and protective teaching ways to children's misbehavior? *We will show you how, in the heat of the moment, to remember that discipline means teaching a child the behavior you want her to learn, leading to self-discipline, self-reliance, self-confidence, and personal responsibility for what she says and does.*

We all try other stress-relieving responses—by giving in when children nag, complain, and whine; bribing them; and shouting or spanking. (See Chapter 2.) These discipline methods may temporarily stop children's behavior we don't like. But they don't work for the long haul. They don't lower our stress, and they also can create a toxic stress response in children. In addition, they don't teach our children life skills and how to reason, problem-solve, and cope with frustration—the ultimate goals of parenting. These *ultimate* goals that we have for our children are the *immediate* goals we have for ourselves—being emotionally strong problem-solvers who can cope when life gets messy.

■ ■ ■

Teachable Moments

In this book, you will learn how to turn tantrums into teachable moments. In fact, you'll learn how to turn all kinds of normal but frustrating behaviors your child does every day into teachable, positive moments that guide her to becoming responsible, resilient, respectful, and resourceful. However, it is predictable, normal, and absolutely understandable that your child will sometimes feel sad, mad, or worried—and sometimes direct that anger or disappointment at you for not letting him do what he wants when he wants to. As the late Fred Rogers, of the award-winning television program *Mister Rogers' Neighborhood*, said, "What's mentionable is manageable." He wanted children to know that all feelings are natural and normal, and that happy times and sad times are part of everyone's life. So he made sure that his work on television and in other settings with children communicated that children have deep feelings that their parents need to understand and respond to. Fears, anxieties, and feelings all make a child feel vulnerable, he believed, so the most important thing is to listen.

He said, "I'm convinced that when we help our children find healthy ways of dealing with their feelings—in ways that don't hurt them or anyone else—we're helping to make our world a safer, better place." We heartily agree. As Rogers did through his work with children, we embrace listening to our children and helping them learn how to calm themselves when their lives are stressful.

Children can't pull themselves up by their "bootie straps," says Jack Shonkoff, MD, the director of Harvard University's Center on the Developing Child. So when we help our child learn how to soothe himself back to sleep, how to clean up his milk when he spills it, and how to problem-solve when he is bullied at school, these are all teachable moments. We love that. And we love that you are reading this book to learn how to make them positive moments for you both.

The takeaway here is this very simple fact: children will behave like children, and although that behavior is often upsetting and annoying, that's not the challenge. The challenge lies in how to respond when they whine, talk back, climb up on furniture, won't eat or go to sleep, and ignore us, so that our responses become teachable moments that help them learn the behavior we want, instead of those we want to stop.

■ ■ ■

So let's review. When we deal with our child's temper tantrums, we are at our best when we not only attempt to restore calm but also teach our child how to cope with frustration and anger in a more appropriate way. And as our children's first teachers, we are their most important role models. We communicate our personal values every day in how we parent, particularly in how we respond to children's normal but frustrating misbehavior.

At the heart of this book is the advice one of our friends likes to give every day, "Everyone, stay calm." In truth, this is actually his own self-talk when he needs to calm down!

When we calm ourselves when stressed, we can think more clearly and respond to others—children and adults—with more patient self-talk, empathy, and teaching. And we can ask for help when we need advice and support, without feeling judged, embarrassed, or that we're bad parents for not having all the answers. We all experience "on the job" learning!

So we hope you think of this book as a sort of GPS to get you where you want to go, with easy directions so you don't get lost. You'll learn how to become a teaching parent who can stay calm when your children seem to be anything but calm—even if you feel unsure of what to do next. As we discuss in the next chapter, by staying calm and remembering a healthy Mind S.E.T. when you are stressed, you can avoid responding using unhealthy discipline.

1 What to Do: How a Healthy Mind S.E.T.® Prevents Toxic Stress

There is nothing either good or bad but thinking makes it so.
—William Shakespeare

Let's assume that you've just told your child to hurry because you're running late to take her to school. But "hurry" is not part of her vocabulary, so she just takes her time getting shoes on, stopping to sing a song to herself, and then just staring off into space. Her usual pace.

By now you are looking at this situation as potentially catastrophic. You are probably saying to yourself, "We'll never get there on time. Everybody there will think I'm not a good parent. My daughter is always dawdling and making us late. I can't stand this." So, given this self-talk, how are you feeling right now? Stressed? Anxious? Depressed? Oh, and let's not forget angry?

Note the key words that exaggerate the situation: "never," "everybody," "always," and "can't stand this." When we use logic, we can see that the word "never," which means "no time in the past or future," is not accurate. In the same way, the word "always" means for "all the past and future or forever." That's not true, is it? See how this kind of exaggeration works?

Let's now change your negative self-talk words to something milder by using positive self-talk. "My daughter dawdles, but we can manage. If we're late, so be it. It doesn't mean that I'm a bad parent. I'm doing the best I can. And I can stand it. It doesn't mean that I'm a bad parent. I should ask her doctor if her behavior is normal and if there's something I can do about it."

Now how do you feel? Maybe a little stressed, but not overwhelmed, and you are far less likely to yell, threaten, or hit your daughter out of frustration, the unhealthy discipline we discuss in Chapter 2.

■ ■ ■

In the over fifty years that we have been working with children and families and from the scientific research that has been conducted during those years on stress, it has become obvious that the mind is the key player. In the Introduction, we described why it is *stressful for us* to care for and nurture a young child. In this chapter, we will look at what happens when a *child is consistently under harmful stress* and how to prevent that stress from becoming toxic to a child.

To understand this fundamental biological process of a toxic stress response, imagine that you've just climbed up on a stool to get something from a top shelf and you start to lose your balance. Your brain screams, "Danger!," and your body mobilizes to *protect* you from that danger. The physical changes that are associated with your brain's response to danger are well understood. When your brain senses danger, adrenaline and cortisol, two hormones that increase alertness, flood the body. These hormones increase your heart rate, dump acid into your stomach, and constrict blood vessels, restricting blood flow to your hands and feet. These physical changes are needed to prepare your body for fighting or fleeing from the danger—in your case, falling off the stool.

If your adrenaline and cortisol levels get high enough or flood your brain and body frequently enough (you keep being exposed to danger), thinking becomes difficult. Problem-solving becomes narrowed to a very few options.

The same process happens in children's brains. Extensive research on the biology of stress now shows that children's healthy development can be derailed by toxic stress—excessive or prolonged activation of the stress response systems in their body and brain. Such toxic stress can have permanently damaging effects, causing a lifetime of learning, behavior, and health problems.

The part of our brain most affected by stress is the prefrontal cortex, which is the decision-making part of the brain. As a result, children who grow up in consistently adverse, stressful environments—including environments in which they are consistently spanked, threatened, or ignored—experience toxic stress. This toxic stress generally makes it harder to concentrate, sit still, rebound from disappointment, and follow directions. And above all, children who experience toxic stress find it harder to self-regulate—that is, exercise self-control. Their brain is always on high alert, not knowing if someone will be there to provide consistent, caring adult support.

Research has demonstrated that supportive, responsive relationships with caring adults to buffer a child's stress as early in life as possible can prevent or reverse the damaging effects of toxic stress. This is one critical reason why it is so important for parents to focus on being caring, supportive, and protective, to consistently and positively teach children what they want them to learn. That way parents can prevent their children from experiencing toxic stress. (We give you the tools to do so, in real time, in Behavior Problems and Solutions, beginning on page 25.) Parents can lay a good foundation for this approach by taking the three steps to a healthy Mind S.E.T.: Self-Talk, Empathy, and Teaching.

Self-Talk, Empathy, and Teaching: Mind S.E.T.

S Is for Self-Talk

It has long been known by cognitive behavior researchers that our words create our emotions. Therefore, to change our feelings, we must first discover the words that drive our feelings and change those words. This sounds simple enough, but it is more difficult than one would think. We lapse into habits that end up making us feel in ways we don't like.

We can divide the words we use into two basic groups: positive self-talk or negative self-talk. Positive self-talk keeps our stress down, keeps depression away, and helps us make clear decisions. Negative self-talk, on the other hand, increases our stress and drives our anxiety and depression.

Here's an example of how we can turn negative self-talk into positive: If our child spills his milk and our self-talk automatically goes to "This is awful! What a mess!," we can shift to positive self-talk and say aloud, "No big deal. Let's get the sponge and clean it up."

Keeping our self-talk calm and constructive will provide a model to help our child avoid the bad habit of exaggerating events as awful disasters instead of treating them realistically as tolerable and fixable. It's bad enough having to deal with problems without making them worse through self-talk that raises our stress, drives our anxiety and depression, and can lead us to make parenting decisions that are unhealthy to our child.

E Is for Empathy

Empathy is the ability to put ourselves in somebody else's position so we can see the world as that other person sees it. Feeling what our child feels, taking on our child's perspective, can help us understand why he is behaving as he is.

When your child hits another child, for example, first put yourself in your child's shoes. How would you feel in your child's position? Would you act in the same way? This is the time for some empathy, so say, "I'm sorry you chose to hit Eric. I know it's frustrating when you want something somebody else has." In this way, we convey understanding and sympathy for the child's position and provide a model for him to use in the future. Then continue the lesson by focusing on the victim, asking, "How do you think Eric felt when you hit him? How would you feel if Eric hit you?" These questions can help the aggressive child understand what it must be like to be on the receiving end of an aggressive act.

Unfortunately, we can also provide a poor role model of empathy when we say such things as, "How could you do that? You know better. That was a mean thing to do." This is not very empathetic language, and it doesn't teach your child how to have empathy for others. By putting yourself in your child's shoes, you can understand how he might feel if you were to respond in such nonempathetic ways.

T Is for Teaching

You want to teach a new behavior that replaces the behavior that isn't good for your child. The teaching strategies in this book are based on applied behavior analysis, the science that is used to identify what is responsible for behavior change. The teaching steps are very simple. First, you show the behavior you want, then you show your child how to do the behavior, and finally you make doing the behavior worthwhile.

The teaching model is the opposite of the punishment model, which is the fallback position most of us think of when we want behavior to change. We have come to believe that if we punish a behavior, it will go away and never return. There are some basic fallacies in this belief. First of all, punishment is only focused on getting rid of a behavior but not on new, replacement behavior. We've all experienced the admonition, "Don't do that!," and we've asked the question, "If I can't do that, what am I supposed to do?" Teaching says, "Instead of doing that, do this."

Behavioral research in punishment has consistently demonstrated that when punishment is used, the behavior often goes underground. In other words, it doesn't go away; it just goes out of sight. Behavior changes only to avoid the punisher seeing the behavior. The thriving business of manufacturing and selling radar detectors is testament to this fact.

Finally, punishment strategies often involve bullying methods and rely on the threat of pain to discourage the unwanted behavior. What happens, however, is an increased stress level that may become toxic to the child, as we discuss at the beginning of this chapter.

Everyone Can Use Mind S.E.T.

Here are some special questions we are often asked concerning whether Mind S.E.T® can be used by single parents, grandparents, and early childhood and preschool programs. We say yes! The more caring, supportive, protective adults, the better.

SINGLE PARENTING AND CO-PARENTING
Q. What if my spouse or ex-spouse or co-parent doesn't use teaching discipline?

Parenting a young child alone—as sole caregiver for a certain number of days a week or all the time—is a difficult job for even the most skilled parent. Not only is parenting a twenty-four-hour, seven-day-a-week job that demands attention and requires patience, but it's also designed to be a team effort. So if parents are separated, divorced, or otherwise living apart, even for a few days at a time because of work or travel, it is best if they work together to plan strategies, share duties, and decide on rules that will let them build independent, self-sufficient, loving, empathetic children. And instead of focusing on trying to control what the other parent does or doesn't do, each parent is best advised to use the strategies that we have outlined in this book.

Keep in mind that children are capable of understanding and following different rules in different settings because the rules are attached to the settings. It is important to note, however, that going to war with the other parent over child-rearing practices will result in the child becoming collateral damage. No one escapes war without damage, so when parents cannot agree on rules, each needs to help the child understand that house rules may be different depending on which parent's house the child is living in at the time—and that is okay.

THE PARENTING GRANDPARENTS

Q. How can grandparents use Mind S.E.T. when emotions run high between grandparents and the parents of their grandchildren?

The strength of the emotional relationships among grandparents, parents, and grandchildren can lead to conflicts around power and control over who's in charge when it comes to making decisions about discipline and parenting.

Grandparents may think that they should be "the boss" because they were always in that role with their children. They also may believe that their adult children should follow their lead when making parenting decisions because they are "older and wiser."

Conflicts can arise between generations over cultural changes, as well, including what constitutes "healthy eating," for example. Parents may be tuned into the health issues associated with diet by demanding that their children eat only organic foods, non-GMO foods, local farm-raised meat and produce, or gluten-free or dairy-free foods. They may require anything from paleo to vegan diets for their children.

Conversely, grandparents may be following different nutritional guidelines (low-fat, low-sugar, and so forth). Either way, for the grandparents to meet their grandchildren's needs without alienating the parents requires a spirit of respectful compromise, conversation, and empathy to bridge the knowledge gap and keep mealtimes from becoming meltdown time.

Jealousy and competition can also cause friction between grandparents and their adult children, as well as between sets of grandparents. Although grandparents may not even realize that they have self-centered expectations about how their adult children should treat them, many keep score regarding how much time and what kinds of presents their grandchildren give to them and to their other grandparents.

They may tell themselves things like, "My son should ask me to come over more. His wife asks her mom to babysit, but not me." "It's awful that my daughter never calls me anymore since she had her baby." "Why do my son and his wife leave and expect me to babysit every time I come over to be with their kids?"

So if you are a grandparent who is upsetting yourself about your relationship with your adult children and your grandchildren, consider what this jealousy and scorekeeping are doing to your relationship with them—not to mention your own stress levels.

Ask yourself these questions:

- How is this helping me?
- How is this helping my children?
- What is my stress level when I say these hurtful things to myself?
- How is this helping my relationships with my children and grandchildren?
- Is this helping me be happy or miserable?
- What is the purpose of playing the "poor me" game?
- Is this the path to being the best grandparent I can be?

It's the messages that grandparents say to themselves that upset them. But when they change their self-talk to say that grandparenting and parenting adult children are not competitive games, they shift their mindset from a negative one to a positive one. They go from "I want to be the favorite!" to "I am happy that my grandchildren have lots of relationships with caring adults."

All of these issues can be managed as long as the grandparents remain flexible and open to the needs of their grandchildren. After all, it's the personal connection and positive relationship with their adult children and their grandchildren that is most important. Having battles over diets, formalities, and expectations will only prevent them from being the consistently teaching grandparents that their grandchildren need them to be.

DAY CARE / PRESCHOOL / EARLY CHILDHOOD EDUCATION / SCHOOL DISCIPLINE

Q. What if my child's day care, preschool, or school does not use these solutions? Can I still use them at home? Yes!

Parents will find many different discipline strategies in place at school, camp, child care, and elsewhere to help build positive behavior. Exposing children to different discipline plans is not a problem. Children learn different rules all the time. (At preschool, for example, Charlie is not permitted to climb on the furniture as he can do at home.) The most important rule is that the discipline plan must not use any violence—emotional, physical, or sexual, including spanking. Mind S.E.T. builds skills of responsibility, resilience, respect, and resourcefulness, skills that a child will use every day for the rest of his life—without creating harmful stress that can become toxic to a child and result in poor health, learning, and behavior outcomes.

2 What Not to Do: How Unhealthy Discipline Creates Toxic Stress

Don't worry that children never listen to you; worry that they are always watching you.

—Robert Fulghum

Six-year-old Marc Johnson was the pride and joy of his parents, Julie and Scott. In their eyes, he could do no wrong, although he had been described by his teacher at their last conference as unruly and difficult.

"He can be a handful," Julie admitted, "but he's so bright, we don't want to do anything that will stop his natural talents from coming out."

Mrs. Miller, Marc's teacher, thought he needed some firm discipline. But the Johnsons were convinced he would be okay. "He'll figure it out," Scott had said. Down deep, Julie was beginning to have doubts about giving Marc so much freedom. She felt as if every day was a major negotiation with Marc as he lobbied for things he wanted to do. He loved his computer games, and when he was asked to find something else to do, he would whine, "Why can't I play? You let me play yesterday. I won't play if you let me have ice cream."

Julie would hold out for a while, and then she would give in. She thought that Marc's negotiation skills would be good in the future if he got into business, so she didn't want to stop him from negotiating. But getting him to do his homework worksheets or his reading assignments was like asking him to jump off a cliff—he'd respond with full-blown tantrums. So to get him to do his homework, she would bribe him with a new toy.

When Scott was home, he would negotiate for a while, but then out of frustration, he would resort to threats of spanking. Julie hated that approach and would try to rescue Marc. Then Scott and Julie would fight while Marc ran around like a wild man.

"What can we do to help our son?" Julie and Scott wondered as they witnessed the chaos that they felt helpless to control. "I'll ask his pediatrician," Julie said. "She may have some ideas."

■　■　■

Indeed, the Johnsons needed some ideas. They had exhausted their discipline strategies and saw that things were increasingly out of control. They needed this book, their "parenting GPS," to help them know what to do to solve Marc's behavior problem. The Johnsons also needed to know that their threatening, bribing, and giving in created stress for Marc that could become toxic. In other words, it's just as important to know what not to do, as it is to know what to do, which is why you'll find "What Not to Do" in Behavior Problems and Solutions, beginning on page 25.

Three Examples of What Not to Do: Giving In, Bribing, and Bullying

In their attempts to reduce their children's stress, as well as their own, parents may resort to discipline methods that not only fail to accomplish that goal but also increase their own and their children's stress in different ways. Here is an overview of three of the most common but unproductive discipline strategies.

1. Giving In

Let's look back at the Johnsons. We know that Julie and Scott's giving in after Marc begs or whines may work to stop the whining and reduce their stress at the moment, but it isn't good for either Marc or them. Giving-in discipline sounds like this: "Okay, I can't stand it. Just stop your whining and crying, and I'll let you have the ice cream." Because the Johnsons wait for a while before giving in, Marc learns to persist until he wins.

This is similar to what gamblers experience, which involves continuing to pull the lever until there is a payoff, even if it only pays off once in a while. Once give-in discipline is used, parents can expect the nagging and whining to persist until it drives their stress level high enough to force them to give in.

2. Bribing

We all know that bribing is an age-old way to get other people to do what we want. Julie and Scott tried it with Marc: "If you do your worksheets, I'll give you a toy." Bribing often has the benefit of working in the short term, especially if the payoff is big enough, but it doesn't work in the long term.

The danger in bribing is that a child learns that everything is negotiable and all behavior has a price. Because it works to get him what he wants, a child will refuse to do anything unless there is a big enough external reward. The constant bargaining creates additional stress for a parent and fails to teach the child to cooperate. He will then hold out on decisions until he gets his way, which can create a problem with friends and others as he stubbornly refuses to cooperate without a payoff.

3. Threatening, Spanking, Shouting, and Bullying

Shouting and threats of spanking failed to teach Marc the behavior Julie and Scott wanted him to learn. In fact, they were teaching the opposite:

- how to shout
- how to hit
- how to be sneaky
- how to fear
- how to be ashamed
- how to take anger out on others
- how to bully

All degrees of corporal punishment, which includes hitting, slapping, spanking, yanking arms, or even threats to do any of these things, damage children's emotional and physical health. The supportive science is well established, as dramatically demonstrated in landmark research by Elizabeth T. Gershoff at the University of Texas at Austin ("Spanking and Child Development: We Know Enough Now to Stop Hitting Our Children," *Child Development Perspectives* 7, no. 3 [September 2013]: 133–137, ncbi.nlm.nih.gov/pmc/articles/PMC3768154), and the stunning results of the groundbreaking Adverse Childhood Experiences (ACE) Study, led by Kaiser Permanente and the Centers for Disease Control (CDC), and related studies. Learn more about the

ACE Study in the book by Nadine Burke Harris, *The Deepest Well: Healing the Long-Term Effects of Childhood Adversity* (Boston: Houghton Mifflin Harcourt, 2018); see also the website *ACES Too High News* (acestoohigh.com) and the section of the CDC's website on ACEs (cdc.gov/violenceprevention/acestudy/index.html).

Other forms of punishment, including threatening and swearing at children, demeaning and insulting them, and withdrawing your love from them are also damaging to children's emotional and physical health. They result in children experiencing a toxic stress response to these dangers, as we described in Chapter 1, because their brain is on constant high alert.

In December 2018, the American Academy of Pediatrics issued an updated policy statement opposing corporal punishment. According to the statement, "parents, other caregivers and adults interacting with children and adolescents should not use corporal punishment (including hitting and spanking), either in anger or as a punishment for or consequence of misbehavior, nor should they use any disciplinary strategy, including verbal abuse, that causes shame or humiliation." Robert D. Sege, a lead author of the policy statement, noted, "The purpose of discipline is to teach children good behavior and support normal child development. Effective discipline does so without the use of corporal punishment or verbal shaming."

Punishment as the primary way to teach children anything is counterproductive. Instead of stopping a behavior, punishment simply pushes the behavior out of sight, so the parent may no longer see it because it's hidden. In fact, children become experts at not getting caught. Parents may even say, "Don't let me catch you doing that again!"

In the hierarchy of moral development, as defined by Lawrence Kohlberg, the lowest level is "following rules only to avoid punishment." The highest level is "following rules because they are right and good." When parents spank children, they stop their children at the lowest level of moral development. Children are interested in avoiding the punishment, not in doing what is good or right.

Spanking is also often the earliest experience a child has with violence. Children learn to behave in violent ways through adult example—a compelling reason to avoid spanking, particularly with the increased exposure children have to violence in the media. It's difficult to justify the admonition "Don't hit!" while you're hitting your child for hitting.

Children see the world in concrete terms. When they see that it's permissible for adults to hit children, they assume it must be permissible for children to hit adults or other children. Hitting begets hitting—as well as anger, revenge, and the breakdown of communication between parents and their children.

The *primary* message given when parents shout or spank is that adults are bigger, stronger, and more powerful than children and can inflict fear and pain if their orders are not followed and they are displeased. This is the definition of bullying. The resulting sense of being a victim and being powerless in the face of greater size and strength creates fear, anxiety, and stress, and over time, that stress will increase the risk of causing a toxic response in the child. In addition, bullying has been found to ultimately lead children to the desire to use violence to get their way.

No positive consequences result from spanking. In fact, the link between the victimization of children and their subsequent problems in managing their anger underscores the argument for creating a zero-tolerance policy regarding spanking in your home, at day care, in preschool, in school, and in other settings, as recommended by the American Academy of Pediatrics. In some countries, their zero-tolerance policy results in criminal penalties for spanking.

In addition, a child who learns to use the bully model to get his way will be rejected and isolated by his peers because he lacks the social skills to work and play well with others. Or the child will gravitate to people who use these same unhealthy behaviors to "bully" their way in the world.

For all of these evidence-based reasons, we believe that it's vitally important for every caregiver of every child to be aware of these dangerous consequences of the use of spanking, shouting, and bullying, either threatened or actually inflicted on a child or other person. If you or someone you know is overwhelmed and unable to respond to a child's behavior without hurting her, we urge you to get help from your child's pediatrician or your own health care provider.

3 How to Use This Book

Disciplining a child includes making rules. I prefer to think of this parenting task as "setting limits." It can be very frightening for a child not to have limits. Not only can the world outside be frightening, but the world inside, the world of feelings, can also be scary when you're not sure you can manage those feelings by yourself.

—Fred Rogers

We designed this book to be a handy reference for resolving behavior that parents find problematic. Under each behavior title in Chapter 6, "Behavior Problems and Solutions," is a list of related behaviors; for example, "Throws toys" is listed under "Aggressive Behavior / Hurting Others: Hitting, Biting, and Bullying."

Also in Chapter 6 we offer advice on how to *prevent* behaviors from becoming problems, how to prevent them from escalating, and how to solve them when they do. We also present case histories that illustrate how families have used the strategies outlined in the book to handle real-life problems.

To get the most out of this book, follow the steps below when you want to find a solution to a child's problematic behavior.

First, use the table of contents or the index to find the behavior problem that you want to solve. Each behavior problem and solution begins with a brief discussion of why a behavior is so common and normal for young children and why children exhibit that behavior.

Second, use this guide to the first three steps in solving a behavior problem using a healthy Mind S.E.T.:

- *S* is for Self-Talk, meaning talking to yourself to calm yourself down, so that you can think clearly and use the two next steps of behavior problem-solving.
- *E* is for Empathy, meaning putting yourself in your child's shoes by thinking about the behavior from her point of view. This step lowers your stress and helps your mind move toward using caring words and tone of voice when teaching, not angrily shaming, blaming, or resenting your child.
- *T* is for Teaching, meaning thinking about what positive behavior you want to teach your child to solve the problem quickly. Also a mentally healthy step to lower stress, teaching positively focuses on what you want your child to learn.

Third, read the section in Chapter 5 "Teaching Tools That Build Emotionally Strong Children." In Chapter 6 you'll find these tools referred to frequently in the advice for solving each behavior problem.

Fourth, follow the advice about what to do and what not to do under each behavior title in Chapter 6. To solve the problem most effectively, think of each "What to Do" suggestion as a tool to teach a new behavior to replace the behavior you want to change. The guiding principle for changing children's behavior is, "Try the simplest tool first." This usually means showing your child what to do and encouraging him to do it. Think about what's most comfortable for you and for your child when using a tool. And if that tool doesn't immediately work, don't give up! It may take lots of days (or weeks or months) of practicing to learn how to use polite language, for example, if your child is used to cursing and swearing. You may also choose to try more than one tool in the "What to Do" suggestions. Just remember: children learn by practicing. Being a consistent teacher is the best way your child will learn the behavior lesson you are teaching—and patience is key.

Learning a new behavior is also an "up and down" process. So don't expect your child to necessarily do the new behavior on Monday, even though she did it on Sunday. And when you change teaching tools—for example, using Grandma's Rule instead of shouting—your child may test you by continuing the old behavior just to see if you will follow through with Grandma's Rule. Be consistent, and practice, practice, practice! As in the case of teaching your child to eat with a spoon, for example, it's a slow, gradual process.

You may find certain words and actions feel more natural than others. Change a word or two if the exact language we suggest doesn't feel comfortable for you to say. Make what you say and do believable to your child. And don't forget that the tone of voice you use can make the difference in motivating your child—stay calm and positive!

It's equally important to know what *not* to do for each behavior that you think of as a problem. Knowing what not to do will help you prevent certain behavior problems from recurring, becoming worse, or creating another problem. (For more, see Chapter 2.)

Fifth, read the case history (names changed) to help you understand how the tool works. Each problem is shared in a real-life situation, so you can consider the stories at the end of each behavior problem and solution as a role play. Think of your child as the main character in the story. Even if your child is in a different age group, notice how the parents change the child's behavior before the child can change the parents'! And notice that it is only over time, with repeated practice, that both the parents' and the child's behavior changes.

4 Encouraging Reminders

> It is only with the heart that one can see rightly; what is essential is invisible to the eye.
>
> —Antoine de Saint-Exupéry

The way you talk about your child is the way she thinks about herself. Calling your child a "slob" when she doesn't pick up her toys when you ask her to won't get the toys picked up or teach her to be organized. Its only effect on your child will be to contribute to her having an unhealthy self-image and thinking about herself as a slob because you said she was.

It's important to separate your child from her behavior. The following list of Encouraging Reminders will help you remember to **love your *child* unconditionally, even when you don't love her *behavior*.** And you will let her know that by what you say and do every single day. It's best to concentrate in specific, constructive ways on teaching the new behavior—always separating *her* from her *behavior*—to help her learn to be respectful, responsible, resilient, and resourceful. Time, patience, and practice are key.

1. **Every child is different from another child, even in the same family.** Understand the temperament and personality of each of your children to best teach them what you want them to learn.
2. **Every child needs reassurance.** It's always important to ask, "Do you need a hug?" Then hug it out!
3. **It's never too late.** You can always start teaching a child a new behavior.
4. **It's not the end of the world if you make a mistake.** Get right back on track with the teaching solutions in Chapter 6.

5. **Put yourself on your child's level.** Crouch down on the floor or sit in a chair or on the couch with your child, so you and your child are able to connect eye to eye.

6. **Think about how you say what you say.** Your tone of voice, facial expression, and body language should communicate that you respect and love your child, even if you don't love her behavior. Your child will learn to treat others respectfully by being treated respectfully.

7. **Avoid being a historian.** Leave behavior problems to history, and don't keep bringing them up. Pay attention to the behaviors you want repeated today.

5 Teaching Tools That Build Emotionally Strong Children

$\mathbf{B}$ecoming a disciplined parent will happen naturally when you use a healthy Mind S.E.T. to teach your child healthy ways to be respectful, responsible, resilient, and resourceful. These Teaching Tools are your stress-free solutions to solve common childhood behavior problems every day. You'll find them scattered throughout Chapter 6. Here's a quick look at each:

BEAT-THE-CLOCK: When your child can walk, he's ready for you to use this tool.

This strategy motivates a child to complete a task within a time limit. Simply set a timer—a smartphone timer works well—and say, "Let's see if you can get that done before the timer sounds. Ready, set, go!" Then, as the child moves toward the goal, offer encouragement, as you would if she were playing on a team sport, saying, "Way to get those blocks in the box! Good job!" When the task is done, compliment her effort, saying, "I like the way you put those blocks in the box!"

CALM TIME ("Time Out"): When your child can sit up for a few minutes, she's ready for you to use this tool.

This strategy—often called "Time Out"—allows everyone to calm down and problem-solve. We like the words "Calm Time" because they reinforce the idea that lowering your heart rate and breathing by relaxing is important.

Whatever you call it, practice giving you and your child a time to catch your breath by saying, "I'm sorry. We both need to calm down. Please sit on the step [stool], and I will sit on the chair [step], while we think about what happened and try to decide a better way to solve this problem. I'll set a timer, so we will know when 'Calm Time' is over." You can decide how long you think that your child will stay and benefit from Calm Time. One method of determining the length of time is to use one minute for each year of a child's age. Calm Time is designed to only be used as a brief break in the heated action—for you and your child.

EMPATHY: When your child is an infant, it's best to begin to strengthen and grow her inborn capacity for empathy.

The most important factor in building and maintaining empathy in children is modeling empathy, understanding, and caring—even your newborn will be learning empathy from what you say and do.

By beginning your response to inappropriate behavior with the statement, "I'm sorry you chose to do that," for example, you're showing your child that you care about his feelings and have empathy for him because he's in the hot seat. In addition, parents can develop their child's potential to be empathetic by pointing out the impact of his behavior on others by asking, "How do you think Andy feels when you push him out of the game?" Conversely, responding with anger to children's behavior erodes their ability to be empathetic.

GRANDMA'S RULE: When your child can walk and follow one to two directions, he's ready for you to use this tool.

Grandma's Rule is a contract that tells the child he gets what he wants when he follows the rule. This motivational strategy is based on the "When-Then" model, as in: "When you have done what I ask, then you may do what you want." This is a strategy many of us use to manage our days as adults: "When we finish our work, then we can play."

IGNORE: When your child begins to be mobile— crawl, scoot, and walk—you can safely ignore

**behaviors that are annoying but not dangerous to
your child or others or destructive of property.**

Whining is a good example of such a behavior and can be ignored by simply pretending that it's not happening. Research has shown that behavior that is ignored tends to fade and go away, which makes this a useful tool in many situations. Your self-talk is: "I don't need to pay attention to this noise. I'll pretend it's not happening."

**PRAISE: When your child is an infant, it's best to begin using
positive praise to build your habit of encouraging learning.**

Praise is given to recognize a desired behavior, such as, "You picked up your blocks and put them away. Thank you for helping," or "You are playing so nicely with your brother." Note that the child's behavior is praised, not the child. Beware of overusing praise. Keep the praise real and meaningful, so that your child understands that positive behaviors get just as much attention as the negative ones.

**THE QUIET GAME: When your child can understand
what it means to be quiet, she's ready to use this tool—
typically around two years old. Start demonstrating
the concept when she can follow a direction.**

This game is played when quiet is desired, such as at bedtime. Simply say, "Let's see how long you can stay quiet. Shhhhhh!" Then periodic praise is given for quiet by whispering, "You are being so quiet. You're going to win the Quiet Game."

**REDIRECT: When your child can understand and follow
your simple directions, this is a basic distraction tool.**

It can be used any time your child is either doing something or about to do something that you know is dangerous, off-limits, or hurtful. For example, let's say your daughter loves to dig in a potted plant. So when you see her reaching for the plant, you can distract her attention by telling her to look at something you have in your hand or to bring you something on the other side of the room.

REPRIMAND: When your child can understand what "stop" means (a command to cease a behavior), this tool can be used—typically starting around age nine months.

Reprimand involves three steps: (1) a command, (2) a reason, and (3) a replacement behavior. For example: (1) "Stop hitting the dog!" (2) "Hitting hurts!" (3) "Touch softly, like this!" Then show how to touch the dog softly.

RULE: When your child can understand what a "rule" means (a boundary to keep his behavior safe), he's ready for this tool.

Rules are limits to set up guidance, spell out expectations, and, when internalized, guide self-control. For example, to teach a child about car-seat safety, say, "The rule is, the car can't move until you are in your seat and buckled in." Rules can also become house rules, as a general code of conduct you want your child to follow. Put them on a poster on the wall, and point them out to your child to remind her of rules you've taught, such as: (1) Talk nicely to everyone. (2) Make safe, good choices. (3) Be a first-time listener.

6 Behavior Problems and Solutions

Call them rules or call them limits, good ones, I believe, have this in common: they serve reasonable purposes; they are practical and within a child's capability; they are consistent; and they are an expression of loving concern.

—Fred Rogers

~~~~~~~~~~~~~~~~~~~~~~~~~~~~~~~~~~~~~

ACTS SHYLY

- Is overly timid or nervous when greeted by adults
- Doesn't want to join in play
- Doesn't want to participate in activities
- Won't go to library, park, or concert
- Freezes up
- Doesn't talk when people are around
- Hides behind adults
- Runs away from people
- Refuses to go places, including parties
- Won't go to school friends' houses or anywhere other people will be

Imagine seeing your neighbor, Kathy, at the supermarket as you're happily shopping with your three-year-old daughter, Corey. Suddenly, Corey clutches your leg and won't answer Kathy's simple greeting, "How are you, Corey?" You're surprised at Corey's sudden shyness, and you ask her, "What's the problem? You love Kathy!"

Children's "freezing up" when greeted by adults confuses many parents. While some children approach the world with unbridled curiosity, others keep a tight rein on their inquisitiveness, choosing to look before they leap. Both tendencies are considered normal, each reflecting an innate style that may or may not stick around as the child ages and matures.

In other words, shyness is not a problem in and of itself. However, it becomes a problem when a child's shyness becomes so powerful that it prevents her from making friends or participating in social activities away from home, such as going to a birthday party or the library. Teaching social skills and role-playing various social situations will help young children reduce their shyness and increase their self-confidence.

NOTE: *Children who act shyly often also have trouble adjusting to change. See also "Won't Adjust to Change," page 200.*

Healthy Mind S.E.T.

Self-Talk. Keep your self-talk positive. Say to yourself, "I accept and love my child as she is. I will decide that nothing is wrong with my child if she doesn't act the way I expect."

Empathy. Put yourself in your child's shoes by thinking, "I want my child to be comfortable being around other people and in new situations, and my child may not be ready to do so. Some children are naturally inquisitive, ready to participate and boldly embrace new situations and people. I can imagine how she feels if that's hard for her."

Teaching. Remind yourself that learning takes time, patience, and practice. Show or explain to your child how to be more comfortable in social situations and how to grow more self-confident as she explores her expanding world.

Solving the Problem

What to Do

Praise Your Child's Behavior

When your child participates in a program at preschool or greets a friend on the playground, say, "I loved your singing in the play!" or "How fun to be friendly to your buddy on the playground!"

Practice Responding to Questions

If your child shifts into shy mode, she's probably telling you that she may need to learn how to answer questions. Practice with her while you're riding in the car or playing in the bathtub. For example, say, "When your teacher asks, 'What's your name?,' say, 'Samira.' That way, she will know who you are. Now, let's practice. When I ask what's your name, what do you say?" Practice with her several times each day until "Samira" is the automatic response. Repeat with other questions, such as, "How old are you?" or "What's your favorite color?"

Practice with Family and Friends

Provide your child opportunities to participate in conversations. For example, say, "What do you think would taste good on our pizza tonight?" or, "Tell your dad about your trip to the zoo today." If you have more than one child, take turns participating in conversations by calling each child by name and asking specific open-ended questions of each child. If one child dominates the conversation, however, use a timer to limit the talkative child's time.

Make Family Time Talk Time

It's helpful to ask your child questions about personal interests and experiences to encourage her to share. When you're reading a book together, ask, "Tell me about the book you're reading." Then give your child a chance to tell the story in her own words. Encourage her to express herself—and tell her how glad you are that she is telling you how she thinks and feels. Notice, too, that the question we suggested is open and requires a lot of information from your child. The question "Are you reading a book?" can be answered in one word. Keep your questions open so your child can learn to use lots of words to answer.

Seek Professional Help If Necessary

If shyness is interfering with your child's happiness and is keeping her from participating in appropriate activities, seek help from your child's health care provider to make sure that a physical problem is not what's discouraging her from being socially confident. Your health care provider can refer you to a mental health professional if she thinks it might help.

What Not to Do

Don't Humiliate or Shame

Even though you may say to yourself, "I am so embarrassed by my child's shyness," shaming or blaming her by telling her that she's ruined Thanksgiving or humiliating her by telling her, "Don't be so silly!," will not help her be more comfortable in social situations. Instead, it will further discourage her from becoming socially confident.

Don't Apologize

Apologizing for her behavior by telling others she's your shy child or she doesn't speak will only deepen her fear of others.

Don't Beg

Although you may be tempted to beg your child to answer your friend when he asks what grade she's in, for example, don't do it. Begging will give her attention for *not* being part of conversations and encourage more refusals to answer questions in the future.

Don't Label

Making excuses to family and friends by saying your child is shy creates a self-fulfilling prophecy that becomes her identity. It also discourages her from trying to behave differently in the future.

Preventing the Problem

Develop Realistic Expectations and Goals

How you expect your child to act around other people may not be realistic, given her developmental stage and temperament. For example, if your two-year-old isn't ready to go to a birthday party, forcing her to go will only create more fear about future social events. Young children overcome their shyness as they gain experience and confidence when interacting with others. However, don't expect changes overnight.

Accept Your Child's Shyness

Children are born with different temperaments. Some are friendly and outgoing, some are more cautious, and some bounce back and forth between the two. But something else could be behind the behavior that you think of as "acting shyly." What may be seen as a shy child might be more accurately called "observant."

Nurture that quality being her comfort zone. Instead of sending your child the message that something's wrong with her because she doesn't act according to your expectations, accept her behavior as part of her unique temperament and more observant style.

Encourage Observation Skills

If you have determined that your child is an observer rather than a child who likes to interact with others, encourage observation by asking questions such as, "What are you seeing?" and "What do you think about that?"

Compliment Your Child

When your child makes a comment during a conversation, pay her a compliment. For example, say, "I like what you said about the puppy, Samira. He does have an unusual white paw."

Be a Good Role Model

Give your child plenty of opportunities to watch you interact with people in social situations. Also, role-play different scenarios with your child, teaching her what to say in certain situations. For example, explain, "When people ask me how I feel, I usually say, 'Fine. How are you?'"

Case History: Getting to Know Gabe

Gabe Bartone was a shy preschooler who would turn his face away when relatives came to visit or bury his head in his mother's shoulder when they would go to play dates with other children his age. His dad, Michael, had also been shy as a child. Gabe's Grandma Leona said that no one outside the family had heard Michael talk until he was almost a teenager.

Gabe's mother, Maria, had hoped that Gabe would outgrow his shyness. But at eight years old, Timid Gabe, as she called him, showed no signs of becoming more outgoing. Michael understood his son and the pain that he felt when he was confronted with talking to neighborhood children he knew but who weren't his friends. So Michael worked out a plan to help his son.

First, he engaged him in conversation by asking lots of questions that required more than a yes-or-no answer. Michael asked, "What are all the things you had for lunch today?" or, "What games did you play at school today?" When Gabe answered with more than one or two words, Michael would say, "Gabe, I'm glad you told me about that," or, "That was a really interesting story about flying the airplanes on the playground."

Michael and Gabe also practiced greeting people. The two would pretend that they were meeting his neighbor, Janice, who was a friend of his mom's. Gabe would say, "Hello, Mrs. Hendler. How are you?" Michael would answer, "Fine, thank you. And you?" Then they would both laugh. After practicing a few times, Gabe was excited to go meet Mrs. Hendler and try out his new line.

Eventually, Gabe began to relax around other children he didn't know well, and family and friends started to comment on how polite he was. Gabe's mom and dad were happy for him. They had expected him to follow Michael's timid path, and they were thrilled to see him being more confident. They decided that they would never again put a label on their son.

AGGRESSIVE BEHAVIOR / HURTING OTHERS: HITTING, BITING, AND BULLYING

- Threatens violence
- Pretends to play with guns
- Creates gun sounds
- Spits
- Scratches others
- Hits others
- Bites others
- Bullies others
- Pinches others
- Slaps others
- Pushes others
- Makes everything a gun
- Throws toys

Focus on teaching your child to treat others with respect—without slapping, scratching, biting, hitting, or threatening. Children are not born wanting to intentionally hurt others, just for the sake of causing them pain and suffering. However, we all are born with the ability to strike out by hurling toys or our teeth or ourselves at our nearest targets when we are frustrated, angry, or just in rambunctious spirits. Why? Because reasoning or compromising is not one of our inborn problem-solving techniques, and throwing toys, hitting, or biting doesn't seem any more wrong than tossing a ball.

So teach your child as soon as he reaches out and hits, slaps, bites, or kicks—and he will most likely do these things before the age of two—that these aggressive behaviors hurt other people. And teach him how to express his feelings without hurting others.

If your child's aggressive behavior is a regular feature of his daily play and is disruptive to friends, family, and yourself, ask your child's health care provider for help in understanding and identifying any underlying physical, mental, or emotional struggles.

NOTE: *Some people may call hitting, biting, and other aggressive behaviors "bullying," so we included that word as a term to describe hurting others. If your child is called a bully or is accused of bullying, focus on teaching him respectful ways to get what he wants or to communicate his feelings. The label itself is not important; changing the behavior that earned him that name is your goal.*

Healthy Mind S.E.T.

Self-Talk. Keep your self-talk positive. Say to yourself, "I don't want my child to hurt someone else, but I can handle her behavior by keeping my cool."

Empathy. Put yourself in your child's shoes by thinking, "I can understand how my child feels. It's hard to be frustrated and want something, and not be able to have it."

Teaching. Learning takes time, patience, and practice. Show or explain to your child that all feelings are okay, and how to express his anger and frustration and get what he wants without hurting someone.

Solving the Problem

What to Do

Remove Your Child from the Situation with Calm Time

When your child bites another child, for example, don't bite him back to teach him how it feels to be bitten. Take him to Calm Time to reduce his anger and help him calm down. In a calm and kind tone of voice, ask him to think about how it would feel to have someone threaten or bully him. This will encourage him to feel empathy toward others. Children are born with the capacity to be empathetic, so from the earliest age, make understanding the feelings of others part of your everyday lessons. Also ask your child to think about ways to get what he wants that will make the other person want to cooperate with him. After Calm Time is over, talk with him about his feelings to help him learn how to express himself in ways that don't hurt others.

For example: "How would you feel if Cameron bit you? You wouldn't like it, right? We don't want to hurt another person, so we don't bite them, even if we are mad. When you are mad, it's important to say how you feel."

Teach Your Child to Apologize and Use Grandma's Rule

Teaching your child to apologize for hitting, spitting, scratching, pinching, slapping, or pushing his friend helps him to practice empathy. "Grandma's Rule" will supply the motivation he may need to follow your request. Say, "When you have told your friend that you are sorry you hit him, then you may go back to playing."

Encourage Cooperative Play

Children who learn to enjoy building things, sharing with others, and engaging in supervised social activities will have less opportunity to resort to violent games for entertainment. Praise your young child when he's getting along with others while playing so he knows you approve of his behavior. Say, "I like the way you're getting along and being kind to each other by sharing toys." Cooperative play is an important social skill that your child will use to build his success now and always.

Make a Rule About Screen Content

It's important to know what your child is watching on electronic devices and what games he's playing. Reduce the amount of violent content your child is exposed to by making a rule about what he can watch and what games he can play, as well as about how long he can watch or play. Put yourself in charge of access to screens to take violence out of your home and out of your child's imagination. (See page 142.)

When Your Child Uses Screens, Watch with Him

To help a child become an educated viewer, it's important for you to be there to discuss what he sees on any screen. For example, if a character is being bullied, it allows you to point out what bullying behavior is, its effect on the victim, and the lesson that bullying someone in real life hurts and is harmful (whether or not that lesson is clear in the show or the game).

Use a Reprimand for Pretending to "Shoot" a Person

When your child tries to "shoot" a sibling or playmate with a ruler, for example, take the ruler away and reprimand your child by saying, "Guns hurt people. The rule is, 'We treat each other kindly and not even pretend to hurt another person.' We don't hurt people; we love people. Please tell Sam you're sorry for pointing a gun at him." When your child follows your directions, say,

"Thank you for being Sam's friend. I like the way you're showing him that you care about him."

Reduce Aggression by Teaching Your Child to Compromise

Help your child learn to resolve disputes peacefully. When you see him threatening to hit his friend for taking his toy, say, "Let's think about what else you could do when your friend takes your toy and you want it back. You could ask me to use my phone timer so you and your friend can time how long each of you plays with the toy. Let the phone timer tell you when it's time to take turns. That way, both of you get to play with it and have fun."

Model Solving Problems Nonviolently

Children who see you getting what you want by using weapons are more likely to imitate those acts themselves. If parents approve of their children's use of weapons or exhibit violent behavior themselves, they serve as negative role models of violence for their children. On the other hand, parents who show their children how to solve problems nonviolently and who consistently praise their children for finding peaceful solutions to conflicts are positive role models of how to be less aggressive.

Make Rules About Pretend Gun Play

When your young child makes pretend guns out of french fries or wants to take his toy guns to school, don't panic, but don't ignore his imaginative play either. Instead, teach the important lesson that even pretending to physically hurt others with a toy gun can upset teachers, police, parents, and other adults, leading to school expulsion or arrest. Make a rule that toy guns stay home, if they are allowed in your home at all. Check your child's backpack to make sure that his favorite water gun, for example, is not going to school with him.

Talk with Your Child About What to Do When She's Upset, Instead of Hurting Someone

Tame your child's hurtful behavior by first explaining that hurting someone—pinching, hitting, biting, slapping, scratching, pushing, or teasing—is wrong. Then show and tell how to ask for the toy, for example, or get help from an adult in order to express her feelings. Ask her to practice these lines and this action a few times until she's familiar with the words and actions. This translates a thought into action. If your child is not yet able to solve problems with you verbally, it is critical that you observe her closely and redirect her to another kind of play before her anger escalates to hurting someone.

Explain What You Mean by "Getting Along with Others"
Saying, "Thank you for playing so nicely together," from time to time while children are playing reminds them that getting along is important. To explain what you mean by getting along with others, tell your child you appreciate her behavior when she shares, takes turns, asks for help, and so on. For example, say, "Good sharing with your friends!" Always be specific about what you are praising. The more you praise your child's behavior, the more that behavior will be repeated. Learning good social skills early will help achieve success now and in the future.

Use Reprimands for Biting, Hitting, Spitting, Scratching, Slapping, Pushing, and Other Hurtful Behaviors
Reprimanding your child helps her understand which of her behaviors you disapprove of and why. It also shows that you respect your child's ability to understand your reasons for disapproving of her behavior. The three parts of an effective reprimand for biting include the following:

1. Tell your child to stop ("Stop biting!").
2. Explain why you disapprove ("Biting hurts people.").
3. Suggest an acceptable alternative to biting ("When you feel angry, go to an adult, and share your feelings.").

Forget the Incident When It's Over
Reminding your child of her previous aggressions doesn't teach her acceptable behavior. On the contrary, it reminds her of how she could be aggressive again.

What Not to Do

Don't Hit, Spit, Scratch, Pinch, Slap, Push, or Bite Your Child Back
No matter how tempting it is to do all of these things to a child to "smack some sense into him" or "teach him a lesson," resist the urge. Although you may be angry and scared when your child hits, spits, scratches, pinches, slaps, pushes, or bites someone, doing the same thing to him sends him a mixed message: "It's okay for me to hurt you, but not for you to hurt someone else."

Don't Spank!
Spanking teaches him it's okay to hurt people to get them to do what you want, as well as many other lessons that you don't want your child to learn, as we discussed in Chapter 2. Even the occasional swat on the behind sends the hurtful

message that if you're bigger and stronger, it's okay to hit to make a point. Studies have shown that *children who are spanked more than twice a month at age three are almost twice as likely to hurt others by age five*, so don't spank!

Don't Overreact

When your child pretends to shoot his little brother with his pencil, remain calm. Instead of simply forbidding the behavior, take advantage of a teachable moment by saying, "I'm sorry you broke the rule about treating people kindly. Pretending to shoot your brother is mean and disrespectful. Tell me the rule about how to treat people, and show me how you can treat your brother with respect."

Don't Threaten

Threatening to hit your child with a wooden spoon when he's pretending to hit his sister with his stuffed animal only teaches him to fear your presence. To your child, a threat is an empty promise and an example of how adults don't keep their word. So instead of threatening a violent consequence, such as, "I'll give you a spanking if I see you pretending to shoot your brother again," simply say, "I'm sorry you chose to break our rule about pretending to hurt someone. Now I want you to think about how scared you'd feel if somebody pointed a gun at you."

Preventing the Problem

Keep Yourself Under Control

Using hurtful behavior—such as spanking, yelling, slapping, or threatening—when you are angry or upset with your child or anyone else only teaches that hurting others is okay. Remember that a toxic stress response results when your child feels threatened by *your* hurtful response to her behavior. Showing self-control when your child seems out of control will not only model positive behavior for your child but also help you teach her what to do besides hurt other people when she is upset. Keep in mind that the behavior of the adults closest to a child encourages him to be kind or cruel. Watch what you do and say—and how explosively you act—in order to help curb your child's appetite for violent play.

Make Caring a Household Rule

When your child hurts others with any form of violence, be it threatening, spitting, scratching, pinching, slapping, pushing, throwing toys at people, or pretending to use a gun, make a rule that tells him what is or isn't allowed regarding using violence in any form. For example, say, "The rule is, 'We treat people nicely to show them that we care.' Threatening, spitting, scratching, pinching, slapping, pushing, throwing toys at them, or pointing guns, even pretend ones, is against our family's rules because it upsets people and makes them afraid." Giving your child rules that guide his behavior builds important social skills that lead your child on a path to success.

Think Before Speaking

Use words and a tone of voice that you wouldn't mind your child repeating. For example, when he breaks a rule, instead of threatening (even in jest) to "knock his head off if he doesn't stop," calmly say, "I'm sorry you decided not to follow the rule about pretending to use a gun. The rule is, 'We treat each other nicely and don't ever hurt or pretend to hurt anyone.'"

Model Kindness

You are your child's first and most important role model. When you listen to, hug, apologize to, and respect your child, he will learn to behave the same way with others.

Learn to Control Your Own Anger

What causes children to "go off" is the same thing that causes adults to explode: anger over something beyond their control. Tell yourself that you hope that you get a raise, the traffic is light, your favorite dress still fits, and so on. But if none of these wishes comes true, don't have a meltdown. By keeping your cool, you set a powerful example for your child of regulating your emotions by using positive self-talk when things don't go your way.

Use Understanding and Empathy

You cannot have empathy for others and be a bully at the same time. When your child hurts others, try to put yourself in her position so that you can understand her motivation. Then help her understand what happens to others when she hurts others. Say, "I understand you were frustrated, but how do you think James felt when you called him a 'dummy'?" Talking about feelings and how hurtful words can be will help your child refocus on the impact her words have on others. Talk about how hurt you felt when someone said something mean to you.

Closely Supervise Your Child's Play

To prevent your child from learning from his peers to hurt others, monitor how she and her friends interact with each other and how they care for their toys. Also respond to your child's friends' hurtful behavior as you would to your own child's.

Avoid Violent Electronic Media

Young children like to imitate what they see on their electronic devices, without realizing that the same hurtful actions really *do* hurt people. Many children have been victimized by playmates who use in real life the kicks and punches that they see their favorite TV or game characters use. Strong identification with a violent character and believing that the situation is realistic are both associated with greater aggressiveness. Watching violent media also provokes a toxic stress response in children, and that is a dangerous brain changer.

Case History: Morgan the Hitter

At three years old, Morgan became known as the neighborhood hitter. He'd had lots of practice on his two older brothers, who had bullied him by teasing him mercilessly.

His mom, Vivian, threatened her youngest child in order to stop his hitting, saying, "If you don't stop hitting people, Morgan, I'm going to spank you." But she knew she couldn't back up her threat. The very idea of hitting a child just made her cringe, and hitting her child to stop him from hitting didn't make sense to her. She was simply at a loss as to what to do about Morgan's hitting.

However, Morgan's five- and seven-year-old brothers' bullying of him didn't seem to bother her. In fact, her family joked frequently about lots of things, and she considered the older boys' insulting and making fun of Morgan in the spirit of not taking yourself too seriously. Besides, it would toughen Morgan up for the cold, cruel world he would have to enter someday, or so she reasoned.

But Morgan's dad didn't agree; he had felt the sting of Vivian's family's insults and teasing. "How do you think Morgan feels about being teased?" he asked one day. Though she didn't want to admit it, Vivian had never thought about this problem from Morgan's point of view—that he got back at his brothers by hitting because he couldn't match their verbal attacks. Vivian had often told him to use words instead, advising him to say, "I don't like to be teased." But it wasn't working. Words simply weren't enough to stop his brothers from bullying him.

So she decided to teach all three boys that hitting, teasing, and throwing things or other aggressive behaviors would not be tolerated. She believed that this was the only way to teach the older boys to model good behavior and to teach Morgan to make better choices about how to deal with his brothers. So the next time Morgan began attacking his brothers after they called him "Little Oscar the Grouch," Vivian reprimanded him first. She said, "Stop hitting, Morgan. Hitting hurts people. We don't hit people." But then she also reprimanded his brothers, saying, "Stop teasing. We do not tease people. It hurts their feelings. We treat people with respect."

The reprimands didn't stop the boys' verbal and physical attacks. So Vivian said, "I'm sorry you're still hitting and teasing each other. I will take you to Calm Time." She then directed the boys to separate chairs and told them to think about what had happened and about ways in which they could avoid it happening again, as well as how they wanted to be treated and treat others.

As Vivian became consistent in her discipline, and as she praised the boys when they got along, they learned what to expect from fighting and from being friendly and treating each other well. Morgan began to hit less often, since he didn't have to tolerate his brothers' teasing, and the older boys became more empathetic as they learned that teasing was hurtful.

BAD MANNERS

- Doesn't say "please" and "thank you"
- Lets the door slam in front of people
- Cuts in front of the line
- Doesn't make eye contact

- Doesn't answer questions
- Doesn't use silverware or a napkin
- Chews with his mouth open

Good manners are important social skills that people use to avoid offending each other, intentionally or unintentionally. In short, using good manners helps people feel comfortable and at ease with each other. You may have found that teaching good manners to your young child is not an easy task, for a variety of reasons. First of all, young children are very egocentric. They generally think only of their own needs and not the needs of others. But even though good manners may not seem important to your child in his me-first mind, teaching your child good manners is part of helping him understand how others feel, and how his behavior affects others, and sets him on a path for positive and healthy relationships. You will find "teaching good manners" within nearly every behavior description in this chapter because using good manners helps prepare a child to navigate the world. For example, see "Plays with Food," page 128.

Healthy Mind S.E.T.

Self-Talk. Keep your self-talk positive. Say to yourself, "I want my child to learn good manners, so he can be respectful of others. I feel better when people treat me with respect, and I want him to learn how."

Empathy. Put yourself in your child's shoes by thinking, "My child doesn't know that using manners is important, so it's my job to teach him."

Teaching. Remind yourself that learning takes time, patience, and practice. Show or explain the manners that you want your child to learn and teach him why they are important.

Solving the Problem

What to Do
Teach Your Child How to Use Screens and Be Polite
When your child has his face in his laptop or his phone screen instead of

looking at you when you are talking, ask him these questions in a calm, kind tone of voice: "How do you think I feel when you don't look at me when I'm talking to you, but are texting or emailing instead? How would you feel if I looked at my phone and kept texting or at my computer and continued to email while you were talking to me?" Say, "It is important to show people respect. Being able to put your phone or computer aside for a moment when someone is talking to you is respectful. You may be able to do two or three things at once, but other people want your undivided attention. That shows them that you care about them so much that they deserve your full attention."

Teach Your Child to Practice Empathy

Children are born with the capacity to be empathetic, so from the earliest age, make understanding the feelings of others part of your everyday teaching. When your child uses bad manners, for example, don't use bad manners to teach him how it feels to be with someone who isn't polite. Instead you can say, "How would you feel if your dad licked his plate after he ate? You would think he had bad manners, right? We want to be polite and make people feel respected, so we use good manners."

Teach Your Child Table Manners at a Non-Eating, Neutral Time

Your child needs to know what behavior you expect her to use in restaurants, in others' homes, and while in your own home. It's best to teach her these expectations when you're not actually sitting down to dinner. For example, have frequent "tea parties," where you show her how to use her spoon, keep food on her tray, keep her hands out of her food, tell you when she's finished eating, and so on.

Set the timer on your phone for a few minutes and say, "When the phone timer rings, you may leave the table. Please tell me when you're finished, and I'll take your plate." Play is life practice for children. So playing "manners" gives her practice in good manners in fun, no-stress play, with you at her side.

Ask Your Child to Do Things—Don't Demand

To make your young child more likely to ask for things politely, show him how to make requests. Say, "When you ask me nicely, then you may play with the blocks." Then explain what you mean by "nicely." For example, teach your child to say, "Please, may I get a fork?" when he wants a fork.

Set Rules for Manners

Keep it simple. Begin manners training by outlining a few rules, such as when to say "please" and "thank you."

Point Out Your Good Manners

It is also good to point out your own good manners when you use them. You can say, "Please put the book on the table. See, I used the word 'please' because that's the rule, and it's a polite way to ask someone to do something. That means I'm using good manners."

Praise Good Manners

When your child follows a manners rule, tell him how nice it sounds when he says "please" and "thank you." Also tell him that using good manners makes others feel respected. Praise his good table manners by saying, "Thank you for chewing with your mouth closed." When he asks you why it's important, explain that it is polite to close your mouth when you chew, just as it is polite to use a napkin to wipe your mouth when you get food on your face.

Correct Bad Manners

When your child forgets the manners rule, say, "Remember the rule: we eat with our fork, not our hands," or "Remember, we say 'thank you' when someone does something nice for us."

Practice Good Manners

When your child crowds in front of you, pushes through the door, and lets it come back to hit you, you know it's time to teach good manners. To teach this new set of behaviors, ask your child to make eye contact with you, so you know he's listening. Then tell him what you want: "It's polite and good manners to open the door, let other people go through before you, and then close the door when everybody is through. Let's practice that." A few practice sessions with lots of praise for each step can teach you child to be aware of others' needs, to look out for others, and to do something unselfish for others. He'll learn good manners that will help his relationships now and for the rest of his life.

What Not to Do

Don't Nag

Don't say, "How many times do I have to tell you to chew with your mouth closed?" Nagging offers no motivation for your child to follow your directions. Nagging only teaches your child to tune you out and to use nagging to motivate others. It doesn't teach him to value manners or show him how to use good manners.

Don't Belittle and Shame

Don't say, "You are eating like a pig," or "Aren't you ashamed you didn't say 'thank you' when Grandma gave you a treat?" Belittling and shaming a child doesn't teach him good manners. Trying to motivate a child by shaming him tells him that your love is conditional, that you only love him when he follows your rules.

Don't Make Dinner a Manners Battle

Rather than continually barking orders at your child to use good manners— saying, "Sit up straight!" or "Use your fork!" or "Use your napkin!"—praise little bits of progress by saying, "I like the way you picked up your fork. It's so nice to see you use a fork instead of your fingers to eat broccoli."

Preventing the Problem

Start Early

Even before your child can say the words "please" and "thank you," set the stage by using these words yourself. When changing a diaper, giving a bath, and feeding your little one, describe your behaviors by using good manners. Say, "Thank you for playing so nicely in the tub, Johnny!" Remember that your child is always listening.

Use Good Manners Yourself

Sometimes we forget that little eyes are on us all the time, so it's important to behave in ways you'd like your child to learn. If you concentrate on using good manners all the time, you are providing a manners model your child will think of throughout her life. Saying "please" and "thank you," holding doors for people, making eye contact with your child when you talk to her, and always using good table manners will teach important social skills needed for success.

Case History: Mia Learns Manners

At two and a half, Mia was beginning to act like a real person, but she was very uncivilized, her parents, Lillian and Thomas, thought. They tried eating dinner with her by placing her in a booster seat so she could be at the table with the adults. But Mia would unbuckle her safety belt and climb onto the table to get more food. And then she'd stuff the food into her mouth until it was so full that Lillian and Thomas feared she would choke. They tried taping the buckle on the safety belt so she couldn't unbuckle it, but then she only screamed. They tried bribing Mia with a sweet dessert, but when she didn't do as she was told, she screamed when they put the dessert away. Dinnertime was a war. Going out to eat was totally out of the question.

"Maybe we started teaching her manners too soon," Thomas suggested.

"Maybe, but she has learned so many new things. Surely she can learn simple manners," Lillian replied.

Mia's parents decided to try again, but they thought a few practice sessions were in order. When Mia was in her booster seat, Lillian stood behind her and guided Mia's spoon-filled hand from the dish to her mouth while Thomas praised the effort.

"Look at that," he said. "Mia is eating so nicely with her spoon."

After Mia began using her spoon correctly, Lillian and Thomas started praising her small bites and then showed her how to ask for more of something and say "please." It took a while, but Mia began learning basic table manners and started receiving praise for her efforts. Dinnertime slowly but surely became something to look forward to, instead of to dread. We're never too old to learn how to teach a child to follow the rules, her parents realized—and to learn a few things from their little student about how having rules is something that makes life less stressful for all.

CAR TRAVEL CONFLICTS

- Demands to play with your phone
- Screams at their sibling
- Needs to use the bathroom constantly
- Kicks the back of the seat

A family trip by car can be stressful even when it's a short trip to school, the park, practices, games, lessons, or lunch, when accompanied by bickering, complaining, fighting, crying, or kicking the back of the driver's seat. It can be worse for long car trips over many hours. What's behind all of this chaos? Your child may miss the sense of security offered by familiar toys, beds, toilets, and foods, making her cranky and anxious. The comforts of home are often absent when you're traveling, so teach your child how to cope with change and how to enjoy the experiences of travel. (Also see "Resists Car Seats and Seat Belts," page 137.)

Healthy Mind S.E.T.

Self-Talk. Keep your self-talk positive. Say to yourself, "It's okay. We will safely get where we need to go, even if my child doesn't always think it's fun to be in the car."

Empathy. Put yourself in your child's shoes by thinking, "I understand that my child may be bored and not want to be restrained or to leave the comfort of her home. I know it's more fun to be able to move around and play. Sometimes I don't want to go anywhere either."

Teaching. Remind yourself that learning takes time, patience, and practice. Show or explain to your child how she can be a happy road buddy in the car.

Solving the Problem

What to Do

Play Car Games to Distract, Educate, and Entertain

Make a list of fun things to do before you leave home. Distract and pay positive attention: Divert your child's attention by singing songs, number games, word games, or Peek-a-Boo. Talk about what you are seeing outside or inside the car. Use in-car "screens" as a last resort, and remember that you're your child's favorite playmate in the car. Count objects, recognize colors, look for animals, and so on to keep your child entertained. To make car rides more special, give him "car only" books or games.

Make Frequent Rest Stops

Your restless young child may be happiest when he's mobile. Restraining him for hours in a car does not suit his adventurous spirit. On long car trips, build in time to let off steam in a roadside park or rest stop, or you may find him rebelling simply because he needs to move.

Monitor Snacks on Long Trips

Highly sugared or carbonated foods or beverages may increase not only a child's activity level but also the chance of your child becoming carsick. Stick to protein snacks or lightly salted ones to keep her healthy and happy.

Use Grandma's Rule

Let your child know that good behavior on trips brings rewards. For example, if your child has been whining about getting a drink, say, "When you've sat in your seat and talked with us without whining, then we'll stop and get something to drink."

Make a Rule About Cell Phone Use

Children who are bored or have had easy access to screens will demand screens when they can't entertain themselves. To stop your child from demanding your cell phone in the car, make it a safety rule. Say, "The rule is, I must have my phone up here with me, so I'll have it in case of an emergency." When your child demands use of the phone, simply restate the rule.

Take Care of Toilet Needs Before You Go

"I need to go potty," your child wails shortly after you leave the house. You know she went just before you left, so you don't think she really needs to go. You also know her bathroom habits and how often she needs to go. If this is a pattern, simply say, "I'm sorry, but you went before we left. I think you can wait until we get there. I'll help you think of something else." This is the time to play find-the-color games. For longer trips, frequent stops are important for more than potty stops. The freedom to move about and be out of a car seat will help keep a restless child satisfied for a while.

What Not to Do

Always Wear Your Seat Belt and Don't Complain About It

Casually telling your friends or family that you hate wearing a seat belt gives your child a reason to resist her belt, too. Make sure to wear your seat belt and point out how your child is wearing one, too, to help her understand that she's not alone in her temporary confinement. If you don't wear a seat belt, your child will not understand why she has to.

Don't Pay Attention to Your Child's Yelling About Being Buckled In

Not giving attention to your child's crying or whining while she's belted in helps her see that there's no benefit in protesting the seat-belt rule. Say to yourself, "I know my child is safer in her car seat and will only fight it temporarily. Her safety is my responsibility, and I am being responsible by enforcing the seat-belt / car-seat rule."

Don't Use Threats or Fear

Telling your child about the grave dangers of being out of her car seat won't teach her how to stay in it. Threatening to take away toys or privileges later in the day won't teach her to follow the rules either.

Don't Spank!

Spanking or threatening to spank her for getting out of her car seat will only hurt you both and won't teach your child how to stay buckled up. You can't be a caring adult and use violence or threats of violence at the same time.

Don't Let Young Children Sit in the Front Seat

No matter how much they fuss and beg to sit next to Mommy or Daddy in the front seat, young children should never be allowed to sit there, even on the shortest of trips. The safest place for young children is buckled safely in a car seat or booster seat in the back.

Don't Make Promises You May Not Fulfill

Don't be too specific about what your child will see on your travels because he might hold you to it. For example, if you say you'll see a bear in Yellowstone Park and you don't, you might hear him whining as you leave, "But you promised I'd see a bear."

Don't Rely Solely on In-Car Media for Entertainment

Even children who love phones, tablets, and other screens may eventually tire of them in the car. That is why word games, puzzles, books, crayons, and other forms of entertainment—including you, of course—are needed even on short trips.

Don't Talk on Your Phone While Driving

Talking on your phone while driving with your child in the car takes your attention away from him and from the road. Using a phone while driving is said to be equivalent to having two alcoholic drinks before driving. It also encourages your child to demand to use the phone when you are using it all the time.

Preventing the Problem

Check the Car Seat or Seat Restraints Before Traveling

The safety measures you take before leaving will determine how relaxed you are with your children when you finally depart. Don't wait until the last minute to find out that you must delay your trip because you lack an essential item: the car seat.

Provide Appropriate Materials for Entertainment

Make sure you pack toys that are harmless to clothing and upholstery. Crayons are okay, but avoid felt-tip pens because they may permanently mark clothing and upholstery. Have age-appropriate materials for hand-held screens or the television DVD player.

Familiarize Your Child with Your Car Trip Plans

Discuss your travel plans with your child so she'll know how long you'll be gone, what will happen to her room while you're away, and when you'll return. Show her maps and photos of your destination. Talk to her about the people, scenery, and events you'll experience. Share personal stories and souvenirs from previous visits to the destination. If your child is anxious about going to an unknown place, compare the destination to one she's familiar with.

Personally Involve Your Child Traveler

Allow your child to participate in the preparation and execution of the trip. Enlist his help in packing his clothing, selecting car toys and media, and picking healthy drinks and snacks.

Establish Rules for Traveling

Before you leave, explain to your child any special rules of the road. For example, you might establish a noise rule, an exploring rule, a pool rule, and a restaurant rule for stops along the way.

Give Your Child Room to Breathe

Make sure she has room to move her hands and legs and still be safely buckled up.

Make a Rule That the Car Will Not Move
Unless Everyone Is Buckled Up

If you enforce this rule from the beginning, your child will become accustomed to the idea of sitting in a car seat and eventually wearing a seat belt. Institute the rule that the car moves only when everyone is buckled in. Be prepared to wait until the passengers are buckled in before you start the trip. Check in by saying, "All buckled in? Let's go!"

Case History: Car Wars

Michael and Andrea Sterling wanted to take their children on a vacation that was just like the vacations they had each enjoyed when they were young. But even short trips in the car with three-year-old Zoe and six-year-old Zachary were more like punishment than a Sunday drive. The backseat of the car was a war zone, with the children's screaming frequently leading Michael and Andrea to issue threats of spankings. But the threats didn't seem to help. The Sterlings, who often felt just as angry after making the threats as they did before, felt nearly hopeless about finding a solution to their car travel problems. Even getting a new car with a built-in TV didn't help: the children began to fight over what to watch.

Eventually, they decided to develop rules for car trips. They found some toys that their kids could play with unsupervised, and they explained the new rules. "Kids," they began, "when we go to school in the morning, we want you to talk with us nicely all the way there. When you do that, you can each pick out your favorite book to read when we get home." They then applied and tested those rules not just on trips to school but on trips to day care, the grocery store, the park, and friends' homes.

Initially, the kids followed the rules, and their parents praised them for it. "Thanks for being so cooperative with each other," they said. But the plan hit a roadblock when the kids returned to fighting about what they wanted to watch on TV in the car. "The TV can come back on when you cooperate with each other" was Andrea's response. It only took two more tests for the children to behave kindly toward each other and follow the car rules during the entire time in the car. They received praise for their efforts, and they were rewarded for their good behavior.

Two weeks later, the Sterling family began its two-hour trek to Grandma's, the longest trip in the car since the practice sessions had begun. The children knew what was expected of them and what rewards were available along the way and at their destination. Between short intervals of viewing TV, they played games and took turns picking shows and new games. The previous ordeal of a car ride had become a pleasant experience for all.

~~~~~~

CLIMBS

- Climbs out of crib
- Climbs on furniture
- Climbs out of bed
- Climbs fences
- Climbs high in trees
- Climbs up on the car

Some children can't resist climbing on anything that looks climbable—even if it isn't. These children will climb on chairs, tables, cabinets, shelves, trees, stone walls, statues, and cars, among other things. Not only can climbing be dangerous, but it can also damage property. It can bring reprimands from librarians whose bookshelves are climbed on or from Grandma when her china cabinet is the Mount Everest of the moment.

As a parent, you realize the problems that climbing can cause, but you may have tried everything you know to do to no avail. Your child heads for anything that he thinks he can climb whenever he sees it. You may have tried scolding, threatening, and Calm Time, and you may even have been tempted to give him a swat to show him the pain he may suffer if he falls. Each climb becomes a test of strength and endurance. Your job as a parent is to not only understand your child's need to climb but also channel that need toward things and places that can be climbed safely.

Healthy Mind S.E.T.

Self-Talk. Keep your self-talk positive. Say to yourself, "I can see how much fun my son has when he climbs all over our furniture. I just need to teach him what is safe to climb and what isn't."

Empathy. Put yourself in your child's shoes by thinking, "I can imagine how it must feel to want to climb up on everything."

Teaching. Remind yourself that learning takes time, patience, and practice. Show or explain how your child can learn to climb safely.

Solving the Problem

What to Do

Be There

When your child is a happy climber, celebrate that fact by encouraging him to climb toys and slides you have at home or in playgrounds. Climbing up on his chair or the couch—those are big steps to be applauded! But the first priority is to let him do so safely. You may need to be there, right beside him, at first. As he grows, you will see how he can climb things without your being close by. The goal is to encourage his independence while not making him afraid. That requires you to know when and how climbing can be fun and safe at the same time.

Play with Climbing Toys, Slides, and Jungle Gyms

If your child loves to climb, take him to climbing areas where he can safely use his energy and strength. Watch him and encourage his safe climbing.

Bell the Cat

When you have a young climber, it's hard to know where he is at all times—he's that fast! So tie bells to his shoes to keep track of where he is. Or if he prefers climbing in bare feet, pin bells to the back of his pants. You can't keep him from climbing unsafe objects if you aren't there to stop him.

Define What Is Climbable and What Is Not

Telling your child what can and cannot be climbed at least puts a framework around his climbing activities. Say, "No, you may not climb the cabinet, but you may climb the couch."

Make Climbing Rules

Making rules about climbing can channel a child's need to climb. Put colored dots on furniture that is okay to climb, and a different color on those that aren't. (This has an added benefit of teaching colors.) Telling him, "Here's the rule about climbing on Grandma's furniture. You are safe to climb everything with a blue dot," will remind him of the rule and help keep the rule in his mind during your visit to Grandma's house.

Remind Your Child of the Rules

When your child begins to climb something that's off-limits, remind him of the climbing rule. Ask him, "What's the rule about climbing here? Does it have a blue dot?"

Remove Your Child from What He Is Climbing

Simply taking him off whatever he's climbing and saying, "I'm sorry, but that is not for climbing," will stop the climb for the moment.

Redirect Your Child Toward Permitted Climbs

When your child starts to climb something that he's not permitted to climb, redirect him to something that he is permitted to climb. Say, "I'm sorry, but you may not climb the dresser. We can go outside, and you may climb on your swing set."

Try a Climbing Wall

Many indoor play areas now have climbing walls designed for children. When your child is old enough, his climbing needs can be satisfied by occasional trips to the climbing wall, which can also be used as a reward for following the no-climbing rule at home.

What Not to Do

Don't Panic

When you see your child climbing something, rather than starting to panic and beginning to yell, stay calm, and quietly remove him from what he is climbing.

Don't Threaten

Telling your child that you will punish him if he climbs again will only encourage him to sneak behind your back to climb something so he can avoid getting caught. Remember: you can't see him climbing if you are not there.

Don't Guilt-Trip

Don't say, "You know that I get so worried whenever you start climbing things. You don't want to upset me, do you?" Using guilt will not motivate your child to stop climbing something, but it will lead him to do the forbidden climbing when you're not around. That way, his thinking goes, he won't feel guilty about upsetting you.

Don't Use Fear

Telling your child, "If you climb up on that couch, you will fall and get hurt," is simply daring him to try to see if that happens instead of keeping him from climbing. But when he climbs and doesn't fall, it will suggest to him that you are not believable and he doesn't need to listen to you.

Preventing the Problem

Anchor Tall Furniture to the Wall

Furniture anchors won't keep your child from climbing, but they will prevent bad accidents if he forgets the rule and climbs his bookcase or dresser.

Provide Places and Things to Climb

Recognizing your child's need to climb and providing climbable things and places will allow him to fulfill his needs and keep boundaries around his climbing.

Case History: Climbing Connor

From the time he was able to walk, Connor tried to climb everything. Climbing up on furniture became too easy, so he began climbing onto the dining table. This frustrated Alyssa, his mother, because no matter how many times she told him to not climb or took him to Calm Time, Connor continued to climb up on the table. Finally, Alyssa and his father, Alan, put the dining room chairs down on their backs so Connor would have to lift them upright to climb them. But the last straw came when Connor climbed his bookshelves and fell. He cried, but soon he was trying to climb his shelves again. Fortunately, Alan had purchased anchors and had anchored all of Connor's furniture to the wall. Then he had to anchor all of the items in the house that were tall enough to climb because Connor was trying to climb them all.

It was when Alan lost his temper and threatened to deliver a swat to Connor's backside that Alan and Alyssa decided that they needed a new plan to teach Connor about climbing. How could they be the kind of parents they wanted to be if they resorted to hitting their child? They told themselves that they would never threaten to hit Connor under any circumstances.

Instead, because they realized that Connor was a climber and that there wasn't a good way to stop him, they decided to closely supervise his climbs. When out of the house, Connor was told the rules about what he could climb and what he could not. "What's the rule about that?" Alyssa would ask, and Connor would answer, "I can't climb that." Alyssa would then praise Connor's answer and offer to take him to the park, where he would be able to climb whatever he wanted. As a result, while Connor still loved to climb, his climbing stopped causing wars between him and his parents. They understood his need to climb, and he was willing to climb what he could and stay off those mountains that were not to be climbed.

CLINGS TO PARENTS / SEPARATION ANXIETY

- Is anxious about what others think
- Fears going to school or playing outside
- Doesn't want to leave Mom or Dad
- Won't play with the babysitter
- Won't let a parent leave the room

The image of a young child clutching her mother's legs—hanging on for dear life while Mom tries to shop, walk out the door, or leave day care—is not make-believe for many parents. It's a real and emotionally draining part of everyday life. If you want (or need) to leave your child with a babysitter or at day care, preschool, or the neighbor's, for example, firmly and lovingly reassure her by telling her that you're proud of her for staying with Ms. Maria and that you will return. Let her know that you're happy she has the chance to play with Ms. Maria.

Even though she may cry when you close the door, your positive attitude will be contagious (as would a negative one). Talk with the caregiver or teacher about embracing your child and engaging in conversation before you leave, so that she is feeling secure when you do. Clinging, unlike hugging, is an urgent demand for immediate attention. (See also "Won't Adjust to Change," page 200.) Your child's independence, self-confidence, and self-sufficiency begin with learning how to separate from you.

NOTE: If from the moment she wakes up until she's asleep, your daughter's forehead has that worried look and her eyes show you that she's walking around anxious all the time, contact your health care provider. Your daughter may say such things as "Everybody at school hates me. I'm afraid that everyone will make fun of what I wear. How come Sally didn't talk to me at lunch? I am such a loser." These expressions of insecurity have the same root as not being comfortable adjusting to change and clinging to parents. Where does all of this anxiety come from? To answer these questions and help your child deal with her anxiety and insecurity in social situations, your child's health care provider may suggest visiting a mental health professional who will be able to evaluate whether this is a serious issue that needs professional help or there is something going on at school or with her friends that she is not telling you.

Some children fear separation so much that they refuse to go on play dates, to birthday parties, to school, or even outside to play. And these fears may not be apparent early in a child's life but may show up later, especially when your child goes to school for the first time or if your family has been personally affected by a school-violence tragedy. In addition, many children experience separation anxiety during their first-grade year if they have not attended a preschool, kindergarten, or day care program for entire days. You know that school is important and even mandatory. So if your child has this kind of fear response, it is important to check with her health care provider to see if a referral to a mental health professional is advisable.

Healthy Mind S.E.T.

Self-Talk. Keep your self-talk positive. Say to yourself, "It's okay. I can do this. I know she misses me. She'll learn that I always come back."

Empathy. Put yourself in your child's shoes by thinking, "My child doesn't want to leave the security of being with me. I understand how she feels."

Teaching. Remind yourself that learning takes time, patience, and practice. Show or explain how your child can learn to become independent and self-sufficient by first feeling good about being away from you and being cared for by others— family, friends, teachers, and other caregivers.

Solving the Problem

What to Do
Play Beat-the-Clock

To teach your child independence, play Beat-the-Clock: Give her five minutes of your time and five minutes to play by herself. Keep increasing the play-by-herself time for each five minutes of time spent with you, until she can play by herself for longer periods. Make sure that you can see her when she's separated from you. For an older child, make sure that you know where she is and that she can safely play by herself while out of your view.

Praise Your Child's Nonclingy Behavior

Say, "You were so brave when you let go of my hand and went into your classroom." When you return to your child after school, say, "It was good that you had fun at school after I left. I knew that you could."

Compliment Your Child When She Can Separate and Play by Herself

Let your child know that you are proud of her ability to play by herself. For example, say, "I'm so proud of the way that you entertained yourself while I worked on the computer." This will further reinforce her self-confidence and independence, which will benefit both of you.

Set Separation Goals

Say, "You're going to the zoo with your class tomorrow. It'll be fun. Let's set a goal of having a good time on your field trip to the zoo." Then periodically remind him of the goal and have him repeat it to you. Ask him, "What's your goal about going to school?" When he says, "I'm going to the zoo with my friends and have fun and learn," say, "That's right. You're going to the zoo to have fun and learn."

Let Someone Else Take Your Child to School or Day Care and Non-School Activities

Because your child has difficulty separating from you, if possible let another caring, responsible adult regularly deliver her to and from school—day care, preschool, or elementary school. She will discover that she can successfully separate and get along when you aren't with her.

In addition, whenever possible involve others in taking your child on errands, to camps, birthday parties, and other activities. Consider asking grandparents or other relatives if they live nearby, your friends, or your neighbors. Your child will learn that you can spend time apart and she'll still be okay.

Use Empathy and Understanding

Put yourself in your child's position as you try to feel the anxiety she may be showing you when she is facing the unknown. In a calm and kind voice say, "I know how you feel. But even though we can't be together for a while, you'll be okay and will have fun with the sitter [your friends]. I will see you later."

Prepare Yourself for Noise When You Separate and Your Child Doesn't Like It

Remember that the noise will eventually subside when your child learns the valuable lesson that she can survive without you for a brief time. Tell yourself, "She's crying because she loves me. But she needs to learn that although I can't always play with her and I occasionally go away, I'll always come back."

Recognize That Your Child Needs Time Away from You

Breaks from constant companionship are necessary for children and parents. So keep your daily routine, even if your child protests your doing something besides playing with her or fusses when you occasionally leave her with another member of your parenting team.

What Not to Do

Don't Get Upset When Your Child Clings

Getting upset with your child for clinging to you won't teach her independence. Tell yourself that your child prefers your company to anything in the whole world, but that it is important for her to learn how to get along with others.

Don't Punish Your Child for Clinging

Instead, follow the steps outlined above to teach her how to separate.

Don't Give Mixed Messages

Don't tell your child to go play by herself while you're holding, patting, or stroking her. This will confuse her about whether to stay or go.

Don't Make Sickness a Convenient Way to Get Special Attention

Don't make being sick more fun than being well by letting your sick child do things that are normally unacceptable. Sickness should be dealt with in a loving way with few changes in routine.

Preventing the Problem

Practice Leaving Your Child with a Sitter

To get your child used to the idea that you may not always be around, practice leaving her occasionally for short periods of time (a few hours) early in her first years of life, if she doesn't attend day care or preschool. These breaks are healthy for both parents and children.

Tell Your Child What You'll Both Be Doing in Your Absence

Telling your child what you'll be doing while you're gone gives her a good example to follow when you ask her to talk about her day's activities. Describe what she'll be doing and where you'll be while you're away, so she won't worry about her fate or yours.

For example, say, "Laura will fix your dinner, read you a story, and tuck you into bed. Your daddy and I are going out to dinner, and we'll be back at eleven o'clock tonight." Or say, "I need to cook dinner now. When I've done that and you've played with your lock-blocks, then we can read a story together." Or say, "While you're in school, I'll be at work. Then I will pick you up at after-school care. I know you'll have a good day."

Play Peek-a-Boo

This simple game gets your child used to the idea that things (and you) go away and, more importantly, come back. Toddlers and preschoolers play Peek-a-Boo in a variety of ways: by hiding behind their hands or some object, watching others hide behind their hands or some object, and (for older children) engaging in a more physically active game of hide-and-seek.

Reassure Your Child That You'll Be Coming Back

Don't forget to tell her that you'll be returning and prove to her you're as good as your word by coming back when you said you would.

Create Special Sitter Activities

"Activity treats" help your child look forward to staying with a babysitter or neighbor instead of being upset by your absence. For example, set aside special videos, finger paints, games, and storybooks that only come out when a sitter comes over.

Prepare Your Child for the Separation

Tell your child that you'll be leaving and plant the suggestion that she can cope while you're gone. For example, say, "You will be having such a good time with Lisa. I know you'll be fine while I'm gone." If you surprise her by leaving without warning, she may always wonder when you're going to disappear suddenly again.

Provide Lots of Hugs and Kisses During Neutral Times

Your showing her that you care will help prevent her from feeling ignored and needing to cling to you to get attention. Giving your child practice with playing near you but not necessarily with you will be helpful to encourage independence.

Case History: "Don't Leave Me!"

Natalie and Rick Gordon loved the party circuit so much that when their four-year-old son, Tyler, clutched both their jackets in horror when a babysitter arrived, they discounted his feelings. They'd say, "Oh, come on, Tyler, honey—don't be a baby! We love you. It's silly for you to feel bad. We go out every Saturday night."

But Tyler wasn't comforted. He screamed at the top of his lungs, "Don't go! Don't leave! Take me!"

His clinging persisted, and the Gordons couldn't understand what they were doing wrong to make their son "punish" them whenever they wanted to leave the house. They asked themselves, "Does he really hate us so much that he wants to embarrass us in front of the babysitter?" They eventually related their frustration to their pediatrician, who reassured them by explaining that Tyler clung to them because he loved them, not because he hated them.

The following Saturday night, the Gordons tried this strategy that the pediatrician recommended: Before leaving, they prepared Tyler for their upcoming departure by saying, "You'll have so much fun playing with Laura while we're at the movies. We'll be back after you're in bed, and we will come in and kiss you when we get home. We'll be here in the morning when you wake up. Laura will make you popcorn in our new popcorn maker and read you a story. Then you'll go to bed. We know you'll have a great time!"

Natalie and Rick didn't drag out their exit with tearful hugs, and they left Tyler while he was only whimpering. After this successful departure, they began to praise Tyler's being quiet during their explanations of where they were going, what they were planning to do, and how long they'd be gone. Whenever they got a good report from the babysitter, they'd let Tyler know how proud they were of his playing nicely while they were gone. "Thanks for being so calm and for helping Laura build your favorite puzzle last night," they'd say with a hug.

The Gordons were also patient. They knew they might have to wait several weeks before being able to leave to the sounds of happy feet, instead of stomping and wailing. But in the meantime, they stopped verbally attacking Tyler for any "babyish" behavior, and they reduced his crying by ignoring it.

CURSES AND SWEARS, USES "BAD WORDS"

- Has a potty mouth
- Swears to get your reaction
- Calls you bad swear words
- Swears to make friends laugh
- Swears when angry
- Swears all the time

Children are, unfortunately, experts at repeating words that they hear in your conversations. Swear words are some of their favorites because of the attention that they get. So when children casually say them at home, in preschool or school, or during a holiday meal, they create quite a stir—drawing either shock or laughter. This encourages them to use those powerful words to get attention from everyone as often as possible. (See also "Name-Calling," page 102.) And let's not forget that children, and especially teenagers, often believe swearing is cool and a way to fit into their peer group. This behavior becomes a teachable moment that can help your child learn how to be respectful in what they say and do.

Healthy Mind S.E.T.

Self-Talk. Keep your self-talk positive. Say to yourself, "It's normal for my child to think that the louder and more powerfully annoying her words are, the more that I'll pay attention to it. I don't like it, but I can teach her to express herself using respectful words."

Empathy. Put yourself in your child's shoes by thinking, "I can understand why she swears—for the same reasons we all do. It feels good just to make a point with an out-of-control word that gets an immediate and emotional response. My agenda is different from my child's. I want my child to be able to use words that are appropriate, show respect, and follow the rules of school and other places a child goes."

Teaching. Remind yourself that learning takes time, patience, and practice. Show or explain how your child can get what she wants—attention, power, control—by using appropriate language.

Solving the Problem

What to Do

Make Rules About Language

Say, "Those words you used, '_____' and '____,' show disrespect and are bad manners. We have a family rule to respect others, just as we want to be respected. So what other words could we use instead of these disrespectful ones?" Then brainstorm new words to use ("Banana Cake" for someone who is not nice, for example). These words give your child something to say that does not engage someone in a war of words but helps express what she feels.

Reinforce Good Coping Skills

When you hear people not swearing when they are mad, point it out. Say, "I feel so good when people are kind and use nice words, like Mr. Wilson. Even when he's mad, he just says that he is angry and explains what is upsetting him. That way, he can solve the problem that's upsetting him without swearing."

Talk About Feelings

If your child uses swear words when she is angry, offer her the same substitute words you use. Then talk about her feelings to help her learn nonoffensive ways of expressing and reducing her anger and tolerating frustration when things don't go her way. Make it okay to express happiness, too, without cursing and swearing. Teach your child by saying, "What could we say when we're excited, without using a swear word?" (Examples: Hooray! Wow! Terrific!)

Teach Your Child Empathy

Tell your child that the word she used is disrespectful and can hurt a person's feelings. Calmly and kindly ask her how she would feel if she heard words that hurt her feelings; then tell her that it is best to do things that make people feel good. Using good manners accomplishes that goal. (See "Bad Manners," page 38.)

Use Grandma's Rule When Language Is Abusive

When older children and teens swear to hurt someone, that act has to be treated as a form of aggression. (See "Aggressive Behavior / Hurting Others: Hitting, Biting, and Bullying," page 30.) Calmly say, "You've chosen to swear at me to hurt me, and that is against our rules. I am taking away your privileges [cell phone, electronic devices, time with friends] until you apologize. The right thing to do is to tell the person you hurt that you are sorry and do something kind for her. When you apologize, then you can have your privileges back."

What Not to Do

Don't Wash Out Her Mouth with Soap

Punishment of bad words simply drives the words underground. Your child will quickly learn that she can use the offending words when you aren't around to hear them.

Don't Shame Your Child

Shaming tells your child that she is a bad person when her only problem is that she has learned some inappropriate behavior. Rather than shaming, tell her that you love her but that you don't love the word she used and that you want her not to use it any more.

Don't Give Bad Words Too Much Power

Making too big a deal of it when your child tries out an occasional bad word can give the word tremendous power. Don't get angry or upset about her use of a swear word, and keep in mind that laughing when a child uses a swear word also gives it power.

Preventing the Problem

Watch Your Language

The most effective way to prevent your child from hearing and repeating in-appropriate language is to clean up your own language. This may be more difficult to do than it seems because swearing is a habit that you might not even notice and can be hard to change.

Monitor Places Where Bad Language May Be Heard

Make sure your parenting team watches the language that they use around your child. If Grandpa swears all the time, see if he will follow your rule about not swearing within earshot of your child.

Don't Expose Your Child to Media Produced for Adults

Adult-oriented programs continue to push the limits of language and violence.

Case History: Jackson Discovers Bad Words

Four-year-old Jackson was bright and busy, both at home and at preschool. He could tell in detail and with much color all about the events that took place during his day. After school one day, Jackson was telling Hannah, his mother, about the game that he and his friends were playing with a ball. He then described what happened when the ball knocked over a glass of water used to clean paintbrushes.

"It made a really big f—ing mess," he gleefully said. Hannah was truly shocked by Jackson's choice of language.

"Where did you learn the word 'f—ing'?" Hannah angrily asked.

"That's what Dad said when he dropped a can of paint in the garage," he answered. Jackson looked frightened—he didn't like to see his mother upset.

"That's a rude word," Hannah explained more calmly. "We don't need rude words like that to say what we want to say. Can you think of another polite word you could use?"

After thinking for a few minutes, Jackson answered, "I could just say it was a big mess. That's what Grandma says sometimes."

"Oh, I like that, and yes, I've heard Grandma say that, too. Jackson, I don't want you using that other word anymore. It is disrespectful and bad manners, and I know you want to show that you use respectful, good manners."

"Okay, Mom, I'm sorry," Jackson said and went off to play.

Hannah made a note to talk to her husband about his use of language.

~~~~~~~~~~~~~~~~~~~~~~~~~~~~~~~~

DAWDLES

- Won't hurry
- Won't get in the car
- Won't get out of the car
- Is slow to get dressed
- Finds things to do instead of what you ask

Because time is a concept that has little or no meaning to very young children, hurrying has no great advantages to them. Getting a child to hurry amid all sorts of exciting distractions—such as toys, TV, or even his own imagination—seems like a lost cause. And often you are urging him to hurry to do something he has little interest in, even though you do!

When you are pressed for time and have to live by the clock, your anxiety can easily become your child's anxiety; but unlike you, he can't understand the stress he's feeling. He just knows that you are upset. Better to let him feel as if he's in control so you can avoid a power struggle. Getting angry because he's dawdling prevents you from becoming the caring adult he needs. So instead, use the following suggestions to motivate him to move to the ticking of your clock.

Healthy Mind S.E.T.

Self-Talk. Keep your self-talk positive. Say to yourself, "It's not awful that my child is dawdling; it's just inconvenient. I can handle this."

Empathy. Put yourself in your child's shoes by thinking, "My agenda is to accomplish something, such as get in the car, and my child's agenda is to do whatever he wants to do. I can understand that he may not want to move quickly—so I need to help him meet my goal of moving faster than he may want."

Teaching. Remind yourself that learning takes time, patience, and practice. Show or explain how your child can stay focused on moving quickly when you need him to.

Solving the Problem

What to Do

Play Beat-the-Clock and Use Grandma's Rule

Set the timer on your phone and say, "I think you can get dressed [or whatever you want your child to do] before the timer sounds." This is a motivational technique that uses your child's competitive nature to encourage him to complete tasks on your timetable. And you can also use Grandma's Rule by saying, "When you beat the timer, then you may play for ten minutes before we leave for school." This lets your child see for himself that good things come to those who stay on a schedule.

Make It Easy for Your Child to Move at Your Pace

Ask motivating questions and play simple games to disguise hurrying. For example, encourage your child to get ready by having him guess what Grandma has waiting for him to eat for lunch at her house. Or ask your child to run to your arms when you want him to hurry along the path to your car. You can also run races with your child to get him from one place to another.

Reward Movement as Well as Results

Motivate your child to complete a task by encouraging him along the way. For example, say, "I like the way you're getting dressed so quickly. Thanks for helping us be on time," rather than waiting until he's done and only saying, "Thank you for getting dressed."

Use Gentle Guidance

You may need to gently move your child through the task at hand (getting in the car, getting dressed, and so on) to teach him that the world goes on regardless of his agenda at the moment.

Use Grandma's Rule

If your child is dawdling because he wants to do what he wants while you want him to move along, use Grandma's Rule. For example, say, "When you've finished getting dressed, then you may play with your train."

Involve Him in Solving the Dawdling Problem

When children are involved in the solution, they feel they have power and control, and they can rise to the occasion. Say, "We seem to have a problem getting ready on time for school. Help me come up with a way for us to be on time." Then praise his suggestions, and tell him how helpful he has been.

What Not to Do

Don't Lose Control

If you're in a hurry and your child is not, don't slow both of yourselves down even more by giving him attention for dawdling (by nagging or yelling at him to get going, for example). Getting angry will only encourage your child to exercise power over you through his easygoing pace.

Don't Nag

Nagging your child to hurry up when he's dawdling only gives him attention for not moving. Disguise a hurry-up technique by turning it into a game, such as Beat-the-Clock.

Don't Dawdle Yourself

Getting your child ready to go somewhere only to have him wait for you tells him that you don't really mean what you say. Don't announce that you're ready to go to the store, for example, when you're not.

Preventing the Problem

Try to Be an On-Time Person

Being an on-time person helps your child understand the importance of meeting time goals and builds his empathy for others. Saying, "We must hurry to get ready, so we can be at school on time and not keep your teacher waiting," motivates your child to move more quickly and helps him make the connection between being on time and preventing the impact of lateness on others.

Try to Allow Lead Time

If you're in a hurry, waiting for your dawdling child may lead you to lose your cool and be that much later. To avoid the anxiety that hurrying can create, make every effort to allow enough time to get ready for outings. Dawdling is a typical response to movement by someone who doesn't understand why hurrying is better than whatever he is currently doing.

Establish and Maintain a Schedule

Since a child needs routine and consistency in his daily life and tends to dawdle more when his routine is broken, establish time limits and a regular pattern of eating, playing, bathing, and sleeping. This will help to familiarize him with the time frame on which you want him to operate.

Case History: Dawdling Allison

Three-year-old Allison had a knack for noticing blades of grass or toying with her shoestrings instead of doing what was necessary at the moment. These behaviors were fine ways to explore her world, of course, but not when she needed to be focused on getting to school.

Grandma Harris, Allison's daily babysitter, found herself getting angry and nearly dragging her granddaughter to the preschool door. "Hurry! Stop dawdling!" she would command, but Allison was oblivious to any encouragement to do things faster than she wanted.

Feeling helpless, angry, and resentful toward her favorite granddaughter, Grandma Harris finally told her daughter and Allison's mom, Joanie, that she could no longer care for Allison. Joanie advised Grandma Harris to praise Allison's attempts at not dawdling and to ignore her when she dawdled. Joanie also encouraged her mother to offer Allison rewards for hurrying—something that came naturally to Grandma Harris, who enjoyed bringing her grandchildren presents.

Grandma Harris worked with her daughter on a plan for dawdling Allison. They decided to use Grandma Harris's smartphone timer; because Allison was only three, they planned to break down the process of her getting ready into small segments. That way, she wouldn't feel overwhelmed by the goal. After Joanie left for work, Grandma Harris said, "It's time to get ready for school. Can you beat the timer getting your pajamas off? Let's see!"

"I can do that!" Allison said, and began pulling off the fuzzy flannels. Then the timer was set for tights, then skirt, then shirt, then shoes. Allison was ready in record time.

"Oh, my!" Grandma Harris exclaimed. "Look at you all dressed and ready, and we have time to play that game you wanted to play."

And so it went. Allison could soon get herself completely ready without any problem. Grandma Harris was pleased with her granddaughter's progress, lavished much praise on her little one, and began to enjoy getting her grandchild ready for preschool again. She felt more in control of the time frame in which they would both operate. And just as importantly, she learned that she and Allison could manage other problems with teaching tools, not temper tantrums!

~~~~~~~~~~~~~~~~~~~~

DESTROYS PROPERTY

- Writes and colors on walls and cabinets
- Tears up books, boxes, napkins, and other household items
- Breaks toys and electronic equipment, such as phones, televisions, computers
- Draws on furniture
- Throws things
- Bangs holes in the walls with toys
- Picks at clothing until it makes a hole
- Paints, colors, draws on "good" clothes

The line between destructive and creative play is not drawn for young children until parents draw it for them. So starting before your child reaches her first birthday and continuing after, draw the line by telling and showing her what she may and may not draw on, tear up, or take apart. The lesson is to help her learn what is a toy and what is not, so she will not destroy property in other situations—at other houses, at school, and so on. However, it will be necessary for you to remind her from time to time of your rules about taking care of things. In general, consistently teach your child to be proud of and to care for her things, and to be creative in appropriate ways, such as on drawing paper (not on walls or cabinets) or with a take-apart play phone (not your real phone).

Healthy Mind S.E.T.

Self-Talk. Keep your self-talk positive. Say to yourself, "It is important for my child to take care of his clothes and toys, and I can teach him how to do so."

Empathy. Put yourself in your child's shoes by thinking, "I can imagine how my child feels. He doesn't understand the value of things and isn't worried about damaging the wall. He just wants to color on it!"

Teaching. Remind yourself that learning takes time, patience, and practice. Show or explain to your child how to take care of his own home, toys, and clothes, as well as things that belong to others.

Solving the Problem

What to Do

Teach Your Child to Ask If Something Can Be Marked On, Cut, or Hit If He's Not Sure

Teach your child to ask you if he can use his drumstick to beat on the refrigerator, for example, if he's not sure if it's okay. His asking serves two learning goals: he gets in the habit of asking questions if he doesn't know an answer, and he doesn't destroy something simply because he doesn't know if it was right or wrong to do so.

Teach Your Child to Practice Empathy

Children are born with the capacity to be empathetic, so from the earliest age, make understanding the feelings of others part of your everyday teaching. When your child destroys things, for example, calmly and kindly say, "How do you think your sister felt when you ripped up her homework? How would you feel if she ripped up something of yours? You wouldn't like it, right? We want to take care of other people's property the same way we would want them to take care of ours."

Supervise Play

By being there, you can guide the play into more gentle activities and stop destruction before it starts.

Praise Care of Things

While your child is playing nicely with his toys, praise him for following the rule and taking care of his things. Take time to say, "You are taking such good care of your farm animal toys. They will last a long time, so you can have them to play with every day."

Use Cleanup as a Consequence to Destructive Play

When your child makes a mess, use Grandma's Rule to get the crayon cleaned off the wall. Say, "When you have scrubbed the crayon off, then you may play with your toys." This approach also teaches her how to clean walls!

Use Reprimands

Briefly tell your child what she did wrong by giving a reprimand. Say, for example, "Stop tearing the book," and then tell her why it was wrong by saying, "We want to keep our books nice so we can read them." Then tell her what she could have done instead, saying, "Books are for reading. Let's read the book."

These statements don't remind her of the unacceptable behavior but teach her the acceptable one.

Take Your Child to Calm Time

If you've given your child a reprimand and she destroys property again, repeat the reprimand, and take her to Calm Time. Tell her to think about how to take care of things rather than damaging them.

What Not to Do

Don't Overreact

If your child breaks something, don't throw a tantrum yourself. Your anger communicates the idea that you care more for your things than for your child. Make sure your degree of disappointment over something being destroyed isn't out of proportion to what happened.

Don't Overly Punish

Just because your child damaged something valuable to you doesn't give you permission to damage your child. Rather than punishing her, put the valuable item away until she's old enough to understand its value.

Don't Confuse by Destroying Things You Said Not To

When you tell your child to take care of something and not damage it, she will be confused if you damage that same thing. For example, telling her not to color on your magazines and then letting her cut pictures out of the same magazines will be confusing. Instead, explain the difference between old and new, and tell her to ask if what she wants to color or cut is old or new.

Don't Replace Broken Toys

If your child deliberately breaks one of his toys, don't replace it. If he knows that a new one will magically appear, he won't learn to take care of the toys he has.

Preventing the Problem

Provide Toys That Are Strong Enough to Be Investigated but Not Destroyed

It's natural for children to try to take apart and put together toys that lend themselves to this kind of activity—as well as ones that don't. To stimulate the kind of creative play you want to encourage, fill your child's play area with toys she can do something with—like stacking toys, push-button games, play workbenches, and so on—in addition to ones that just sit there, such as stuffed animals, for imaginative play.

Give Her Plenty of Things to Wear and Tear

Provide lots of old clothes and materials for crafts, dress-up, painting, or other activities, so your young child won't substitute new or valuable items for her play projects.

Make Rules About Caring for and Playing with Toys

Young children don't innately know the value of things or how to play with everything appropriately, so teach them, for example, to use crayons to draw in coloring books, instead of on books and newspapers. Say, "Your coloring book is the only paper you can color on with markers right now." Or, "The toy golf club is for hitting a ball, not a person or the wall or furniture."

With regard to other potentially damaging behavior, say, "Books are not for tearing. If you want to tear paper, ask me, and I'll give you some to tear," or, "This remote control car won't run anymore if we take it apart. You can take the screws out of this broken toy to see what's inside."

Be Consistent

Don't confuse your child by letting her damage or destroy something she shouldn't. Also, she won't know what to expect and won't understand if you stop her fun by reprimanding her for something that was formerly okay.

Teach Her the Importance of Caring for Things

Increase your chances of keeping destruction to a minimum by letting your child know when she's taking wonderful care of her toys. This reminds her of the rule, helps her feel good about her behavior, and makes her proud of her possessions.

Model Caring for Things

As you take care of your own possessions, point out to your child what you are doing to make sure that your computer doesn't break, your books aren't used as a holder for a coffee cup, or your phone doesn't get damaged.

Case History: Tim the Terror

Walt and Becky Brady knew they had a destructive three-year-old long before the preschool teacher called them in for a conference. They could have bent the teacher's ear with tales of purple crayon on the yellow dining-room wallpaper, cars and trucks with wheels ripped off, and mosaics made out of pages from hardcover books. The last straw for them was when Tim used indelible markers on Becky's computer screen.

When the Bradys arrived home from their conference, the babysitter reported that Tim had drawn on the tile floor again with his crayons. "When are you going to stop all this destruction, Tim?" Walt screamed as he sent Tim to his room. A little later, the Bradys discovered that Tim had torn up three of his picture books while he was in his room.

The Bradys decided to change their approach. Instead of yelling at Tim, they focused on teaching him to take care of his belongings. The next time they found Tim tearing a page from a book, they said, "Now you have to fix this book, Tim." They took him by the hand to the tape drawer and helped him tear off the appropriate amount of tape to repair the book.

In addition, Walt began to satisfy his son's curiosity by having Tim help him fix things around the house. Tim was now learning about screwdrivers, wrenches, and other tools, and he was being a helper instead of a destroyer. And then an interesting thing happened: Tim seldom repeated a destructive behavior once he'd fixed the damage.

They taught him to ask them if something was okay to hit or tear up, if he wasn't sure. And whenever he did damage something, his parents explained again what he was allowed to cut, mark on, or tear. The Bradys also encouraged Tim to be as responsible for his possessions as they were for theirs. Eventually, Tim began to embrace this responsibility. He beamed with pride when his parents praised his caring for his books, toys, and stuffed animals in a responsible way. And he was quick to fix what he accidentally broke. As Tim's behavior became less destructive, his parents still didn't expect him to care for his toys as they did for their adult possessions. But they were careful to model neat behavior, so Tim could see that they practiced what they preached about respecting property.

EATS TOO MUCH

- Overeats
- Focuses almost constantly on food
- Asks for more of the same food without eating other foods
- Sneaks food
- Wants to eat all the time
- Eats too fast
- Eats everything and asks for more at each meal

Because overeating is a symptom of a problem, not the problem itself, try to discover the reasons behind your child's seemingly bottomless pit of a stomach. Possible explanations include habit, emotional comfort, boredom, mimicry, or the desire for attention. Help him find ways to satisfy his needs and wants without overeating. However, it may also be confusing for you to be able to differentiate between what is overeating and what is a child's hunger needing to be satisfied. It can be hard to tell, even for us adults. Ask for help from your child's health care provider if you are not sure if his eating is normal. Avoid putting a child on a diet that is not medically supervised.

NOTE: See also "Not Eating," page 107, and "Plays with Food," page 128, for other food-related issues.

Healthy Mind S.E.T.

Self-Talk. Keep your self-talk positive. Say to yourself, "I don't like it that my child eats too much, but I can help her learn healthy eating habits."

Empathy. Put yourself in your child's shoes by thinking, "My child does not understand that eating more after she is full is not a healthy habit. I still have trouble practicing that myself. Eating makes her feel good, so finding other ways to feel good is important."

Teaching. Remind yourself that learning takes time, patience, and practice. Show or explain to your child how to recognize when she is hungry or full, eat slowly, and enjoy other activities besides eating.

Solving the Problem

What to Do

Teach Your Child How to Eat Slowly and Recognize When He Is Hungry or Full

Appetite is a complicated topic. Some children don't know how to understand the feelings of hunger instead of being full—they both feel the same in some children's minds. In addition, a full stomach is only part of what causes someone to feel satisfied after a meal. The brain must also receive a series of signals from digestive hormones. Eating slowly doesn't always work, but it is helpful to give time for these signals to reach the brain.

Ask your child to describe the feeling when he says he's hungry. Then ask him the same questions after he's eaten. This ongoing conversation also helps set up the habit of you and your child talking about all of his feelings, physical and emotional—a healthy habit for both of you in creating a relationship built on love, empathy, and trust.

Use Grandma's Rule

To help your child focus on moving, rather than on eating, say, "When you have played outside for half an hour, then you may have a snack."

Provide Healthy Meals

Providing meals made up of vegetables, fruits, proteins, and whole grains is important because they not only are good for overall health but also satisfy hunger.

Change Time at the Table as She Grows

Toddlers may not have the attention span or the desire to sit at the table with you for as long as you would like. So feeding your toddler more just to get her to stay there is often the remedy! Observe how much your child usually eats at a certain age, and when she is done, offer the chance to play near the table while you continue to sit. That way, she is not set up to continue to eat, but you can keep an eye on her while you have fun chatting. As she grows, her attention span for sitting will, too. And she will learn from your modeling what social skills look like at the table.

Provide Pleasurable Activities Other Than Eating

Get to know what your child likes to do besides eat. Suggest these activities after a meal or snack to change his focus away from food. It takes about twenty minutes or so for his brain to let him know that he's not hungry anymore. Say, "I love it when you draw me a picture. I'll get the markers and paper." Give him positive attention for things that are not food related, such as his artwork.

Provide Nutritious Between-Meal Snacks

A well-timed snack can prevent your child from getting overly hungry and gorging at mealtime when it finally arrives. Avoid salty or sweet foods and carbonated soda. Vegetable, fruit, and protein snacks, such as peanut butter on celery or on an apple are nutritious ways to accomplish this goal.

Watch When Your Child Overeats

Try to discover why your child overeats by seeing if he turns to food when he's bored, mad, sad, watching others eat, or wanting attention from you. Help him resolve his feelings by talking with you about what's on his mind. Listen to his feelings, and help him come up with solutions to solve the problems, instead of using food to help soothe his upset feelings.

Praise Wise Food Selections

You can mold your child's food preferences by your tone of voice and by encouraging him to eat foods that you want him to favor. Whenever your child picks up an apple, for example, say, "That's a great choice you made for a snack. I'm glad you're taking care of yourself so well by eating yummy treats like apples."

Encourage Exercise

Overweight children often don't eat any more than normal-weight children; they just don't burn off enough calories through exercise. If you live in a cold climate, suggest physical activities to do inside in the winter, like dancing or jumping rope. In the summer, try activities such as swimming, walking, baseball, soccer, and swinging. All these not only are good for your child's physical development but also relieve tension, give him fresh air, and build his coordination and strength. Your participation will make exercise even more fun for your child.

What Not to Do

Don't Brag About How Much You Could Eat When You Were Younger

Doing so models overeating as a goal to be proud of, which encourages your child to overeat.

Don't Reward with Food

Don't offer food as a present or reward. This helps you avoid teaching your child that eating means more than satisfying hunger.

Don't Give In to His Desire to Overeat

Your child may keep asking for another hot dog, for example, after he's eaten two. Use common sense about quantities of foods that you give your child to consume at a sitting. This is your job as a caring, supportive, protective parent.

Just because your child wants more food doesn't mean he should have it at that moment. Satisfying his hunger is important, so say, "I think two hot dogs are enough for now. Let's play for a few minutes, and then we can talk about whether or not you are still hungry." In this way, you are teaching him what is an appropriate amount of a certain food while showing respect for his desires and wishes.

Don't Give Treats When Your Child Is Upset

Your child may begin to associate food with emotional (rather than physical) nourishment if you consistently offer treats to comfort him when he's upset.

Don't Consistently Allow Food While You're Watching TV

Avoid teaching your child to associate food with TV. It's a good idea to limit his screen time for many reasons (see "Screen Time / Screen Addiction," page 142), including because television advertising bombards your child with food-related messages. If possible, record his favorite shows and zip through the commercials.

Don't Give Junk Food as Snacks

What you allow for snacks and meals is what your child will expect. Food preferences are learned, not inborn, and empty calories are designed to make us crave more of the same.

Don't Make Fun of Your Child If He Overeats or If He's Overweight

Calling him a name, such as "Chubby," doesn't solve the problem of overeating. It does create another problem: it becomes his identity, so he thinks that chubby is who he is rather than the result of his eating too much food, eating too quickly, and eating unhealthy food.

Preventing the Problem

Model a Healthy Attitude About Food

Your relationship with food is contagious. When you complain about dieting or being too fat, or brag about how much you can eat, for example, your child learns that food has power beyond being enjoyable and making him healthy. Since moderation is the key to health, moderate your talk as well as your behavior. Eating disorders in young children have become much more prevalent, in part because of our talking about food all the time, watching it being prepared in TV programs, and finding food everywhere that may not have anything to do with hunger (think of mindlessly eating doughnuts and snacks during work meetings). Being in a dieting- and body-image-obsessed culture adds to the risk of our children developing eating disorders.

Become Informed About the Appropriate Amount and Kinds of Foods for Your Child

Since most children don't make the buying decisions—they don't go to the grocery store or have food delivered at home—it's up to you to establish healthy eating habits, the earlier the better. Consult your child's health care provider for answers to specific nutrition questions or recommendations about your child's food and drink that are right for his age, developmental stage, and health needs. For more information about recommended guidelines for young children's nutrition, go to "Ages and Stages" on the website Healthy Children (healthychildren.org/english/ages-stages/pages/default.aspx), and select the "Nutrition" link under your child's age group.

Only Have Healthy Foods in Your Home

Keep candy, sweetened drinks, and other foods and drinks that have little nutritional value out of your overeater's reach so he won't be tempted to choose them. If you don't have unhealthy foods around, your child can't eat them, and you won't be tempted to use those foods as a bribe.

Teach When, How, and Where Eating Is Allowed

Restrict eating to the kitchen and dining room only. Slow down the pace of eating, and teach your child that food is eaten from a plate or bowl, instead of directly from the sack, package, or refrigerator. That will help him take the time to eat with a focus—and actually think about what he's eating and notice what it looks like on the plate. Slowing down and being mindful of the process of eating aids in digestion, keeps us from taking big mouthfuls or stuffing food in our mouths, and helps us focus on eating, not simply rush through the experience. Taking more time between mouthfuls also allows our brains to get the message that we're full before we've eaten more than we need.

Control Your Own Eating Habits

If you snack on empty-calorie junk foods all day, your children will be inclined to do the same. The same is true for eating the whole pizza (that is meant to serve four) or the entire bag of potato chips (which also serves four).

Case History: "No More Cookies!"

Three-year-old Olivia Hanlon was getting a reputation at preschool and family functions for being a "walking bottomless pit." If food was in sight, Olivia ate it. She never seemed to be full.

"No, you can't have another cookie, Olivia!" Eva Hanlon would scream every time she caught her daughter with her hand in the cookie jar. "You've had enough cookies to last your lifetime!"

But neither angry outbursts nor the threat of taking away her tricycle lessened Olivia's desire to finish every morsel in a box or on a plate. Eva decided to consult her pediatrician to learn how to change Olivia's eating habits. The doctor provided a nutrition plan and recipe suggestions specifically tailored for Olivia. The doctor also explained that when children eat very fast, as Eva had said Olivia did, their brains don't tell them they are full until later.

The next day, Olivia wolfed down the suggested amount of oatmeal and asked for more, but Eva finally had an answer that wasn't angry or insulting: "I'm glad you liked the oatmeal, Olivia. We can have some more tomorrow morning. Let's go read that new book now." Eva knew that the amount that she had given Olivia was nutritionally adequate and that her stomach would eventually send her brain the message that it was full. This made it easier for Eva to stand firm when Olivia begged for more oatmeal. It was also easier for Eva to plan each meal, because she knew what amounts were enough to nourish her daughter.

At meals, Olivia's parents engaged her in conversation and praised her slower eating pace. They also ended their steady supply of cookies, so Olivia started to try new foods that were tasty and more nutritious. Eva praised Olivia's choices every time she chose a healthy food, saying "That's great that you picked carrot sticks for a snack."

FIGHTS CLEANUP ROUTINES: BATHING AND DIAPERING

- Won't get in the bathtub
- Won't get out of the bathtub
- Fights washing her hair
- Throws water out of the bathtub
- Fights diapering
- Takes off her diaper
- Didn't bathe or shower when he said he did

From a no-more-tears formula shampoo to disposable diapers, products abound to make bathing, diapering, and shampooing as painless as possible for children and their parents. It's predicted (as these manufacturers know) that little ones will find cleanup routines distasteful, so don't feel alone as your child fights rinsing and soaking and changing. Making the tasks into fun time with you—singing, playing with toys, rubbing your child's back—will turn the attention to the play, instead of the "work" of getting clean. A win-win for you both.

Make the distinction between what products irritate your child physically (does it burn his eyes? irritate his bottom?) and mentally (are all soaps and diapers undesirable?) by seeing whether his protests are telling you more than just that he doesn't like the bath or diaper change. Switch from products that irritate the skin to those that are better for your child, after consulting with your child's health care professional.

NOTE: *Older children may do the opposite—fight getting out of the tub. When you think that time's up for the bath and your child doesn't, teach your child that getting out of the tub is sometimes as important as getting in by using "Beat-the-Clock" and other problem-solvers here.*

Healthy Mind S.E.T.

Self-Talk. Keep your self-talk positive. Say to yourself, "My child may not like getting his diaper changed, taking a bath, or getting out of the tub, but I can make it fun and not a power struggle."

Empathy. Put yourself in your child's shoes by thinking, "It's not important to my child to get clean; he doesn't want to stop having fun in order to get cleaned up. I get that. I sometimes feel the same way!"

Teaching. Remind yourself that learning takes time, patience, and practice. Show or explain that being clean feels so good, that your child is doing something good for himself, and that getting out of or in the tub and getting a clean diaper can be fun.

Solving the Problem

What to Do

Play Beat-the-Clock to Get in the Bath

For those children who slow to a crawl and find a pile of things to do in order to avoid getting cleaned up, getting changed or bathed, or brushing their teeth, playing Beat-the-Clock can save the day. Say, "Let's see if you can get ready for your bath before the timer rings." Then set your phone timer for a few minutes. Say, "The timer is going. Can you be in the bath before the timer goes off?" While your child hurries to the bathtub, praise his effort, and when he beats the clock, reward him with a hug.

Make Sure Your Child Has Really Taken a Bath or Shower When He Tells You He Has

Many children, particularly in the eight- to twelve-year-old age group, don't want to stop what they're doing and see no reason to shower or bathe, so they fake it. A head that's gotten wet under the sink faucet may look like a shower was taken when the body odor tells a different story. When your child fakes a shower, tell him that you will come into the bathroom to supervise. Many children want to avoid that close supervision, so they negotiate for trust. The sniff test will verify that they have indeed taken a shower or bath. And here's another test: clean skin is slick; dirty, sweaty skin is sticky. So do the touch test!

Remain Calm and Ignore the Noise

A calm mood is contagious when dealing with your upset child. So don't pay attention to the noise—just keep caring for and loving your child while you bathe or diaper him. He will learn that noise doesn't stop the process of getting clean, which is the opposite of what he wants. Say to yourself, "I know my child needs to be diapered. If I don't pay attention to his noise, I'll get this done faster and more effectively."

Have Fun in the Process

Distract and pay positive attention: talk to your child, recite rhymes, and sing songs as you describe what you are doing that is so good for your child— diapering or bathing him.

Encourage Your Child by Praising His Help

Ask your child to wash his own tummy, rub on the soap, or open the diaper to give him a feeling of controlling and participating in his personal hygiene. Even the slightest sign of cooperation is a signal for praise.

Also, pour on the words of encouragement. The more your child gets attention for acting as you'd prefer, the more he'll repeat the action to get your praise. Say, "I really like how you put that shampoo on your hair," or, "That's great, the way you're sitting up in the tub," or, "Thanks for lying down so nicely while I diaper you. It's so nice that you are helping with your bath."

Use Grandma's Rule

Let your child know that when he's done something you want him to do (take a bath), he can do something he wants to do (read a story). Say, "When your bath is over, then we'll have a story," or, "When we're finished with your diaper, then you may play with your blocks."

Compliment Your Child When Cleanup Is Finished

Tell your child how delightful he looks and smells. Ask him to go look in the mirror. This will remind him of why he needs to have a bath or have his diaper changed. Learning to take pride in being clean will help him make cleanliness a priority.

Bathroom Cleanup

Some children love their bath so much that they want to share it with everybody, so splashing water all over becomes the game of the day. Depending on your bathroom, you can let water be splashed all over and clean it up, with your child's help of course, after the bath. But if you want it to stop, use

Grandma's Rule. When splashing starts, say, "I'm sorry you're splashing water all over. The water needs to stay in the tub. When you keep it in the tub, you may stay and play. If you can't, bath time will be over." Remember, Grandma's Rule is a contract that tells the child he gets what he wants when he follows the rule.

What Not to Do

Don't Demand Cooperation

Just because you demand that your child get diapered doesn't mean he's going to lie still while you do it. Don't punish lack of cooperation. Acting rough and tough yourself only teaches him to be rough and tough, too.

Don't Make Cleanup Painful

Try to make cleanup as comfortable as possible for your child. Provide towels he can use to wipe his eyes, make the bathwater temperature just right, wrap him in a robe after you're done, and so on.

Don't Avoid Cleanup

Just because your child resists doesn't mean you should back down. Resistance to cleanup can be overcome by persistence, practice, and patience.

Preventing the Problem

Compromise on Cleanup Times and Places

Be flexible about cleanup routines, such as where you diaper your baby or toddler (for example, on the couch or standing up), when you wash his hair, or when he bathes. To avoid your child fighting cleanup routines, fit them into his schedule as much as possible, so he won't have to stop a favorite activity just to clean up.

Involve Your Child in the Process

Help your child play a part in the cleanup or diapering routine. Ask him to bring you things he can carry (according to his age, skill level, and ability to follow directions). Let him pick a favorite toy or towel, for example, to give him a feeling of control over the bath time routine. Letting your child help with the shampoo or hold the washcloth over the eyes helps her feel that she's not the victim but an active participant in an unpleasant activity.

Prepare Your Child for the Cleanup Event

Give your child some warning before a bath, for example, to make the transition from playtime to bath time less abrupt. Set your phone timer for a few minutes and say, "When the timer rings, it will be time for the tub," or, "In a few minutes, we will change your diaper," or, "When we finish this book, it will be time for your bath."

Gather Materials Before Putting Your Child in the Tub

If your child is too young to help you prepare, make sure you get things ready before beginning the cleanup. This helps avoid unnecessary delays and prevents your needing to leave him alone in the tub (never do that!).

Develop a Positive Attitude

Your child will pick up on the dread in your voice if you announce bath time as if it's a prison sentence. If you sound worried or anxious, you're telling him it must be as horrible as he thought. Your attitude is contagious, so make it one that you want imitated.

Make the Bathtub an Ocean of Adventure

Lots of water toys and pouring cups and pitchers can make tub time more fun. Beware, however—if a young child has a cup, he's going to try to drink the bathwater!

Case History: Bathtub Oceans of Fun

Carol and Phil Porter bathed and shampooed their two-year-old daughter, Lauren, just as they thought most parents they knew did. But they feared something was wrong with Lauren when she screamed and fought her way through these normal cleanup routines. The Porters never had experienced this problem with their older daughter, Elizabeth, and none of their friends had ever complained about it.

The Porters talked to their pediatrician, who assured them that the soaps, water, and towels were not harmful or irritating. Phil thought stricter discipline was needed, but they eventually agreed that the best approach was to make cleanup more appetizing to Lauren. The only water-related activity Lauren had enjoyed was swimming in the ocean during their summer vacation. So the Porters decided to call bath time Oceans of Fun.

That evening, they set the phone timer to sound when it was time to get in the "ocean." (Of course, they kept the phone far away from the water!) During their trip, they had always set the phone timer to sound when they could go in the real ocean, because Lauren was always begging to get in the water. They hoped this technique would prove helpful at home in Minneapolis, too. "When the timer sounds, it will be time to play Oceans of Fun," Carol told Lauren. "Let's finish this book while we're waiting."

When the timer went off, Lauren and her mother gathered towels and soap, and Lauren excitedly asked questions about the new game. Lauren smiled with delight as her mom led her to the bathroom, where she found the bluest "ocean" she'd ever seen (the result of blue bubble bath) and jaunty boats cruising around a toy ship holding a container of soap (toys Carol bought to add to the experience).

Lauren jumped in without a push or an invitation and began playing with the ocean toys. Her mother started singing a song about a tugboat, and she gave Lauren a handful of shampoo to wash her own hair for the first time. The cleanup continued without yelling or screaming—and with just a little too much splashing. Carol began bathing Lauren in the ocean at least once a day, to give her opportunities to learn how to splash less, wash herself more carefully, and enjoy the experience.

GETS INTO EVERYTHING

- Plays with your jewelry, makeup, plants, and items in your desk and kitchen drawers
- Plays with the water in the toilet
- Pulls everything out of kitchen cabinets
- Crawls under furniture, unplugs lamps, and so forth

Just getting into first gear in their first year or so, children feel the joy of exploration from their toes to their teeth. They don't automatically know what's off-limits and what isn't, but by about age two or so, they're able to make the distinction if you've set them straight. While restricting the adventures of your little explorers, keep in mind the balance you're trying to strike between letting normal, healthy curiosity be expressed and teaching what behavior is and isn't appropriate. The only way children will know that dry pasta stays in the package (even though it's fun to play with all the "sticks"), for example, is if you teach him that pasta is for eating, not playing. Those are simple lessons—but important ones that speak to parents being teachers of small and large lessons.

Healthy Mind S.E.T.

Self-Talk. Keep your self-talk positive. Say to yourself, "This is what normal, healthy, curious children do. This teachable moment helps me understand that my child hasn't learned yet what he may or may not explore to keep him safe."

Empathy. Put yourself in your child's shoes by thinking, "My agenda is to keep my child safe. Her agenda is to do what she wants and explore when and where she wants to, without recognizing the potential danger. I can understand why she likes to investigate drawers and cabinets—I'm glad she is curious!"

Teaching. Remind yourself that learning takes time, patience, and practice. Show or explain what is and isn't okay to play with or explore.

Solving the Problem

What to Do

Teach Your Child to Touch with Her Eyes, Not Her Hands

Tell your child that she may look at the big potted plant in the living room with her eyes but not with her hands. In a calm and kind tone of voice, say, "Stop. Touch with your eyes, not your hands," and show her what you mean by "touch with your eyes." This allows her the freedom to explore the item in a limited, controlled way. And it helps if you explore with her while describing what you see.

Keep the Bathroom Door Closed, Unless You Go There with Him

Young children love to play in water, so to prevent them from playing in the toilet water, keep the bathroom door closed until you are able to go there with your child. When you are there, teach him what the important things in the bathroom are for—toilet for going potty, sink for washing hands, tub for taking a bath. They don't know that it's not okay to flush the toilet over and over again, to unroll the toilet paper for yards and yards—the bathroom holds lots of adventures for young explorers. This teachable moment accomplishes a double lesson: learning the important skills of getting clean that happen in a bathroom and keeping your bathroom equipment (and your child) safe.

Make a Rule

Rules act as predictable guidelines for children. Telling your child the rules gives her boundaries that she needs. If your child gets into your jewelry, desk drawer, or makeup, for example, teach her to come to you first before playing with it. Say, "The rule is, if you want something, please come ask me if it's okay if you play with it."

Use Reprimands and Calm Time

Consistently reprimand your child for a repeated offense to teach her you mean what you say. Reprimand by saying calmly in a kind tone of voice, "Stop opening my desk drawer. Those things in there are not for you to play with. I'm sorry you're getting things out of my desk. The rule is that if you want something out of my desk drawer, you need to ask me."

If your child repeatedly gets into your makeup or desk drawer (and if that's against your rule), reprimand her again and take her to Calm Time to think about how to follow the rules and how to ask you if she wants to play with your makeup or things in the desk drawer.

Compliment Your Child When She Follows the Rules

Tell your child how proud you are of her for following the rules. Giving her that compliment will reward the behavior you want with attention, which will encourage her to do the right thing again. Say, "Thank you for coming to ask me if you could get the markers out of my desk," or "Thanks for asking if you can look at my makeup. Let me show you all the fun stuff in my makeup bag."

Pay Attention

It is impossible to know whether your young child is following your rules and staying out of danger if you are totally engrossed in your own activity. Keep your eyes on your child so you can be ready to guide her toward what is safe and not safe to explore.

What Not to Do

Don't Leave Guns or Knives Where Children Can Reach Them

No matter how much safety training children receive, the allure of weapons is too great to resist. Keep all guns locked up, each with its own approved trigger lock, and lock up the ammunition in a separate place that is inaccessible to children. Also, keep all knives locked away in a childproof place, no matter how old your child is. Just hiding guns and knives is not enough. Children are experts at finding hiding places. Better safe than sorry.

Don't Make Forbidden Things More Inviting by Getting Upset

If you become angry when your child breaks a rule, she'll see that she can get more of your attention from misbehavior and be encouraged to get into trouble more often. Even if she's not looking for attention, she will learn to sneak in her rule-breaking explorations if you overreact.

Don't Punish

Rather than punishing your child by spanking her for being naturally curious and getting into things, teach her how to use her curiosity safely—a skill that will serve her well her entire lifetime. Instead of trying to stamp out inappropriate behavior, emphasize the positive by teaching the behavior you want.

Preventing the Problem

Childproof Your Home

Keeping doors closed, stairways blocked, cabinets locked, and dangerous areas fenced off will reduce the number of times you have to say no to your child. Young children are busy establishing their independence and making their mark on the world, and they can't understand why they can't go wherever they want. Above all, lock up guns, knives, and other dangerous possessions where your child can't reach them.

Decide What's Off-Limits

Decide what your child's boundaries will be, and communicate this information early and often. For example, say, "You may play in the living room or in the kitchen, but not in Mommy or Daddy's office. I will keep the door closed to help you remember. When you want to go there, come get me, and we'll go there together."

Put Away Valuable Items You Don't Want Broken

A toddler or preschooler will not understand the difference between an expensive vase and a plastic one. Play it safe by removing valuable items until your little one won't grab for everything despite being told not to. Even older children (and adults!) can break valuables when engaged in rambunctious play, of course.

Teach Your Child How and When She Can Go into Off-Limits Areas

Explain to your child the acceptable ways of playing in off-limits areas. Never allowing her to go into a room, for example, makes her want to do it even more. Say, "You can go into Mommy's office, but come get me first." Know what your young child is doing and where she is doing it at all times, so she can safely explore her world.

Create a Special Place for Your Child's Things

It will take time for your child to learn what is okay to touch and not. So designate a special drawer or cabinet where her things are kept, to make it special for her to play with her toys freely and openly.

Case History: "Do Not Touch!"

"Curiosity killed the cat" was the line Sophia Stein remembered her mother saying to her when she rummaged through her mother's office desk, an off-limits place when Sophia was a youngster. Now she found her fifteen-month-old son, Sam, exploring off-limits lamp cords and plants. She knew he wasn't being intentionally naughty; he was behaving like a normally curious child.

But Sophia didn't think her reactions to his curiosity showed much self-discipline. "No! Do not touch!" she would shout whenever he got into things she had told him not to touch. She would spank him as punishment, but she eventually realized that Sam was only learning to avoid the spanking by committing his "crimes" behind her back.

So she decided to lock up things she didn't want him to touch, put breakable items out of reach, and keep an eye on him as much as possible.

"Stop! This is Mommy's! Touch with your eyes, not your hands," she said to Sam one particularly active morning when he had started taking everything out of a jewelry box she had forgotten to put on the top shelf. She removed the box and guided her son back to the kitchen, where they both had a good time taking the pots and pans out of the cabinet. They also played with a toy key and lockbox and several other toys that provided stimulation for his imagination and curiosity—toys that were appropriate for his age and appropriate for him to take apart and explore.

Once the dangerous and expensive things were removed from Sam's reach and replaced with things he could play with safely, the Steins' household became more pleasant. Sophia knew she would have to continue monitoring her son's curiosity even though her house was childproofed, but she let him have more freedom than before.

Months later, Sam demonstrated that he was learning the rules when he pointed to her tablet computer, which he knew was off-limits, and said, "Stop! Mommy's! Touch with eyes!" To reward his good behavior, Sophia gave him a sealed box of rice, which he loved to shake like a rattle. Everyone's "toys" were safe!

INTERRUPTS

- Demands your attention
- Talks to you while you're talking on the phone, texting, or checking email
- Won't let you work
- Interrupts you to ask a million questions

Our lives today are full of many ways to be interrupted at any time of the day or night—via social media, phone calls, emails, and texts. We can wait to answer the screens that ding and ping, but when our child interrupts what we are doing by saying, "Mommy, look at me!" or "Daddy, I want a drink!," it can stress us out more than the electronic messages. We want to pay attention to her, but we cannot immediately do so. She doesn't know that it's rude and disrespectful to interrupt us when we are talking with someone else or in a meeting. She just wants our attention!

This is the time to teach our child that it is not polite to interrupt, and that it is also disrespectful to ignore people who are standing right in front of us. Teaching her what we want her to do when she wants attention—practice patience and empathy—is the name of the game.

NOTE: *When you need to talk with your child because it is an emergency but he is talking to a friend, politely but firmly tell him you need to talk with him for a minute. Say, "Excuse me, Sam, I need to ask you a quick question." Modeling what you would like him to do when he needs to talk with you is a powerful way of showing, not just telling, him what you want to teach. It is important for your child to know that you can be interrupted if it is urgent to do so. Tending to your child when he* *absolutely needs you—he feels sick or is hurt or in danger—is your first responsibility, as is making sure you can get his attention when you need it.*

Healthy Mind S.E.T.

Self-Talk. Keep your self-talk positive. Say to yourself, "It's annoying when my child interrupts me, but I can teach her respect, patience, and empathy."

Empathy. Put yourself in your child's shoes by thinking, "I understand that my child thinks that the world revolves only around him. I also want to interrupt people sometimes to say what I want to say."

Teaching. Remind yourself that learning takes time, patience, and practice. Show or explain how to be patient and not interrupt someone, as well as how to do so with respect, if he needs immediate attention.

Solving the Problem

What to Do

Teach Your Child to Practice Empathy

Children are born with the capacity to be empathetic, so from the earliest age, make understanding the feelings of others part of your everyday lessons. When your child interrupts, for example, use a calm and kind tone of voice to say, "How do you think I feel when you interrupt me when I'm talking to Dad? How would you feel if I interrupted you when you were talking to your friend? We want to be polite and make people feel respected. Being able to wait until someone finishes what they are doing before paying attention to you is hard, but it's a polite way we show respect."

Provide Him with Special Toys, Activities, and Other Alternatives

Because a young child's most priceless possession is his parents' attention, he'll try anything to get it back when they are on the phone, computer, or tablet, or if another person takes his parents' attention away. To limit the tricks your child uses to get your undivided attention, make sure you're prepared with the box of special toys and activities that are reserved for those times when you're chatting with "the competition." This will keep your child busy without you, while you're busy without him. Tell your child, "I'm going to meet with Sally. Here's your special fun box of toys just for you to play with while I'm busy with Sally."

Thank Your Child for Not Interrupting

After you and your child have your separate "playtimes," praise his respectful behavior, and reward him by giving him your undivided attention. Say, "Thank you so much for playing with your toys while I had a meeting. That was so helpful to me to get some of my work done. Now we can play your favorite board game."

Whenever Possible, Involve Your Child in Your Conversation

When a friend visits, try to include your child in your conversation for a few minutes by asking him questions. This will reduce the possibility of his interrupting you to get attention.

Use Grandma's Rule

Use the timer on your phone to let your child know that your attention will soon be all his again. He can earn your attention and have fun at the same time. Tell him, "When you've played with your toys and the timer sounds, we can play school."

Reprimand and Use Calm Time

When your child continually interrupts you when you are talking to a friend, use a reprimand such as, "Please stop interrupting. I cannot talk to my friend while I'm being interrupted. Instead of interrupting, please play with your cars."

If your child does not stop, use Calm Time to remove him from the possibility of getting attention for interrupting. Say, "I'm sorry that you're continuing to interrupt. Let's have some Calm Time while you think of ways to keep from interrupting me when I ask you. When Calm Time is over, we'll talk about what you can do instead of interrupting." Then tell your child that it is important to be learn to be patient when he wants your attention. It's something that you and he will work on together.

What Not to Do

Don't Get Angry and Yell at Your Child for Interrupting

Yelling at your child about any behavior only encourages him to yell and doesn't teach him how to give you interruption-free time.

Don't Interrupt People, Especially Your Child

Even if your child is a constant chatterbox, show him that you will not interrupt him while he's talking. Be a role model of the behavior you want him to learn.

Preventing the Problem

Provide Him with Special Toys, Activities, and Other Alternatives

Because a young child's most priceless possession is his parents' attention, he'll try anything to get it back when they are on the phone, computer, or tablet, or if another person takes his parents' attention away. To limit the tricks your child uses to get your undivided attention, make sure you're prepared with a box of special toys and activities. This will keep your child busy without you, while you're busy without him.

This may not always prevent your child from trying to interrupt you but will be a ready tool to use when she does. Get the box ready ahead of time so you can pull it out quickly!

Case History: "Not Now, Riley!"

Whenever Amelia Wilkens was in a meeting or having coffee with a friend at home, her three-year-old daughter, Riley, interrupted with requests for drinks or toys from the "high place." She also asked questions such as, "Where are we going today?"

Although Amelia wanted to answer, she tried to explain calmly at each interruption, saying, "Sweetheart, Mommy is busy right now. Please don't interrupt." But Riley continued to interrupt, so one day Amelia started screaming in frustration and anger, "Stop interrupting me! You're such a bad girl!" Not only did the yelling fail to stop Riley's interrupting; it angered her into crying and screaming so loudly that her mother couldn't continue her own activity. The more her mother yelled, the more Riley interrupted by crying—a cause-and-effect situation that Amelia finally understood and decided to reverse.

She realized that she needed to give her daughter attention for *not* interrupting instead of for interrupting. The new plan started when Amelia's coworker, Maria, dropped off a package, as she did every Monday morning.

Amelia was talking with Maria, but she took a moment to notice how Riley had begun playing with the toys that Amelia had gathered around the sofa where she was sitting. "Thanks for not interrupting!" she said to Riley, giving her a big hug.

When she finished meeting with Maria, Amelia again praised Riley's behavior, saying, "Thanks for not interrupting me while I talked with Maria. These puzzles are here for you." The puzzles were especially fascinating to Riley because they were called special-time toys—ones she was allowed to play with only when her mother was busy at home and nearby.

~~~~~~

JEALOUS

- Envies someone
- Is angry over someone's success
- Resents someone
- Is spiteful of someone
- Hates someone who has more or has what she wants
- Wants to cause someone harm because she has more attention, friends, or popularity

Young children live at the center of their own universe. This self-centered view of life is the source of sibling rivalry and jealousy. When the attention they demand isn't there because it's being given to a new baby, another sibling, a friend, someone they don't even know, or even a parent, young children often sulk, sabotage, scream, or solicit more attention any way they can. This might come in the form of hitting their siblings (see "Sibling Rivalry and Fighting with Siblings," page 150), breaking toys, or throwing tantrums.

As children get older, someone getting more attention, having a better phone, more "likes" on a social media account, or even a bigger piece of cake, for example, can create the same jealous feelings. Children have more ways than ever today to hurt someone else—or themselves—by using social media to try to get validation, acceptance, recognition, power, or control. Your job is to teach your child how to cope with her feelings and problem-solve how to turn jealousy into admiration for others.

Healthy Mind S.E.T.

Self-Talk. Keep your self-talk positive. Say to yourself, "I don't like it when my child is jealous, but I can help her learn to accept and be grateful for what she has."

Empathy. Put yourself in your child's shoes by thinking, "I understand jealousy because I have been jealous of my friend's new car and my cousin's new house. It feels so bad to be jealous that I want to help her turn that jealousy into being happy for someone else—but that's hard."

Teaching. Remind yourself that learning takes time, patience, and practice. Show or explain to your child how to be grateful for what she has and be happy for someone else. Also support your child's emotions of sadness and anger when she feels jealous by teaching her that all feelings are okay—and that she can learn how to deal with them.

Solving the Problem

What to Do
Respond Immediately to Threats
If your child is jealous of someone, whether a classmate, a friend, or a sibling, and wants to harm them in some way, it's time to take action to manage that threat. Talk with her health care provider and school counselor immediately.

Show Empathy and Praise Helping
Say, "I know that caring for our baby takes time that you would like to have with me, but let's take care of her together. You are such a good helper. Now, please get a diaper for me."

Talk About Your "Likes" and Feelings
Be aware of what your older child is saying on social media. She is likely becoming tuned into the competitive nature of that medium of communication. She may make jealous comments about friends in school or online, such as "Everyone has more 'likes' than I do" or "I wasn't invited to the party" or "I hate Sarah for not asking me to spend the night Friday. She posted a picture of Leah and Harper. Why wasn't I invited?" This constant comparison, although natural for those who are trying to figure out their identity as preteens and teenagers, is creeping down into the world of young children. Keep your communication with your child open and comforting but not judgmental of

her friends. Give her support as you teach her how to feel good about herself; help her shift her focus to positive self-talk and empathy to steer her away from feeling jealous.

Teach How to Use Self-Talk to Replace Jealousy with Appreciation

Self-talk is powerful. When your child tells you she's jealous of someone else, ask her to talk about what she's saying to herself to make her feel jealous. That opens the conversation about how what we say to ourselves—our self-talk—affects our attitude about life. When we tell ourselves that it is awesome that Sara was elected president of the class, for example, we feel happy for her instead of jealous of her. Ask your child how it feels to tell herself that she is happy for another person instead of feeling jealous—those good feelings will reinforce her using positive self-talk as a habit when she is upset and feeling bad about herself and the world.

Teach Gratitude

Help your child learn to be grateful for what she has by reminding her from time to time. If she's jealous of a friend's new coat, ask her to think about what her friend is missing, such as the song you sing every night together. A bedtime prayer can be a listing of things for which she is grateful: a mom who loves her, a grandma and grandpa she gets to visit, and so on. Ask her to name what she is grateful for. Developing a sense of gratitude will shift her focus from what she doesn't have to what she does.

Monitor Your Time and Create Special One-on-One Time

To a child, feeling unconditionally loved matters most. Consider how much time you spend with your child reading stories, answering questions, sharing meals, playing games, and so on. When your child feels secure in your love, her jealousy meter stays low because she knows she's a high priority for you. Create special outings just for you and each of your children, to ensure that you build a special bond with each one and each child feels valued and important. And don't forget to tell each of your children, "I love you," many times every day, as well as show that you do with your hugs.

Turn Jealousy into Helpfulness

A young child wants her world to exist for her alone, but she also wants to be independent. By teaching young children to be helpful toward siblings and others when they are feeling left out and jealous, you're helping them turn negative behavior into something positive and praiseworthy. Say, "I know you want me to play with you now, but first I have to take your brother to soccer practice. Come help me put the oranges in the sack, so the boys will have a treat. You can have one, too."

Praise Sharing

Point out her willingness to share by saying, "That was so nice of you to let your friend have the bigger piece of cake. Thanks for being so generous."

Make Deals; Don't Punish

When your child gets out of sorts because she wants your undivided attention and is jealous of her sister getting it instead, punishing her for being upset will only increase her sense of alienation. Show her how she can cope with not getting the attention she wants when she wants it. Say, "I'm sorry you're so upset because I can't play right now. Let's make a deal. I'll play with your baby sister for a while, and when the phone timer rings, I'll read your book to you. Next time, we'll switch, and you can go first."

What Not to Do

Don't Compare Your Child to Siblings or Others

Saying "I wish you could be as helpful as your little brother," or "Why can't you be as sweet as your big sister?" only tells your child that she's not living up to who you want her to be. To children, that translates into not being as lovable as other family members, which is a surefire way to create jealousy.

Preventing the Problem

Keep Your Child Involved

While you're changing your baby's diaper, for example, enlist your other child's help by asking her to get a new diaper, hold the lotion, or entertain the baby. If your young child becomes jealous while you're hugging someone, a bigger hug to include her can prevent jealousy.

Help Your Child Feel Special

Allow your older child to help open the baby's gifts and show them to the baby. Encouraging friends and relatives to bring gifts for both children helps the older child feel special.

Monitor Social Media

Managing your child's social media usage will help you manage the flare-up of jealousy over what's being said, potential put-downs, and taunting about what someone has and others don't. When you know what your child is hearing and seeing, you are in a better position to channel potential jealousy into positive self-talk.

Case History: Green-Eyed Grace

Grace Goodman was really excited when she learned that she was going to have a baby brother or sister. She loved the idea of having a new playmate, which seemed to her like a new toy. Her parents, CJ and Christine Goodman, were convinced that Grace wouldn't have any problems accepting the new baby. But were they in for a surprise!

Everything went well the first few days after the baby, Jayden, was brought home, because Grammy was there and Grace got lots of attention. Grace told her mom and dad that she thought Jayden looked funny, didn't smell very good sometimes, and wasn't able to play with her the way she wanted. But she reassured her mom by saying, "I guess it's okay if he stays. Let's keep him."

However, when Grammy left to go back home—a thousand miles away—Grace realized that her mom had to spend way too much time taking care of Jayden. Grace decided she needed to reassert herself as the number one kid in her house. She tried whining for a while, but that didn't make her mom leave Jayden and come play with her. Then she tried pouting, but nobody seemed to pay any attention to that, either. So she started refusing to do what her mom and dad asked, like putting away her toys or brushing her teeth. Her mom was exasperated by this change of attitude and said, "Grace, what's gotten into you?"

When CJ came home that evening and heard what Grace had done, his first response was, "Oh, yes. Your mother warned us that Grace would be jealous of Jayden."

So the Goodmans developed a plan to involve Grace in caring for Jayden. Grace became Mommy's Little Helper and was eager to assist when Jayden was being changed or fed. She even held the storybook so Christine could read to her while feeding Jayden.

When Grammy came to visit, she brought Grace a little gift, as well as one for Jayden. Grace got to open Jayden's gift so she could show him what Grammy brought. Grammy also spent plenty of time with Grace, so she didn't feel so left out when Grammy was holding Jayden.

Like a miracle, Grace became a much more pleasant child to have around. The Goodmans knew that their empathy for Grace helped her accept the new family member and the important responsibility of being a big sister.

~~~~~~~~~~~~~~~~~~~~~~~~~~~~~~

LIES

- Avoids the truth, even when confronted
- Makes up stories that aren't true but says they are
- Tells about events that aren't true
- Is not truthful about what she does or says
- Denies doing something, even when confronted
- Makes excuses

Your job is to understand what your child's trying to accomplish by lying and help him learn the benefits of telling the truth. Knowing that the truth is important to you will make being honest more important to your child. It is easier for your child to tell the truth when she knows she can trust you when she does, even if it's something tough to share.

It's helpful to understand the reasons why children (or adults) lie, in order to know how to best teach them to tell the truth:

Reason #1: To talk about their make-believe world: "My magic wand lets me do everything, and it broke the lamp."

Reason #2: To avoid consequences for their actions: "No, I didn't take the last cookie."

Reason #3: To get out of doing things that they don't want to do: "Sure, Mommy, I brushed my teeth."

Reason #4: To try to make themselves seem better in someone else's opinion: "Sara, I have three horses that I get to ride every day. I might ride one to school."

Young children live in an interesting world where fantasy and reality mix. They enjoy cartoons, pretend play, Santa Claus, wicked witches, flying capes, make-believe on demand, and so on—as do some adults who continue to have a rich fantasy life.

But as far as parenting is concerned, it's important to help your child learn to tell the truth, even when it may mean that she has to accept personal

The Seattle Public Library
Central Library
www.spl.org

Checked Out On: 2/4/2020 13:26
XXXXXXXXX8178

Item Title	Due Date
0010100134526	2/25/2020
Jake _Emma's island getaway	
0010101472628	2/25/2020
Poof! a bot!	
0010100271443	2/25/2020
I voted : making a choice makes a difference	
0010101377256	2/25/2020
Discipline with love and limits : practical solutions to over 100 common childhood behavior problems	

# of Items: 4

Renew items at www.spl.org/MyAccount
or 206-386-4190
Sign up for due date reminders
at www.spl.org/notifications

responsibility for her actions. The lesson becomes twofold: it's important to tell the truth and to be responsible for your actions.

Healthy Mind S.E.T.

Self-Talk. Keep your self-talk positive. Say to yourself, "I don't like it when my child lies. Instead of getting angry, I want to understand why he lies and teach the value of telling the truth."

Empathy. Put yourself in your child's shoes by thinking, "It's hard to tell the truth sometimes because you have to face the consequences. My child may think that lying is the better option."

Teaching. Remind yourself that learning takes time, patience, and practice. Show or explain to your child the benefits of telling the truth and how to take responsibility for his actions.

Solving the Problem

What to Do

Teach Your Child to Practice Empathy

Children are born with the capacity to be empathetic, so from the earliest age, make understanding the feelings of others part of your everyday lessons. When your child lies to you, for example, calmly use a respectful tone of voice while you speak to him: "How do you think I feel when you lie and don't tell me the truth? How would you feel if I lied to you? We trust that what another person says is true, which shows that we respect the other person and ourselves. Telling the truth is polite and helps everyone feel comfortable that they can believe what someone says."

Model Being Empathetic Yourself

Understanding why your child is lying helps you teach her to not lie. For example, when your child tells you that she didn't mark her bedroom wall with crayons even though you know she did, tell her, "I understand that you don't want to tell me the truth about what you did. I want you to know that you can always tell me the truth, so we can fix the problem together." Your child will feel more comfortable telling the truth when she knows you'll be sensitive to her feelings.

Teach Accepting Responsibility

When you catch your child lying—by saying that she didn't use a pencil to draw on the walls when she actually did, for example—don't punish her for lying. Instead, teach her how to accept responsibility for making a mistake and to fix the problem it caused. For example, say, "I'm sorry the wall has marks on it. Now we're going to have to learn about taking care of walls. Let's get the cleaning stuff and start cleaning. I'll get the cleaner while you get the paper towels."

Think About Whether Your Child's Storytelling Reveals Hidden Fears

For example, "Mommy, there's a monster in my room! Come save me!" may be your child's way of telling you she's afraid of the dark. Also, young children can be convinced of almost anything. If they want to believe something badly enough, they can convince themselves of the truth in even the biggest lie. Say, "Let's leave a light on in the hall, so you can be sure that there are no monsters. You will then be sure that they are not living here."

Look for Honesty

Look for people and events that demonstrate honesty and truth. Point these out to your child to reinforce your message that being honest is important. And remember to praise your child's honesty.

Praise Telling the Truth

When you know your child told the truth, offer praise. Say, "Thank you for telling me the truth. When you are truthful, I can trust you. But no matter what, I will always love you."

Recognize Make-Believe

When your child tells you a made-up story, say, "I love the story you made up. Let's write it down and save it. You are a good storyteller."

Teach That Lying Destroys Trust

When your child is caught in a lie, say, "I'm sorry you chose not to tell the truth. Let's work on telling the truth so I can always believe that what you tell me is true. Believing what someone says is important, so you know that they will do what they say they will do."

Explain the Difference Between Lying and Telling the Truth

Young children don't always know that what they're saying is a lie because it might seem like the truth to them. Help your child understand the difference between reality and fantasy by saying, "I know you want your friend to like you, but telling him that you have ten dogs living at your house isn't truthful. The truth is that you'd like to have all those dogs, but you only have one dog named Molly. She's a really nice dog, and you love her a lot."

Teach Your Child to Accept Responsibility for What She Says and Does

When you ask your daughter to do a chore, such as putting the toys away in her room, she might lie to get out of doing the job by telling you that she already did it. Say, "I'm so glad you did what I asked. I'll go see what a great job you did."

If she says, "Oh no, Mommy, not yet," you can be reasonably sure she's avoided her responsibility. Check it out! If you discover that she lied, say, "I'm sorry you chose not to tell me the truth about doing what I asked. I know you didn't want to put all those toys away and didn't want me to be disappointed, but doing what I ask and telling the truth are important. Now let's go get the job done. I'll watch while you pick up."

Practice Telling the Truth

When your child lies to you about turning off the TV when you asked her to do so when the show she's watching is over, she's letting you know she needs practice telling the truth. Say, "I'm sorry you didn't tell me the truth when I asked you if you had turned off the TV. Let's practice telling the truth. I'll ask you to turn off the TV when the show is over. Then you say, 'Yes, Mommy, I'll turn off the TV when this show is over.' Then you do it. Now let's practice."

Play Make-Believe with Your Child

To help your child understand the difference between truth and fiction, set aside time for her to make up stories. Then contrast this *story time* with *truth time*, in which she's asked to tell the truth about what happened. When your child tells you something that you know isn't true, say, "That's an interesting make-believe story you just told me. Now tell me a true story about what really happened."

What Not to Do

Don't Test Your Child's Honesty

If you know your child has done something wrong, asking her a question to which you already know the answer forces her into a dilemma: tell the truth and get punished, or lie and maybe get away with it. Don't make her choose.

Don't Model Lying

Avoid exaggerating or making up stories to impress people, to avoid consequences, or to get out of doing what you don't want to do. For example, telling your child that there isn't any ice cream at home when she knows that there is tells her that you also lie, which makes it okay for her to do.

Don't Overreact

Even if you've said to your child a hundred times that you can't stand a liar, going ballistic when your child lies only increases her need to avoid telling the truth to keep you from getting mad.

Don't Label Your Child a Liar

Don't make lying a self-fulfilling prophecy. A child who's called a liar will come to believe that what she does is who she is. Your child isn't what she does. She's a child. You might not love her behavior, but you'll always love her unconditionally.

Don't Take Lying Personally

Little Dana isn't telling you an exaggerated version of her morning at day care just to irritate you. She may actually believe that the classroom's pet snake got out of its cage because she was scared that it would. Listen to her story and tell her, "That's an interesting story, sweetheart. I'm sure having the snake loose in the room would be really scary. Do you want me to talk to Ms. Laura about keeping the snake safely locked up in its cage?"

Don't Talk a Lot About Lying

Talking about lying just keeps what you don't want in front of your child instead of what you do want. Talk about telling the truth, which is the behavior that you are trying to teach your child.

Preventing the Problem

Reinforce Telling the Truth

Offer praise when you know you're hearing the truth, whether it's about something bad that happened or something good. This helps your young child begin to understand the difference between what's true and what's not.

Model Telling the Truth

When your young child asks for a cookie right before dinner, you might be tempted to say, "We don't have any more cookies," instead of telling her the truth, which is "I don't want you to eat a cookie before dinner." By lying to her, you're telling her that it's okay to lie when she wants to get out of doing something unpleasant. She knows where the cookies are, so don't pretend that she doesn't! Say, "I know you want a cookie now, but when you've eaten your dinner, you can pick one out yourself."

Although Ryan Kirk had just turned seven years old, his parents had already tagged him as a liar. He'd come home from school and tell Julie, his mother, the most fantastic stories about how his friend Adam had brought his pony to school. Every day it was something new, and Julie was becoming afraid that Ryan's fantasies were getting out of hand.

Lawrence, Ryan's dad, had also heard Ryan's tall tales. He had recently confronted his son about some juice that had been spilled in the kitchen, and the answer he got astonished him. Ryan tried to convince his dad that someone broke into the house to steal stuff and must have spilled the juice on the floor. "But son, it's the same grape juice that you have in your cup right now. How do you explain that? Now don't you lie to me!" When Ryan didn't have an answer, he was taken to Calm Time so Dad could calm down and Ryan could have some time to think about how to tell the truth.

Julie and Lawrence soon realized that this consequence would not teach their son to tell the truth, because the more they took him to Calm Time, the more he lied. He even tried to lie his way out of Calm Time. Ryan's parents loved him and needed to help him understand that they would love him no matter what happened. They also knew that their son didn't have to lie to impress them or to stay out of trouble, but they weren't sure if he knew that. When they thought about how the world seems to little children—a confusing blend of fantasy and reality—the Kirks understood that they could help their son by teaching him the difference between fact and fiction. They decided to change their problem-solving strategy.

"Tell me about school today," Julie said when Ryan got into the car after school the next day.

"Well," Ryan began, "today was real neat because the football team that plays in the stadium came and showed us how to play football. But Josh got hurt and they had to take him to the hospital in an ambulance . . . "

Then Julie stopped him. "Wow!" she exclaimed. "That must have been exciting. Is this what you wanted to happen today at school, or did this really happen?"

"Well . . . ," Ryan said, "I wished it had happened. Then school would have been more exciting."

"Ryan, your story was very interesting, but I really want to know the truth. You don't have to make up things about school so I'll think your day was exciting. You can tell me about the games you played, who sat next to you at snack time, what Ms. Sharon talked about, and all sorts of things that I'd like to hear about. I have an idea. You like to make up stories, so let's have story time when you can make up stories, and then let's have truth time when you can report what actually happened during your day."

So Ryan got into the habit of saying, "Story time, Mom." Then he'd launch into a fantastic tale about his day at school, and they'd both laugh. Julie would rave about how much she enjoyed story time.

"Now it's truth time, Ryan," his mom would then say, and he'd report on the real events of the day. Julie would tell Ryan how much she loved his truth-time tales, too. This allowed Lawrence and Julie to accomplish three goals: they taught their son lessons in honesty, they taught him how important telling the truth was to them, and they supported his budding storytelling creativity.

NAME-CALLING

- Belittles
- Threatens you and others
- Bullies by calling hurtful names
- Teases
- Insults
- Puts down
- Humiliates
- Shames

When frustration turns to anger in struggles for acceptance, validation, recognition, power, and control, name-calling is often the result. Name-calling is meant to dominate, hurt, and belittle the other person. After all, an enemy who is shrunk in the mind of the angry child is less of an opponent. Children—and adults for that matter—often resort to name-calling because by putting someone else down, they feel better about themselves—although only momentarily. The real lesson to be learned is that name-calling doesn't feel good for anyone, either the one calling names or the person who is called the name. Instead of name-calling, teach your child how to deal with his anger and frustration without putting someone else down. (See also "Curses and Swears, Uses 'Bad Words,'" page 58.)

Healthy Mind S.E.T.

Self-Talk. Keep your self-talk positive. Say to yourself, "I don't want my child to hurt someone else by calling her names, but I will keep calm while I teach her why and what else to do when she's angry."

Empathy. Put yourself in your child's shoes by thinking, "I can understand that my child calls people names when she's upset. I sometimes want to do that, too!"

Teaching. Remind yourself that learning takes time, patience, and practice. Show or explain how to cope with her feelings when she is angry, instead of name-calling. Your ultimate lesson will serve her well for a lifetime: how to feel empathy for another person when she's upset, so her responses become helpful, not hurtful, to herself and others. Getting along with others takes lifelong practice.

Solving the Problem

What to Do
Teach Your Child to Practice Empathy
Children are born with the capacity to be empathetic, so from the earliest age, make understanding the feelings of others part of your everyday teaching. When your child calls another child a name, for example, don't call him a name to teach him how it feels to be called names. But do calmly and kindly talk to him: "How would you feel if Jean called you a name? You wouldn't like it, right? We don't want to hurt another person's feelings, so we don't call them names, even if we are mad. When you are angry, it's important to tell a teacher or other adult that you are upset and tell them why. They can help you cope with your feelings without name-calling."

Take Your Child to Calm Time
Remove your child from the fun she's having for a specific length of time by saying to her that when she calls people names, or belittles, teases, or insults them, she loses her chance to play. Say, "I'm sorry you called CeCe a dummy. I'm taking you to Calm Time so you can think about how to get along." Set your phone timer for about one minute for each year of your child's age. When

Calm Time's over, talk with her about playing without name-calling. When she is calm, ask her to apologize to CeCe and rejoin the play activity.

Teach Your Child to Apologize and Use Grandma's Rule

Say to your child, "I know that you are frustrated, but you need to tell your friend that you are sorry." Learning to apologize gives your child practice in using empathy to see things from another's point of view and encourages getting along with others.

Use Grandma's Rule by saying, "When you have told your friend, 'I'm sorry that I called you a name and hurt your feelings,' then you may go back to play."

Teach What Words and Names Are Appropriate and Inappropriate to Use

Make sure you've educated your child about using hurtful words and names before expecting her to know what they are. For example, even though she may hear her friends at preschool, day care, or school or online calling someone "stupid," your rule is that calling people hurtful names like "stupid" or telling them to shut up is not acceptable.

Teach How to Self-Calm

Say to your child, "When you *want* to call someone a name to let him know he hurt you or to put him down, say, 'Stop,' and then count to ten. That will help you calm down, so you can cool off and think better. Then you can talk with your teacher or me about how to feel better about the situation that caused you to feel angry." Practice this routine in a neutral calm time to role-play how it works together.

Notice Nice Talk

Praise your child when she uses kind, friendly words and doesn't call people hurtful names. Doing so shows her what language you do and don't approve of her using. Learning to use kind words with playmates is developing the kind of social skills that will help your child get along well with others today and in the future. Kindness is contagious: the more kind words your child uses, the more others will do so in return.

What Not to Do

Don't Model Road Rage

Cursing at a driver who cut you off will tell your child that it's okay to call people names when she's angry. To reduce your own anger, and model empathy and safe driving for your child, say, "Cutting me off while I was driving was dangerous. I hope that other driver doesn't have an accident before she gets where she is going."

Don't Name-Call Because You Were Called a Name

Because being insulted or called names is so irritating, it's easy to shout back to your child the same ridiculous words she says to you, such as, "You are so stupid! You should know better than to call names." This gives your child permission to use the kinds of names you did. Channel your rage into an explanation of how and why you feel so upset, to teach your child when her words or actions make you happy or unhappy and how you'd like her to respond when she feels like name-calling. Respond calmly to being called a name to burst the bubble of influence your child hopes name-calling will achieve.

Don't Use Punishment for Name-Calling

If you punish your child for name-calling, he will only use the names when you are not around. Using punishment for remedying misbehavior teaches your child how to avoid getting caught. Punished behavior does not go away; it just goes out of sight.

Don't Shame or Put Your Child Down for Name-Calling

Shaming and using put-downs when you are angry with your child only teaches her to use those same words when she is angry. Remember to use positive self-talk to calm yourself before you respond to your child's behavior.

Preventing the Problem

Think About What You Call Your Child

Avoid calling your child nicknames that you wouldn't want her to call someone else. Saying, "You're a crazy little dude!" may not offend him but may be hurtful to others, if your child uses that name.

Teach How to Respond to Being a Name-Calling Victim

Suggest desirable ways for your child to respond when she's the victim of a name-caller. Say, "When your friend calls you a bad name, tell her that you don't want to play with her when she calls you names." Encourage your child to talk with you if she is a victim of name-calling, so you can help her learn how to cope with her feelings.

Case History: Aiden, the King of Insults

Six-year-old Aiden loved to be the leader in any activity. He wanted to dictate the rules of the game, to play with the most coveted toys, and to be first in line at school. When he couldn't have these things, Aiden would often resort to putting someone down, belittling, insulting, and name-calling. All that was tolerated by the adults in his world until one day out of frustration over a struggle for first in line, he called Mrs. Anderson, his teacher, a "dummy."

Of course, Mrs. Anderson did not take Aiden's word kindly, so his parents were sent an email about the incident. His parents were not surprised because they had also been victims of Aiden's anger and insulting names. At first, they thought his calling them names was cute and would make it a contest to see who would win the name-calling contest. "You poo poo head," hurled by young Aiden, would be met with "No, you're a poo poo poo head," from one of his parents. However, after Mrs. Anderson's email, his parents decided they had to do something to curb Aiden's insulting habit.

Steve, Aiden's dad, was all about using soap in the mouth, something he remembered from his own childhood, but Jane, his mom, wouldn't have any of that. They decided to have a discussion with Aiden about his anger and name-calling.

Realizing how short a six-year-old's attention span was, they made it brief. "We know that when you get mad at someone, you want to get back at him, so you call him a name. We understand that, but it's hurtful to others and needs to stop. When you are angry and want to call somebody a name, don't. Instead, say to yourself, 'Stop,' and then count to ten. Every day we will ask you how many times you told yourself, 'Stop.' Now let's make-believe that you are mad at someone, and before you call him a name, you tell yourself, 'Stop.' Let's practice."

Of course, Aiden wanted to argue with them, and began by saying, "But you call me names back!" His parents agreed that they shouldn't do that and promised to clean up their act by telling themselves, "Stop," when they felt the urge to name-call. They also contacted Mrs. Anderson with their plan, and she promised to keep track and praise Aiden's self-control. Aiden was rewarded with an outing at the end of the week for the number of times he reported stopping himself from name-calling. And Aiden got better at cooling his need to win by putting others down.

NOT EATING

- Doesn't want to eat
- Is made fun of for not eating
- Cries during meals
- Pushes food away or on the floor
- Wants something else to eat
- Says, "I hate this food"
- Will only eat one food
- Demands different food
- Throws food
- Uses food as a toy
- Won't stay at the table
- Won't sit in his chair

Not eating, overeating, playing with food—all test the patience of parents, teachers, grandparents, and caregivers. As in the case of sleep, questions and worries around what, how much, when, and if children are "eating right" top the list of topics that stress everyone who is raising a child. Indeed, whole books and websites, product lines, and clinicians focus only on those subjects.

When responding to your child's not eating, look for solutions here and in "Eats Too Much" (page 71) and "Plays with Food" (page 128). All focus on eating as an enjoyable way to take care of ourselves. Learn different ways to make mealtimes teachable moments as your child grows from infancy through adolescence in order to help eating become a low-stress experience—not a power struggle.

NOTE: *A Special Word About the Drama of Not Eating*

Eating is a subject that taps into emotional issues as well as physical ones—and breastfeeding, in particular, is a subject that touches on being able to provide for one's child in a uniquely personal way. For some parents, wanting children to grow up strong and healthy becomes connected to whether or not they are "good eaters."

Therefore, how much, what, where, when, and how they feed their children are all questions that families often have difficulty answering. So much information is available today about the best ways to handle feeding children to prevent obesity, encourage good eating habits, and boost optimum health that it's no wonder parents are confused. On top of that, feeding children literally changes as they grow and become better able to chew solids, drink from a cup, and master all the skills involved in eating and drinking. Families want to do the right thing by their children, but it can be overwhelming.

"How do we know what's best?" parents ask, particularly if they are still struggling with food issues themselves. Many new moms are tired of the weight gain from pregnancy, don't like their own body image, or are trying to sort through all their emotional feelings leftover from their own childhood weight worries, just to name a few of the big factors that make feeding stressful.

It's so hard to know what is normal and what is not when children don't want to eat or to know why children don't want to eat or make a fuss about food. We will try to answer these questions by giving a brief overview of a few common problems parents have and how to solve them. Your child's health care provider is someone who knows your child's health best, so trust her to help you work through the eating questions that are most important to you.

Healthy Mind S.E.T.

Self-Talk. Keep your self-talk positive. Say to yourself, "It is okay if my child doesn't eat everything all the time. He isn't going to starve. When he's hungry, he'll eat. And when he's not, it's okay. He can choose. It's best if I don't make a fuss about eating or not eating. I know my child will eat a balanced diet if I provide that when it's mealtime."

Empathy. Put yourself in your child's shoes by thinking, "There may be several reasons why my child may not want to eat: She may not be hungry. She may be occupied with other activities and doesn't want to stop what she's doing. She learned that she gets my attention by not eating or by playing with food. She is afraid of gaining weight or being fat, or feels fat, or is teased for being fat. She has problems with swallowing or chewing food."

Teaching. Remind yourself that learning takes time, patience, and practice. Help your child learn that eating nutritious food is an enjoyable, stress-free experience.

Solving the Problem

What to Do

Motivate with the Timer

Children do best when they have a routine and know what will happen next. Set your phone timer and say, "When the timer rings it will be dinnertime. So when you hear the timer, let's see how fast you can get to the table."

Set Mealtime Rules

Children need rules to tell them what is expected of them. Typical rules are: stay seated, use utensils instead of fingers, keep food on plates, say when you're finished eating.

Praise Mealtime Behavior

Calling attention to appropriate behavior at the table not only helps that behavior stay around, but also gives your child attention so she doesn't have to not eat to get attention. Say, "You are sitting so nicely and using your spoon." Or, "Thank you for trying the broccoli."

Make Sure Your Child Has a Balanced Diet over Time

At snacks and meals, offer a variety of foods for good nutrition. Small and more frequent food offerings in a greater variety and with a balance of protein, carbohydrates, and fruits and vegetables ensure your child gets a balanced diet over meals during each day and every day.

Provide Less Food More Often for Toddlers and Preschoolers

Although you may want to provide breakfast, lunch, and dinner at particular times of day, when children are in the early years of starting solid foods and into the preschool years, their stomachs can't hold enough food to last four or more hours between meals. Let your child eat as often as she likes, within limits. Say, "Whenever you're hungry, let me know, and you can have carrot sticks or an apple." Make sure you can follow through with your suggestions, based on your child's age, what foods are available, and what time a main meal is coming.

Be Mindful of the Transition to Solid Food from Only Breast or Bottle-Feeding

As your infant and then toddler transitions to eating more solid food after their first year of life, be mindful that bottle- or breastfeeding doesn't interfere with eating solid food. Keep a reasonable interval between liquid feedings and solid food offerings. When you start mealtime with food, instead of a bottle or glass of milk or juice, she may be more interested in eating.

Let Your Child Choose Foods

Let your child choose her between-meal snack or lunch food (with your supervision). When she feels she has some control over what she's eating, she may be more excited about food. Offer her only two choices at a time, so she doesn't become overwhelmed with the decision-making process; praise her choices with comments like "I'm glad you chose that orange. It's really a delicious snack."

Provide Variety and Balance

Children need to learn about proper diet, which involves a wide range of foods. Expose your child to the various tastes, textures, colors, and aromas of nutritious foods. Remember that children's tastes often change overnight, so don't be surprised if your child turns down a food today that was a favorite the day before.

Grow Your Own Veggies

If you have space for a small garden or can use large pots for planting, try growing a few vegetables. Children who have a hand in growing food are often more willing to try foods they ordinarily turn down.

Let Nature Take Its Course

A healthy child will naturally select a balanced diet over a week's time, and pediatricians say this will keep her adequately nourished. But she will do this only if a wide variety of healthy foods is available. Make a note of what your child has eaten from Monday through Sunday before becoming alarmed that she's undernourished.

Establish Regular Mealtimes

Because your child is not on the same eating schedule as you are, she may often want to play outside or finish an art project when your mealtime arrives. Identify the times when your child seems to get hungry to learn what kind of hunger clock she's on (which you could switch to, if possible). She may need to be trained to switch to your schedule for sitting together, or you may choose to switch to hers. The bottom line is this: meals are healthiest, emotionally and physically, when they are fun times for family interaction.

Table-Time Rules

Encourage your child to interact with you at the table for a reasonable amount of time for the child's age. Say, "The phone timer will tell us when dinner is over. The rule is that we want all of us to stay at the table until the phone timer rings. Tell me when you're finished eating, and I'll remove your plate."

This is an important distinction: your child doesn't have to keep eating to stay at the table with you—just as adults don't. The point is that you want your child to be at the table to get her accustomed to this healthy habit that she will follow for the rest of her life. Mealtime is a time to satisfy social hunger as well as physical hunger. Include her in conversation, and offer praise for appropriate behavior while at the table to keep her there and happy.

What Not to Do

Don't Bribe or Beg
When your child is not eating, don't bribe or beg her to clean her plate. This makes not eating a game to get your attention, which gives your child a feeling of power over you.

Don't Get Upset When Your Child Won't Eat
Giving your child attention for not eating can make it much more interesting to her than eating. On the other hand, she may not have an appetite because she is not feeling well. So check to see if she has a fever or is struggling with an upset tummy to see if these may be the reasons for her not eating.

Don't Skip Meals Yourself
Skipping meals gives your child the idea that not eating is okay for her since it's okay for you.

Don't Emphasize a Big Tummy or Idolize a Bone-Thin Physique
Even a three-year-old can become irrationally weight conscious if you show her how to be obsessed with her body.

Preventing the Problem

Learn the Appropriate Amount of Food for Your Child's Age and Weight
Consult your child's health care provider for answers to specific nutrition questions about your child. For information about recommended guidelines for young children, see "Nutrition & Fitness" in the preschool section on the Healthy Children website (healthychildren.org/English/ages-stages/preschool /nutrition-fitness/Pages/default.aspx).

Make Sure She Has the Skills Required for Eating

Learning how to swallow, bite, and chew solid food are all skills that take practice. Your child's not eating might be related to the fact that she really doesn't know how to do those basic skills. So practice with a few soft and mushy foods that she can pick up (no fork or spoon to learn how to use) and learn how to chew and swallow before graduating to other solid foods that are bigger and need more sophisticated skills to be able to eat. Talk with your child's health care provider about what foods to start giving your little one and when, so she can learn how to handle solid food in her mouth.

Make Mealtimes Happy Times

Children who learn to enjoy close family time with conversation and good food are happy to stay at the table and follow the mealtime rules. To make mealtime a happy time, talk to your children, ask open questions about their day, praise them when they follow the rules, and refrain from judgment and criticism.

Case History: "I Won't Eat!"

When Owen Rowland turned seven years old, his appetite dropped to zero. His parents, Leo and Lillian, didn't know why, and neither did his pediatrician, who checked him over physically at the insistence of Owen's fretful mother. They nagged him, threatened him, begged him, and made deals with him to get him to eat. One night, after Lillian had begged him to eat just one pea, Owen threw an especially loud and violent tantrum, shoved his plate off the table, and shouted, "No, I won't eat!"

Leo decided to take over this mealtime battle. "Now, Owen, listen to me. If you don't take a bite of macaroni, you'll have to leave the table," he threatened, firmly letting his son know the rule of the moment. But he never guessed that Owen would take him up on the offer and get down from his chair. "Owen Rowland, you will not get down from this table!" Leo yelled. "You will stay and eat your dinner if you have to sit here all night," he said, changing the rules and thoroughly confusing his son.

Later that night, after they had kissed and hugged their son and put him to bed, the Rowlands decided that something different had to be done. They did not want to yell at their little boy for not eating. They wanted to turn mealtime back into what it used to be—a time for food and fun exchanges of stories and the events of the day—because they understood how important family mealtime is. So the next night at dinner, they shifted their attention away from food and pretended to ignore Owen's lack of appetite.

"Tell me about how you were the helper at school today, Owen," his mother began (with all the sincerity and calmness she could muster) as she passed the broccoli to her husband. Owen perked up as he told the story of how he was chosen to hold the flag. In between his excited explanations, he just happened to swallow a forkful of mashed potatoes. "That was so nice of you to be such a good helper today," Lillian said. "I'm glad you like the mashed potatoes, too," she added. The Rowlands ate their meal and didn't push their son to try a few more potatoes.

The next morning, they discussed the evening's more pleasant mealtime and decided to continue what they were doing. They also remembered what Owen's doctor had said: "Owen may eat only small amounts, judging from his normal but slight body size, and he may eat those more than three times a day, as many people do."

Dinnertime became less of a daily preoccupation for Lillian. She began creating fun carrot-stick boats and cheese-and-raisin faces for Owen to eat for his lunch and as snacks. Owen developed a whole new interest in eating more during the day, though he still only took a few mouthfuls at dinner. But the Rowlands appreciated those minutes Owen did spend eating, and they let their son dictate when he was and wasn't hungry.

OVERLY ACTIVE

- Fidgets constantly
- Can't stay at the table
- Runs or climbs excessively
- Has problems playing quietly
- Is constantly on the go
- Is overly talkative
- Blurts out answers before the question is completed
- Has trouble waiting in lines or taking turns
- Doesn't sit still
- Doesn't pay attention

- Is easily distracted
- Loses things

"Jackie's so hyper," her grandmother exclaimed after two hours of grueling babysitting with her young granddaughter. "She wouldn't sit down once—not even to eat!" Jackie's mother had heard the term "hyper" used before to describe her daughter, but when Jackie's grandmother started complaining about Jackie's behavior, Jackie's mother asked herself, "Is Jackie a normal, busy three-year-old, or is she hyperactive?"

Clinical tests must be done to obtain a proper diagnosis of hyperactivity, but even this may not be definitive for young children. If you see four of the symptoms below in your child on a daily basis for at least six months, or if your child's "hyper" activity starts making it hard for her to sleep, eat, get along with friends, and learn in a classroom, for example, get help from your pediatrician for medical, psychological, and academic testing:

- Fidgeting constantly
- Leaving her seat
- Running or climbing excessively
- Having problems playing quietly
- Being constantly on the go
- Being overly talkative
- Blurting out answers before the question is completed
- Having trouble waiting in lines or taking turns
- Interrupting or intruding on others

The important lesson here is that those trained in diagnosing Attention Deficit and Hyperactivity Disorder (ADHD) can help you understand the difference between a "hyper" active child and a hyperactive child—and she can help you manage the behavior of both. Because these behaviors often describe the average young child, it's very difficult to attach the label "hyperactive" to a little whirlwind.

Hyperactivity is considered part of a larger disorder commonly referred to as ADHD, which comes in three forms: (1) ADHD, Predominantly Inattentive Type; (2) ADHD, Predominantly Hyperactive / Impulsive Type; and (3) ADHD, Predominantly Combined Type. All forms of ADHD are difficult to diagnose before children enter formal schooling at about age five, when they're first required to sit and pay attention for longer periods of time, work while remaining seated, and memorize material that they'll be tested on later.

Healthy Mind S.E.T.

Self-Talk. Keep your self-talk positive. Say to yourself, "I am not sure if my child is hyperactive or just has lots of energy. Either way, I will help him learn how to live with his unique self."

Empathy. Put yourself in your child's shoes by thinking, "It must be difficult to try to live in a world that demands that a child be quiet and focused when his body screams to move. To my child, many distractions are demanding his attention, so it's hard to stay focused on only one thing."

Teaching. Remind yourself that learning takes time, patience, and practice. Show or explain how your child can sit still, slow down, and focus when he needs to.

Solving the Problem

What to Do

Provide Quiet Activities

Schedule breaks during your child's day to have quiet activities, such as reading, listening, and playing thinking games, such as chess. Playing chess has been found to be helpful for children by giving them practice in focusing attention and learning to plan ahead.

Practice Slowing Down

Give your child opportunities to practice walking—not running—from Point A to Point B. Say, "Show me how to walk from the kitchen to the bedroom. I know you can do it. When you walk instead of run, you keep yourself safe."

Provide a Variety of Activities

Born-to-be-busy children flit like houseflies from one activity to another and have trouble staying in one place. Give your overly active child several choices by saying, "You can color on your drawing table, play with clay in the kitchen, or play with your building blocks. I'll set the timer on the phone, and you can do one activity until the timer rings. Then you can choose something else if you want." Providing many options lets your child fulfill her need to be busy without driving you to distraction.

Exercise

Your high-energy child needs constructive outlets for her need to be on the go. Let her run in the park or in your yard whenever you can, or make sure her school or day care provider gives her some running time.

Although it may be tempting to sign her up for the neighborhood sports team that all her buddies are on, beware of starting your young child too early in sports that can injure her growing body or cause her to burn out on that sport. Young children need the freedom to rev up their newly charged engines without being corralled in an organized, competitive setting. Highly active children often do better in individual sports, such as tennis, than in team sports.

Have Quiet Times

For children who love to talk, setting aside periods when quiet is mandated is helpful. Begin with short periods and gradually expand to longer periods of time as your child learns to keep his thoughts to himself. Begin by saying, "We need some quiet right now. I'll set my phone timer for five minutes, and during that time, we will both be quiet. That means no talking. Let's start now." If five minutes is too long, reduce the time until your child can be successful. Praise his quiet when he meets the goal and continue until you can have a reasonable amount of quiet time with no talking.

Teach Relaxation

When your child learns to relax her body, her motor slows down, and she feels less frantic. Help her avoid constantly pushing to do more, go faster, or get there sooner by keeping your voice soft and soothing, by rubbing her back to help her relax, and by talking to her about how calm and relaxed her body feels.

What Not to Do

Don't Punish

When your overly active child accidentally collides with your most precious vase, take a deep breath and say, "I'm sorry you chose to run instead of walk. Now you have to practice walking in the house, so I'll know you can do it. Then we'll clean up the mess." In this way, you'll reach your ultimate goals of teaching your child to walk instead of run, respect property, and be responsible for her own actions.

Don't Ground

Your busy child needs daily opportunities to play in the great outdoors, so grounding her to the house or her room can cause two problems: (1) her physical need for activity will swell to explosive levels, and (2) she will continue to be overly active in the house instead of outside.

Don't Rely on Medication Alone

Relying on medication alone to control hyperactivity won't teach your child self-control. Get a thorough evaluation from a professional experienced in assessing your child before you decide what medications are necessary for your child's well-being.

Preventing the Problem

Suggest Quiet Activities

If your child regularly runs instead of walks and screams instead of talks, introduce calm activities to slow her breakneck speed. For example, play the Quiet Game (see Chapter 5), read to her, or have a tiptoe-and-whisper time to teach her that "slow and calm" is a refreshing change of pace.

Watch Your Own Activity Level

Does hyperactivity run in families? Research has shown that when a parent is diagnosed with hyperactivity, it's highly likely that his or her child will be, too. Look at your own life: Do you ever sit down? Do you talk fast and constantly? Is your pace always rushed? If you're a high-energy, always-on-the-go person whose overly active lifestyle doesn't get in the way of your success and happiness, then your child may simply have your inborn, high-speed temperament. Since young children are such great imitators, slowing down your activity level will show your young child how to savor the moment.

Provide Plenty of Activity Options

Young children have short attention spans and seem to flit from one activity to another, always demanding something new to do. Overly active children need even more play choices because they are always on the hunt for something to stimulate their ever-hungry brains. Being able to guide your child to a new exciting activity before she has an energy explosion will eventually help her learn to guide herself.

Avoid Overly Active Screen Time

When your child is in constant motion, her entertainment shouldn't be. Violent television programs and video games model behavior you don't want her to imitate, for example. Depending on your child's age, limit her exposure time to screens. (See "Screen Time / Screen Addiction," page 142.)

Case History: Wild About Ethan

When Jane and Russell Anderson attended Ethan's teacher conference at school, they weren't at all surprised at Ms. Sharon's comment that their five-year-old son was very active.

"He even kept me awake at night when I was pregnant with him, he was so restless and busy," Jane told her. "When Russell is out of town, I sometimes let Ethan sleep with me, and it's the same thing. I don't get much sleep because he's so restless. He never walks; he runs. He's just like his dad." Jane put her hand on Russell's knee, which had been in constant motion since he first sat down for the conference.

"Yeah, I was a hyper kid," Russell grinned. "Mom had to go to school lots to bail me out because I was always in trouble for being out of my seat, talking, or doing something stupid. I had to take medication to calm down. Do you think Ethan needs medication?"

"Well, it's not such a big problem in school now and doesn't seem to be interfering with his learning. He's learning quickly and easily, so I don't think he needs to be tested for ADHD. But it would be good to keep an eye on him," Ms. Sharon told them. "When he's in first grade next year, you should work closely with his teacher to see if something more needs to be done. In the meantime, here's a list of things you can do to try to slow him down a bit, as well as the best places you can go for a full evaluation if you choose. We believe that children should have a thorough evaluation before starting any kind of medication or treatment program."

Jane and Russell took the list home and began working with Ethan. Several times a day, they had quiet time during which they read stories to him or relaxed with him. At first, Ethan couldn't sit still for more than fifty or sixty seconds, but gradually he began to sit for ten minutes at a time. They also cut out most of the TV Ethan liked to watch and imitate—from wrestling mayhem to martial arts—after his teacher suggested limiting his exposure to such frantic fare.

His mom and dad also made a new household rule: "When you're in the house, you must walk. Running is for outside." To teach him the rule, they had Ethan practice navigating the house by walking. This was new to Ethan.

"But what if I'm in a hurry? Why can't I run if I want to?" Ethan whined.

Jane smiled inside at Ethan's question. She remembered having to help Russell learn how to slow down after he knocked over a lamp one night trying to get to the kitchen and back before a TV commercial was over. "Because it's against the rule to run in the house," she answered. "Running is for outside, where you have lots of room to run and won't bang into the furniture."

Jane also started doing simple relaxation exercises with Ethan at bedtime. She rubbed his back while softly saying, "You're feeling quiet and relaxed. Your feet feel heavy and relaxed. Your legs, your tummy, your back, your arms, and your hands all feel relaxed and comfortable. Your whole body is relaxed and warm. Your mind is quiet, and you're comfortable and still. Now, Ethan, think of being in your bed all quiet and snuggly while you're feeling so calm and quiet."

Ethan gradually became calmer and quieter and somewhat less active. It wasn't always easy for him to keep his body quiet, but he worked at it with his parents and his teacher, which helped prepare him for making a smooth transition to the less active world of the first grade.

OVERUSES "NO"

- Answers no to every direction or suggestion
- Saying no even if he means yes

"No" ranks as the most-likely-to-be-used word among children. Why? They are great at imitating what they hear. To keep our children safe, we say, "No! Don't touch!" or ,"No! Don't open!" or, "No! Don't do that!" or just, "No, no, no!" from the time that our little ones are about eight months old and start exploring their world.

Whenever they start scooting, crawling, and doing things that we don't want them to do, such as trying to touch a hot stove burner, for example, we say no! So children learn quickly that *their* saying no can be a useful tool to get their own power and control over what they don't want to do—get dressed, clean up their toys, or get in the car, for example. It is absolutely normal for children to say no. Now it's your job to teach them when and where that word is useful.

NOTE: *See also "Temper Tantrums," page 170; "Want My Own Way," page 186; and "Won't Do What You Ask / Won't Listen / Ignores You / Doesn't Follow Directions," page 220.*

Healthy Mind S.E.T.

Self-Talk. Keep your self-talk positive. Say to yourself, "I don't like it when my child says no to me, but I know that he's showing that he's growing up and trying to become independent. That is a good thing!"

Empathy. Put yourself in your child's shoes by thinking, "I understand that my child says no for many reasons—power, control, independence. I sometimes say it, too, for those same reasons."

Teaching. Remind yourself that learning takes time, patience, and practice. Show or explain to your child how he can learn to cooperate, compromise, and do things you want him to do without a power struggle. Your job is to teach him how to get what he wants without saying no to your every request.

Solving the Problem

What to Do
Redirect Your Child's Behavior
You usually want your child to stop a behavior when you say no to her. So instead of saying no, teach another behavior to replace the one you want stopped. For example, if your toddler is digging in the potted plant, instead of saying no, simply say, "Please stop digging in the plant. Let's play with the dollhouse instead." This redirection moves her to a new behavior and avoids the use of the dreaded "no" by replacing it with "stop."

Get to Know Your Child's Personality
If you're familiar with your very young child's needs and wants, you'll know when her no means she doesn't want something. She may be saying no because it gets so much attention from you or because she likes the sound of saying the word "just for fun." A good example of this behavior is when a child says no to

the question "Are you hungry?" as she's reaching for a snack. In other words, don't always take her literally when she says no to every request.

Let Your Child Say No, and Use Grandma's Rule
Even though you want her to do what you want (or need) her to do, your child is entitled to say no, of course. Let's say she wants to play with markers, but you have asked her to pick up the crayons off the floor. If she says no when you ask her to pick up the crayons, say, "I understand that you don't want to pick up your crayons. When you've picked up the crayons, then you may play with the markers."

Using Grandma's Rule in this way—"when you have done what you need to do, then you may do what you want to do"—teaches your child that you've taken her feelings into consideration. But she still needs to do what you've asked before she may do what she wants.

Some Things are Nonnegotiable
Although it would be nice if young children could say no and we could let them do whatever they want, one of the most important missions of discipline is to teach a child self-discipline. Being self-disciplined means that sometimes we have to put off what we want to do or tolerate frustration. Say, "I know you don't want to get in the car. I'm sorry about that. But it's time for school. You can get in by yourself, or I can help you get in. You choose which way."

Teach that "No" Can Be an Important Word
Teach your child that saying no is sometimes what she needs to do. If your child says "No, I don't want to wear that," simply answer by saying, "I understand that you don't like this. That's okay—we'll get something else to wear." This shows her that you don't mind that she says no sometimes. In addition, allowing a firm no when something is unpleasant or dangerous needs to be encouraged. Teach her to say no when a playmate tries to hit or bite her. "Stop" is another word that can be useful to ward off aggressive acts by others, such as biting or hitting.

What Not to Do
Don't Laugh at the Use of "No"
Laughing or calling attention to your child's overuse of the word "no" only encourages her to use it more to get your reaction.

Don't Get Angry
The saying-no stage is normal in children and will soon pass. Getting angry gives your child attention for saying no. Getting angry will tell your child that

"no" is a bad word to be avoided at all costs, which is not a message you want to deliver. As stated above, there are many times when "no" should be encouraged, such as to express an opinion or to protect against an aggressive act by someone.

Preventing the Problem

Limit Your Use of the Word "No" to Limit Your Child's

The best way to reduce the frequency of your child's overuse of the word "no" is by limiting the number of times she hears you say it, as well as by limiting her opportunities to use it as an answer. For example, use the word "stop" instead of "no" when your child is doing something that you don't want her to do. She will also learn to use "stop" to keep herself safe from aggressive acts by others.

Limit Yes-No Questions

Avoid questions your child can answer with no. For example, ask her how much water she wants, not whether she wants some. If you want her to get in the car, don't say, "Do you want to get in the car?" Say, "We're getting in the car now," and then do it!

Case Study: Brooks Gets Positive

Twenty-month-old Brooks Chumley's favorite word to say was his parents' least favorite word to hear: "no." Because little Brooks used that word to answer every question asked of him, his parents started to wonder about his mental powers. "Can't you say anything besides no?" they'd ask their son, only to get his usual response.

So the Chumleys tried to reduce the number of times that they used the word during the day to see if that would have an effect on their little one's vocabulary. Instead of saying, "No, not now," whenever he demanded a cookie, they'd say, "Yes, when you've eaten your dinner, you may have a cookie." And while they were still, in effect, saying no to his request, Brooks didn't react negatively in return. Instead, he took his parents up on their promise and got his cookie immediately after dinner.

As his parents traded in their nos for yeses, Brooks started to increase his use of "yes," a word that was immediately met with smiles, hugs, and compliments from his delighted parents. "Thanks for saying yes when I asked you if you wanted to take a bath," his mother would say. They were delighted that their son was decreasing his nos in direct proportion to how much praise he got for saying yes.

The Chumleys also tried to limit the number of yes-no questions they asked Brooks. Instead of asking him if he wanted something to drink with his dinner, they said, "Do you want water or milk?" He would happily make a choice between the two. Their efforts were painless ways to manage their son's negativity, and they soon found their household taking on a more positive tone.

To keep him safe when he was headed for the stairs or was climbing on his dresser, his parents said, "Stop," instead of no—that word said exactly what they wanted him to do!

PLANE TRAVEL STRESS

- Kicks the back of the seat
- Screams at sibling
- Unbuckles the seat belt
- Won't stay in the airline seat
- Screams during the flight
- Needs to use the bathroom constantly
- Won't get strapped in the seat

Flying with young children to visit grandparents or just for a family vacation can lead to high stress for everyone. Managing your restless, active child and his equipment (car seat, backpack, luggage, toys, electronics, favorite foods eaten without silverware) while being corralled in the small space of an airplane seat is good to think about long before you pack anyone's bags.

You are allowed to take your child's car seat on board, but ask the airline how old your little one needs to be before he must have his own ticket or boarding pass, and any other rules. The adventure will be less stressful with helpers, so think about who might come along to support you, your child, and all of the items you will need—and share the challenge of airline travel from start to finish.

Healthy Mind S.E.T.

Self-Talk. Keep your self-talk positive. Say to yourself, "My child will sense my mood, so I need to keep telling myself, 'This is okay. I can handle this. This is no big deal.' This affirmative self-talk will reduce my anxiety and won't panic my child about flying."

Empathy. Put yourself in your child's shoes by thinking, "The excitement of the airplane and all the people can overload her, just as it does me. I understand why she's unable to sit still in the chair while we wait to get on the plane. It's hard for me, too."

Teaching. Remind yourself that learning takes time, patience, and practice. Show or explain to your child how she can keep busy in the small space of an airplane seat for the flight, as well as during the waiting time in the airport.

Solving the Problem

What to Do
Use Empathy
At the first sign of rebellion or loud talking or screaming, stop what you are doing and begin talking calmly to your child. Say, "I understand you don't want to sit any longer, but that's the rule. The pilot will tell us when we can get up. I know you can wait. You are being so patient."

Make Travel Rules and Praise Following the Rules
Simple rules, such as those you have for any outing, will establish boundaries of behavior. So give your child rules, such as: stay close, listen to instructions, hold my hand, keep your seat belt buckled. You could even write those out together, so you have a list to check when your child follows these rules and praise to give for doing so.

Walk It Off
Tour the waiting area to keep from sitting too long before the flight. During the flight, walk the aisle to keep your child busy. Even taking many trips to the bathroom, although tedious, will keep little ones occupied. When a young child won't stay in his seat, invoke the airline rule. Say, "I understand that you want to get out, but the rule is that you must stay seated while that light is on. See the light? When it goes off, we can walk to where those nice people who helped us are."

Praise Your Child's Empathy

Keep complimenting your child's good behavior throughout the trip. Say, "You are sitting so quietly. That is so respectful of the other people on the airplane [in the airport]." Or say, "We want to be polite and show people respect. Being able to use a quiet voice on an airplane is respectful of other people's privacy and need for quiet." Another example is saying, "Thank you for playing with your puzzle box so quietly. That doesn't interrupt the people in the seats next to us on the plane. They can hear better when we are quiet near them."

Use Grandma's Rule

To motivate your child to sit in his seat and to use a quiet voice, say, "When you sit down in your seat, you and I can sing softly to each other."

Kick the Shoes Off

When you can't book the bulkhead seat so no one is in front of you, to prevent your child from kicking the back of the seat in front of him, first take his shoes off. Use your phone timer to make a contest of keeping his feet still. Say, "Let's see how long you can keep your feet still. I'm setting the timer." Children love challenges, so while his feet are still, praise his stillness. If kicking begins, put your hands on his feet, and focus his attention on something else, such as your phone or the book you are reading to him. If all interventions fail, holding him in your lap so you can control his feet may be necessary, or walk the plane aisle so he'll use his feet for walking instead of kicking.

Traveling with Two Children

We recommend that parents of twins book seats in separate sections when both parents are traveling and in a section with three seats when only one parent is traveling. Keeping the children separated prevents a lot of bickering and competing between siblings. This plan works equally well with any two children. If bickering starts and is getting loud, play the Quiet Game. Say, "Let's see who can stay quiet the longest. I'm setting the timer." Children love to compete, especially for their parent's attention, so give lots of attention to quiet by saying, "You are staying so quiet. I'm thinking you may both win a prize when the plane lands." Prizes can be as simple as stickers to wear proudly on a shirt.

What Not to Do

Don't Offer Food Rewards

When your child gets restless on the plane or while awaiting its departure, don't use food as an incentive for him to follow the airplane rules. Food can be given during the flight as part of the experience, just as reading a book or playing a game can be part of it.

Don't Threaten

Making threats only creates a response in your child that can be toxic, as he will worry about being on the receiving end of your anger. Saying things in the airport, such as, "If you don't behave, we'll just go home," won't teach him appropriate behavior, even if you are willing to give up your flight tickets. In addition, you will become the source of your child's stress, not the source of caring and support. Using praise and activity as rewards keeps your behavior caring and encouraging for your child.

Preventing the Problem

Take Along Games, Toys, Books

Keeping children's minds occupied requires a lot of entertainment. So bring along as many fun travel-friendly items as possible, such as books, small toys, little puzzles, electronic devices, and so forth. For older children, help them pack what they want to use on the plane as well as during the time waiting for the flight to take off.

Use a Bottle to Help Prevent Baby's Ear Pain

When traveling with a baby, give him a bottle or breastfeed him when the plane is taking off and landing to relieve pressure on his ears. Much screaming can be eliminated by keeping pain out of your child's ears.

Use Gum to Prevent Ear Pain

If your child can chew gum safely, offer him some during takeoff and landing to avoid pain from ear popping.

Practice Before Traveling

If this will be your child's first trip, it's good to first practice everything you'll do on the way to Grandma's house, for example. Your dining chairs can become airplane seats, doorways can be metal detectors, and kitchen counters can become X-ray conveyers. Walking through the boarding routine and seating will at least partially prepare your child for what is in store. When you go on your trip, you can remind him of what he's learned by saying, "Remember, we practiced doing this at home."

Get Your Child His Own Luggage

Children love to imitate adults, so a wheeled carry-on bag with toys and games inside can help your child feel as if he is a fellow "big" traveler. It will also motivate him to exhibit more grown-up behavior to match how he's feeling.

Use Your Car Seat

Airlines recommend taking your child's car seat on board as an extra safety measure. Not only is it safer, but it is also familiar to your child and more comfortable for him than sitting low in an airplane seat with a lap belt. He is more likely to stay buckled in because that's the rule you have in your car.

Take the "Red Eye"

If possible, think about whether it is a good idea to schedule a flight at night so your child could stay on his sleep schedule during most of it. Some little ones, including infants, will do well with that schedule, as will their parents. If you are not up for that kind of flight, don't do it—you may have to stay up all night, if your child does. Again, a car seat can help because it will probably be more comfortable for him to sleep in a seat that he's familiar with.

Case History: Travel Trouble

Anya was a bright and energetic two-and-a-half-year-old, and her grandparents wanted very much to see her. So they gave her mother, Serena, tickets for a flight to their retirement home in the warm, sunny South. Although Serena wanted to see her parents and spend a week in a warm place because of the fierce winter they were suffering through, she was worried about taking Anya on a plane trip. And she would have to do it alone because her husband couldn't get off work to go with them.

Serena worried about the trip for a whole week but then decided to accept the offer. "What's the worst that could happen during a three-hour flight?" she asked her husband. To find out what it might be like to travel with a young child, Serena began asking their friends about their experiences, and the answers she got didn't put her at ease. They heard stories of out-of-control children, screaming adults, cranky passengers, and lost favorite toys. Serena was about to back out of the trip until she said to herself, "I've handled worse than what I've heard about traveling with kids. I can handle this trip."

Serena began planning what Anya would need to keep her happy on the flight. Serena borrowed the cutest carry-on bag from her friend, and Anya wheeled it around the house for days, filled with things she wanted to take to "Bama and Papa's." Every day, mother and daughter would set up chairs in a row and pretend to be flying.

When the day to fly came, Anya was cooperative and followed the rules that they had made about getting through security and into the waiting area. Wheeling her carry-on, the two travelers explored the terminal. Finally, they boarded. Serena buckled Anya's car seat into the airplane seat, and Anya climbed in. During the flight, Serena began handing out toys, books, and games as her daughter requested them or got tired of the one she had. By the time they arrived at their destination, Anya had napped and was fresh and ready for her visit. Serena was also relaxed after a good trip. The worst that had happened through the whole time was what this mom's wild imagination had conjured up in a week's worth of worry *before* the trip!

PLAYS WITH FOOD

- Throws food on the floor
- Uses food as a toy, paint, or weapon
- Makes a mess at mealtimes
- Spits food on the table
- Mixes milk on the plate with food
- Practices chewing

Take a young child, mix her with food she wants to explore or doesn't want to eat, and presto! You have an instant mess on your hands, her hands, and probably the floor and table, too. Children are little researchers who sometimes like to experiment with food to see what happens. It is fun to watch peas roll across the kitchen floor, and the mashed potatoes make such nice snowflake designs when dropped on the floor. And oh, the milk! Such a glorious mess!

When your child starts playing with her food instead of putting it in her mouth, it may mean that she's exploring and seeing what happens if a meatball is smashed. Be patient. Instead of playing with it, she may eat all the meatball when it's in smaller pieces. As she grows, you will learn that she is playing with food because she:

- is practicing chewing and swallowing
- is no longer hungry
- wants smaller pieces of food
- has fun seeing what food does when she plays with it or
- is finished eating, whether she can say the words or not

Be present at meals, so you will know if your child has finished eating or is simply playing with food because of one of the reasons above.

The lessons you are there to teach: it's important for children to learn how to eat, how to use manners, and how to communicate when they are finished eating. Also see, "Bad Manners," page 38, and "Not Eating," page 107.

Healthy Mind S.E.T.

Self-Talk. Keep your self-talk positive. Say to yourself, "It's normal for my child to want to play with food if she's not hungry or is excited that squishing macaroni or throwing peas is fun."

Empathy. Put yourself in your child's shoes by thinking, "It's easy to understand that squishing tomatoes makes a colorful mess or peas can be thrown like balls. I want her to have a good time eating and not make a mess, but I understand that my child wants to play and have fun."

Teaching. Remind yourself that learning takes time, patience, and practice. Show or explain how to make mealtimes less messy by teaching your child that it's okay to explore food (within limits) and that using good manners, cleaning up, and telling you when she is finished eating are good habits to practice.

Solving the Problem

What to Do
Make Food Rules and Cleanup a Team Effort
When your child is able to walk, she is able to help clean up. Calmly and kindly say, "I know that peas look like balls, but they are a food that stays on the plate or is put in our mouths. Let's clean up the peas that you threw."
Make Eating Time a Fun and Happy Time to Be Together
Even if she cannot yet talk, you can do the talking or repeat her babbling,

which also keeps her attention focused on eating, not playing with food. For older children, compliment good manners by saying, "It's great that you are using your spoon so politely. It's so fun to eat together."

Ask Whether Your Child Is Finished When She Starts Playing with Her Food

Don't immediately assume that your child is just being playful with her food. Ask, "Are you finished eating?," when she is playing with her meat loaf, for example. Instead of asking, "Do you want more?," teach your child to tell you when she is finished eating. For the toddlers and new talkers, ask, "All done?" And for the older child, teach her to say, "May I please be excused?" to end her meal.

Lengthen the Time for Sitting at the Table as Your Child Matures

Keep the length of time that your child sits at the table reasonable for her age. If you want to keep sitting, but you know she is finished, provide an area near the table where you can see her while she plays. If possible, give her a special toy just for this purpose, to make her mealtime as fun as yours. As she grows, she will be able to sit longer. The idea is to keep mealtimes as stress-free as possible.

What Not to Do

Don't Overreact

Though you may be disgusted at the mess and annoyed because you have to clean it up, focus on teaching your child to let you know when he's finished eating, instead of waiting for him to make a mess.

Don't Let Playing with Food Become a Way of Getting Attention

Ignore any food play that is not harming anyone else and that you feel comfortable accepting at the table. So, for example, ignore arranging peas into a smiley face, but don't ignore throwing food.

Preventing the Problem

Dress for the Mess

When your child starts eating solid food with his hands all the way through the time that he is able to use forks and spoons easily, making a mess is part of mealtime. So think about how to make cleanup afterward as easy as possible. Just as you might take off your more expensive clothes when you are eating or making food (so you don't spill anything on them), take off your child's best outfits and change him into something that won't be a big deal if he ruins it with red sauce stains, for example. Put a mat under the high chair or booster seat in order to have an easier cleanup job later. Some children are great at wearing bibs; some fight it. Changing your child into clothes you don't mind having to clean up afterward is a good alternative to making a big deal about a bib.

Don't Play with Food Yourself

If you play with the food on your plate while talking or after you've finished eating, your child will assume that she can do it, too.

Serve Food in a Form She Can Handle

To reduce the likelihood of a mess, cut her food into bite-size pieces that are easily handled and chewed, and gradually make them larger as she grows.

Keep Bowls of Food out of Reach

To avoid messes, steer playful young children away from the temptation to serve themselves from a larger serving dish or pitcher.

Talk to Your Child at the Table

If you make conversation with her, she will be less likely to spend time there looking for other ways to get your attention, such as playing with her food.

Case History: Dinnertime Disasters

Dinnertime at the Webb's house was looking more like art class than mealtime since five-year-old Nick had begun smearing food around his plate and spitting out what didn't tickle his taste buds. His parents, who were disgusted with their son's wasteful and messy games, tried to stop him by screaming, "Don't play with your food!" But even after his mother threatened, "If you do that with your peas one more time, I'll take you down from the table," Nick tried to roll one more pea down the slope of his fork and flick it on the floor. Clearly, threatening to take him from the table didn't stop him from playing with food.

So the Webbs decided that Nick must not need to eat all of the food that they put on his plate. When he was full, he simply used his leftover food for entertainment! His parents began to anticipate when Nick was full. They trained themselves to notice when his playful eyes and hands started to find new things to do with his french fries and green beans, and they quickly removed his plate. At each meal, Nick's parents also reminded their son to ask,

"May I please be excused?," which they made a rule to signal when he was finished eating.

Both of Nick's parents were relieved after experiencing three straight weeks without any food art at mealtimes. But then Nick chose to try his hand at making a river of creamed corn on the table. Fortunately, they had decided what the rule would be for slipups, and they calmly explained it to Nick: "Whenever you make a mess, you must clean it up." Instead of yelling at Nick, they calmly demonstrated the process.

Nick didn't get any attention for having to clean up his mess by himself, and it took only three wipe-up nights for him to start saying, "May I please be excused?" Those words worked like magic, he discovered, and he appreciated the hugs and kisses from his parents, who would say, "Thanks for asking to be excused. I know you're finished with your dinner, and now you may go play with your trucks."

The whole family seemed relieved that more time was spent talking about how nicely Nick was showing good manners at the table, instead of about how destructive he was with his food. Dinners with their son were shorter, but sweeter than ever before.

POTTY PROBLEMS

- Screams when changing training pants
- Won't tell you when she needs to go potty
- Has many toileting accidents
- Doesn't care if underwear is wet
- Won't take time out to go potty
- Hides when having a bowel movement
- Won't use potty except at home
- Has accidents at preschool or day care

Toilet training is one of the first major battles of wills between parents and young children. The war breaks out when parents ask their independence-loving offspring to give up doing something that has been natural for them to do. Instead, parents want their children to begin doing something that is new, takes away playtime, and is often undesirable.

To most children, what is desirable about toilet training is pleasing their parents. So foster the least accident-prone toilet training possible by putting more attention on what you want to teach your child to do (keep his pants dry, go potty in the potty) than not do (go potty in his pants). Help your child feel proud of himself while you lessen the likelihood that he will have an accident just to get your attention and reaction. For more tips on toilet training, see "Toilet Training" on the Healthy Children website (healthychildren.org /English/ages-stages/toddler/toilet-training/Pages/default.aspx).

NOTE: *If your child is having continuous toilet-training accidents after the age of four, consult your child's health care provider. She will check to make sure that your child is physically okay and help you understand what might be causing him to have accidents.*

Bed-wetting is not related to toilet training but to a pattern of deep sleep. Many children wet the bed occasionally, but it is not considered bed-wetting until after age six. If your child is six or older, and has three or more wet nights each week, ask your child's health care provider to help you understand what might be the cause and how to treat it.

Healthy Mind S.E.T.

Self-Talk. Keep your self-talk positive. Say to yourself, "It is annoying that my child keeps having potty problems, but I know that he will soon be potty trained."

Empathy. Put yourself in your child's shoes by thinking, "I understand that it is hard for my child to take time out from play to use the bathroom, especially since he doesn't care if he's wet. I sometimes don't want to find a bathroom either."

Teaching. Remind yourself that learning takes time, patience, and practice. Show or explain how to make being dry important to your child, so he will feel good about using the potty.

Solving the Problem

What to Do
Ask Her to Check Her Pants
Although you may want your child to tell you when she needs to go potty, that may not happen for a while. Instead of waiting for her to tell you, ask her to

check her pants to see if she's still dry. The goal is to go potty to stay dry, with dryness being most important.

Use Grandma's Rule at Home

Set your phone timer for fifteen minutes and then say, "When you have been clean and dry until my phone timer rings, then we can read a story." Keep resetting the timer until you think it would be time for a trip to the potty.

Praise Being Dry as Well as Correct Use of the Toilet

Teach your child to keep himself dry by telling him how good staying dry is. This increases his awareness of what you want him to do (stay dry) while wearing training pants. While your child is in training pants, say to him about every fifteen minutes, "Check your pants. Are they dry?" This gives him the responsibility of checking his dryness, which makes him feel more in control of the process. If he's dry, tell him you're glad. Say, "How nice that you're staying dry."

Remind Your Child of the Rule for Going Potty in the Wrong Places

Many young children occasionally go to the bathroom in an inappropriate place (outside, for example). When your child does this, remind him that the rule is, "You go potty in the bathroom potty. Let's practice." Then proceed with practicing correct potty procedures. If you are concerned about your child's repeatedly having new accidents on the playground at preschool (when he was not having accidents for a long period of time since being trained), for example, check with his health care provider to ensure that he is physically okay.

React Calmly to Accidents

If your child is wet, say, "I'm sorry that you're wet. Now we need to practice staying dry." Then practice five times going to the toilet from various parts of the house. (Pants down, sit on the toilet, pants up. Then repeat these steps from the next part of the house.) In practice, it's not necessary for your child to urinate or have a bowel movement, but only to go through the correct motions for getting to and using the toilet.

Use Grandma's Rule in Public

When your child wants to go only in his potty when you're in a public place, try Grandma's Rule. Say, "We need to keep dry. We can't use your potty because it's not here. When you've used this potty, we can stay here at the zoo." If you prefer, take your child's potty with you, and Grandma's Rule still applies: "When you've used our potty, we can stay at the zoo."

About Bowel Movements

Some children are reluctant to have bowel movements in the potty because it is uncomfortable or scary to do so, and it interrupts their play. To solve the problem, try making the goal to have a clean, as well as dry, diaper. Ask your child: "Check your pants. Are you *clean* and dry?" Also, because bowel movements are usually fairly regular, plot the time of day your young child has his. Often the need to have a bowel movement is accompanied by agitation and scurrying around to find a hiding place. That's the time to take him to the potty and ask him to sit for a few minutes, even if he objects. Have fun things that aren't available at other times on hand in the bathroom to divert his attention and make sitting more pleasant. Keep practicing until bowel movements are regular potty occurrences. If the problem persists, check with your child's health care practitioner for ideas about changing your child's diet to soften his stool, for example, to make it more comfortable for him to have a bowel movement.

What Not to Do

Don't Punish Toilet-Training Accidents

Punishment only gives your child attention for going potty in his pants (or another wrong place). It doesn't teach him how to toilet appropriately and stay dry.

Don't Ask the Wrong Question

Saying, "Check your pants," increases your child's awareness of what you want and puts him in charge. It's a good substitute for "Do you need to go potty?," which is generally answered with a no. Help your child feel responsible for checking his dry-wet condition and doing something about it.

Don't Shame

Don't try to get your young child to stay dry by saying, "Shame on you! You are too old to have accidents." This will only make him hide accidents from you, and it won't teach him how to stay dry.

Preventing the Problem

Look for Signs of Toilet-Training Readiness (Usually Around Two to Three Years)

The generally accepted signs of readiness include a child's awareness of the fact that he's urinating or having a bowel movement (or is about to do so); more regular and predictable elimination patterns; the ability to pull his pants down and climb on the toilet or potty chair (and do the reverse); the ability to understand toilet-training terminology and follow simple directions; an interest in using the toilet; and a general dislike of having a soiled diaper and being changed.

Don't Train Too Early

Early training simply teaches children to depend more on their parents than on their own ability to manage using the toilet. Children who are forced before they're ready may take longer to learn how to use the toilet.

Model Correct Potty Behavior

Familiarize your child with the potty and how it's used by showing him how you go to the bathroom (and how he can when he's ready).

Make It as Convenient as Possible for Your Child to Use the Potty When He Needs to Go

During toilet training keep the potty chair in the kitchen for easier cleanup after accidents, for example. Take the potty with you in the early stages, to help your child feel comfortable about using the potty outside your home. Portable folding toilet seats can be a comfort for children who are reluctant to use toilets in strange places.

Choose a Toilet Training Procedure, and Stick with It

Many resources (books, DVDs, videos, and websites) are available to help you toilet train your child. Find one that feels comfortable to you and consistently follow through with the methods it recommends. For ideas, see "Toilet Training" on the Healthy Children website (healthychildren.org/English /ages-stages/toddler/toilet-training/Pages/default.aspx). Whatever method you choose, consistency and patience are the keys to success.

Case History: Kaylee's "Accidents"

Nearly four years old, Kaylee Winter started to have occasional toilet-training accidents, signaling that she was waiting too long before heading for the bathroom. Kaylee had discovered that she could relieve the physical pressure of having to go by releasing only a small amount of urine into her pants and still be acceptably dry. When her mother, Claire, would scold her for wetting her pants, Kaylee would point out how she had wet "just a little." Claire realized that Kaylee was just too preoccupied with her activities to take time out to run to the bathroom, and to her, just a little wet was no big deal.

After analyzing the situation, Claire decided to reinstate the routine they had used to toilet train her daughter the previous year. She once again began praising Kaylee's dry pants instead of getting upset when she had wet ones. "Check your pants, Kaylee. Are they dry?" Claire said the next morning after breakfast. She was delighted when Kaylee happily said yes with a big grin.

"Thanks for keeping yourself dry, honey," Claire then said, giving her daughter a hug at the same time. "Let's keep them dry all day!"

After a few days of periodically asking Kaylee to check her pants (Kaylee always found herself dry), Claire thought her problem was behind her—until the very next day, when Kaylee was wet again. "It looks like you've forgotten how to go potty. Let's practice five times going to the potty," she told her glum-looking daughter, who seemed very disappointed that she now had to spend her valuable playtime practicing. Kaylee also missed her mother's praise when her pants were dry. But Kaylee soon learned that it was easier to go to the potty and get the praise for dry pants than it was to practice when her pants were wet.

Kaylee continued to follow through with keeping her pants dry for several months. For the rest of the year, Claire occasionally praised Kaylee for staying dry, as a reminder. Instead of becoming angry and frustrated when her daughter was wet, she kept in mind that it was better to help Kaylee firmly reestablish a love of dry pants.

RESISTS CAR SEATS AND SEAT BELTS

- Won't get in the car seat
- Won't get out of the car seat
- Kicks the back of the seat
- Demands your phone in the car
- Screams at sibling
- Unbuckles the belt on the car seat
- Needs to use the bathroom constantly

Car seats and seat belts are the enemies of millions of freedom-loving young children—adventurous spirits who don't understand why they must be strapped down. But they can understand the rule that the car doesn't move until they're strapped into their car seats or the belts are on. So ensure your own and your child's safety every time she gets into a car by enforcing the belts-on rule. The seat-belt habit will become second nature to your child—a passenger today and a driver tomorrow—if you're not wishy-washy about this life-or-death rule.

And for your own safety, a wild child bouncing around unrestrained in the car is a dangerous distraction. Also, every state now requires that infants and children be buckled up when riding in a motor vehicle. Approved car seats and seat belts have weight and age specifications to make car travel as safe as possible for your child, and new standards recommend rear-facing seats for as long as possible, until the child reaches the highest weight or height allowed by the car seat manufacturer. Finally, the leading cause of death for American children is trauma from automobile accidents. The risk of this happening can be lowered by making sure children are properly restrained. Never compromise the rule about being buckled up, or you may be compromising your child's life. (See also "Car Travel Conflicts," page 43.)

Healthy Mind S.E.T.

Self-Talk. Keep your self-talk positive. Say to yourself, "I love driving, even if my child is not always happy in a car seat or using a seat belt."

Empathy. Put yourself in your child's shoes by thinking, "I understand that my child may sometimes not like to be strapped into the car seat or a seat belt. I don't like it sometimes, too."

Teaching. Remind yourself that learning takes time, patience, and practice. Show or explain how your child can feel good cruising along in his car seat or seat belt.

Solving the Problem

What to Do
Give Choices for Refusing to Get in the Car Seat
It's okay if your child screams as you put him in the car seat. Say, "Here are your choices: you can climb in yourself, or I can put you in. You choose."

Use Grandma's Rule

Make getting into the car and buckled in the signal for the car fun to begin. Provide favorite in-car-only music and handheld toys after your child is safely buckled in. Say, "When you're safely in your seat and we hear the 'snap,' then you can play with your special car toy, and we can sing the car songs." Keep telling your child how much you like the way he got buckled in, so you can share the fun of a car trip with him. Your excitement will be contagious!

Buckle Yourself Up

Make sure to wear your seat belt and point out how your child is wearing one, too, to help her understand that she's not alone in her temporary confinement. If you don't wear a seat belt, your child will not understand why she has to.

Praise Staying in the Seat Belt

If you ignore your child while she's riding nicely, she may look for ways to get your attention, including trying to get out of her car seat or seat belt. Keep your child out of trouble in the car by talking to her and playing word games, as well as by praising how nicely she's sitting.

Redirect Your Child's Attention

Try activities, such as number games, word games, Peek-a-Boo, singing songs, and so on. This will help to prevent your child from trying to get out of her seat because she needs something to do. Conversation with you is much more valuable to her than what she can watch on TV, so avoid entertaining her only with the in-car TV.

Potty Before You Go

To prevent your child from using the excuse that he needs to go potty to get out of his seat or prevent him from getting in, make sure to have a potty stop before leaving the house. You know your child's potty habits, so having to go every five minutes is probably not necessary. Simply say, "I know you went potty before we left the house, so I don't think you need to go now." Then turn on your entertainment voice and keep him distracted. If your child needs to potty very frequently, check with your health care provider to make sure there isn't a urinary tract problem.

What Not to Do

Don't Complain About Having to Wear a Seat Belt

Casually telling friends and family that you hate wearing a seat belt gives your child a reason to resist her belt, too.

Don't Pay Attention to Your Child's Yelling About Being Buckled In, Unless She Gets out of Her Seat Belt

Not giving attention to your child's crying or whining while she's belted in helps her see that there's no benefit in protesting the seat-belt rule. Say to yourself, "I know my child is safer in her seat belt and will only fight it temporarily. Her safety is my responsibility, and I am being responsible by enforcing the seat-belt rule."

Don't Use Threats or Fear

Telling your child about the grave dangers of being out of her car seat or seat belt won't teach her how to stay in it. Threatening to take away toys or privileges later in the day won't teach her to follow the rules, either. In addition, telling your child that the police will arrest her if she gets out of her car seat or seat belt will only make her fear the police and won't teach her how to stay in her seat, safely buckled up.

Don't Spank!

Spanking or threatening to spank her for getting out of her car seat will only hurt you both and won't teach your child how to stay buckled up. You can't be a caring adult and use violence or threats of violence at the same time.

Preventing the Problem

Give Your Child Room to Breathe

Make sure she has room to move her hands and legs and still be safely buckled up.

Make a Rule That the Car Will Not Move Unless Everyone Is Buckled Up

If you enforce this rule from the beginning, your child will become accustomed to the idea of sitting in a car seat and eventually wearing a seat belt.

Make Your Child Proud to Be Safe

Tell your child why she's graduating to a booster seat or using only a seat belt. This will make her proud of being strapped in. For example, say, "You're getting to be so grown-up. Here's your new safety seat for the car!"

Conduct a Training Program

Let your child know how you expect her to act in a car. Take short drives around the neighborhood with one parent or friend driving and the other praising your child for sitting nicely in her car seat. Say, "You're sitting in your car seat so nicely today."

Check the Car Seat or Seat Restraints Before Traveling

The safety measures you take before leaving will determine how relaxed you are with your children when you finally depart. Don't wait until the last minute to find out that you must delay your trip because you lack an essential item: the car seat.

Case History: Unbuckled Jacob

Stephan Brenner loved to take his four-year-old son, Jacob, on errands with him—until his son figured out how to get his father's undivided attention by unbuckling his seat belt and jumping around in the backseat. "Don't you ever undo that belt again, young man!" Stephan ordered when he saw that his son had gotten free. But simply demanding that Jacob stay put didn't solve the problem, so Stephan decided that harsher, more threatening punishment was necessary. Though he had not spanked his son before, he threatened to give him a swift swat on his bottom whenever he found him roaming unbuckled in the backseat.

However, Stephan didn't feel good about threatening his son, and it didn't stop the problem. Jacob began to cry every time they had to go to preschool because he didn't want to wear a seat belt. The next time they had to get in the car, Stephan tried another idea: redirecting Jacob's attention to the world outside his window. He started to include Jacob in a conversation about the trees, asking him to name colors he saw and to count how many cars were on the road.

It was amazing! Jacob and his dad actually had more fun in the car than he had ever imagined they could because it was just the two of them—special time to bond over all the fun things to see that were more exciting than Stephan had ever realized. Seeing the world through his child's eyes opened Stephan's eyes to how even the simplest car ride can be an adventure when shared. And Jacob was so engaged with his father that he didn't focus on the belt—just his father's love.

SCREEN TIME / SCREEN ADDICTION

- Loses the phone or other device
- Cyberbullies
- Demands latest version of games or other items
- Won't put the phone or screen down
- Is addicted to his phone response—how many "likes," texts, and so on
- Is overly emotional when the screen is restricted or off
- Refuses to do anything but use a screen
- Wants TV on all the time
- Sneaks screen time
- Demands to use your phone
- Watches or wants to watch screens all the time

Young children are growing up in a world flooded with an ever-expanding variety of electronic media—including TV, computers, tablets, smartphones, and video games. These media can become addictive because of the fast-paced, emotionally charged words and images that they produce. This subject has begun to alarm researchers and child development experts, who warn that too much screen time is harmful not only for our children's brains but also their bodies, self-worth, and confidence. Websites, apps, and other tools are available for free or a fee to help parents monitor their children's screen time and create a plan for electronic devices used in their family. These are just two ways of addressing children's screen use.

Although your child may be quiet and happy while engaged in screen time, research has demonstrated the danger of letting him become addicted to watching screens, instead of having some screen time as only one of his many activities. In addition to screen time, your child needs active play outside to build his healthy mind and body and prevent obesity, time to read a book to help him create images in his mind based on words he's reading, and creative play with nonelectronic toys to build his gross-motor and fine-motor skills.

A child's brain develops rapidly during his first years. "The early years matter because, in the first few years of life, more than 1 million new neural connections are formed every second," according to the Center on the Developing Child at Harvard University. "Neural connections are formed through the interaction of genes and a baby's environment and experiences, especially 'serve and return' interaction with adults, or what developmental researchers call contingent reciprocity. These are the connections that build brain architecture—the foundation upon which all later learning, behavior, and health depend." (Read more in the article "Serve and Return" on the website of Harvard University's Center on the Developing Child, developingchild .harvard.edu/science/key-concepts/serve-and-return.)

In short, young children learn social skills by interacting with people, not screens. Rather than the stimulation of screen time, what young children really need is face time with a caring adult and peers. Dimitri Christakis of Seattle Children's Hospital was the lead author of the American Academy of Pediatrics (AAP) guidelines for screen time. The AAP now recommends parents "avoid digital media use, except video chatting, in children younger than 18 to 24 months." Interviews and data from an ongoing study of the effects of screen time on more than eleven thousand American children by the National Institutes of Health show that those who spent more than two hours a day on screens got lower scores on thinking and language tests. Other studies have also shown that excessive media use can lead to attention problems, school difficulties, sleep and eating disorders, aggressiveness, and obesity. In addition, media can provide platforms for illicit and risky behaviors through cyberbullying and dangerous connections with strangers posing as friends.

Children would rather be older than their age because they see the freedom and privileges that are granted older children and adults, and they don't understand why *they* can't have that freedom. That desire to be older can drive them to seek out content on their devices that is geared toward teens and young adults, such as programs about dating, parties, first kiss, and sexual and drug abuse behaviors. Such advanced content may push young children and preteens into reacting to the world as if they, too, are much older, but without the judgment and experience to deal with those adult themes. It is therefore important to monitor the content of the programming your child is viewing. That also gives you the opportunity to discuss what you and your child think about content on screens and to guide your child's thinking in an appropriate direction.

NOTE: *For more information on talking with your child about screen time, see "How to Make a Family Media Use Plan" on the Healthy Children website: healthychildren .org/English/family-life/Media/Pages/How-to-Make-a-Family-Media-Use-Plan.aspx.*

Healthy Mind S.E.T.

Self-Talk. Keep your self-talk positive. Say to yourself, "I don't like it when my child gets upset when I tell him he cannot watch television, play on the phone, and use the computer. But I know I can handle this. I can provide and suggest other activities. Even though I know we live in a wired world, my child needs other stimulation."

Empathy. Put yourself in your child's shoes by thinking, "I understand that the stuff on screens is amazing. It talks to you and takes you on exciting adventures that you can repeat over and over."

Teaching. Remind yourself that learning takes time, patience, and practice. Show or explain to your child that he can experience other adventures that are just as stimulating and exciting as those he watches and listens to on screens—and how good it feels to do other things than look at a screen.

Solving the Problem

What to Do

Use a Phone Basket During Mealtimes

During mealtimes or other times that you decide are important, put a basket in the center of the table, and have every family member place their electronic device in it. That way, everyone understands that a screen-free meal is important, the time when the contact between people is the in-person, face-to-face kind.

Limit Screen Time

It is important for children to spend time in outdoor play, reading, hobbies, and using their imaginations in free play, as well as in developing language through interacting with other children and adults. The American Academy of Pediatrics (AAP) has guidelines for healthy use of electronic devices by children of all ages. These guidelines are in constant review, based on new science that is revealing the dangers of too much screen time for a child's health, learning, and behavior.

Research has been helpful in forming guidelines that make sense. Toddlers who watch more TV are more likely to have problems paying attention at age seven. Video programming is constantly changing and constantly interesting, and it almost never forces a child to deal with anything more tedious than an infomercial. Also, for your child who is between two to five years of age, the AAP says that even with high-quality content, you should cap his TV time at one hour a day. Remember, too, that TV is still TV whether he actually watches it on a television screen or on a mobile phone or computer.

Enforce Screen-Free Zones

Create screen-free zones in your home: no TVs, computers, or video games in bedrooms and eating areas. Make sure that you and your children do not use phones or tablets in restaurants or while eating at home. This is an easy way to reduce being online and on screen all the time, and automatically reduces the risk of your child becoming addicted to screens.

Go Screen-Free When You Are Interacting with Your Child

When you are playing, diapering, feeding, bathing, or simply talking with your young child, turn off the TV, put away your smartphone, and power down your tablet. He doesn't need the distraction of electronics while you and he are having fun together.

Enforce Your Rules

When your child sees that his favorite screen is not on, demands you turn it on, and throws tantrums when you don't, stick to your rules about how much screen time is healthy for a child of a certain age, and maintain the screen-free zones that you have established. Giving in whenever he demands screen time does not teach him frustration tolerance, the ability to delay gratification, or the importance of following rules.

Become Your Child's Companion

When you make yourself available to your young child for one-on-one time, he will want less time with electronics. Young children love having the undivided attention of a caring adult—be grateful for it while he still wants you near.

If Your Older Child Needs Earphones, Monitor the Volume

If earphones are the only way you can manage screen time use in your house, the rule about volume is important to teach your child so he keeps the audio at a safe level. Monitor the volume as best you can by frequently checking the level or by helping your child learn that the earphones get taken away if they are used at high levels. Both will help avoid hearing loss for your child.

Teach Your Child to Practice Empathy

Say to your child, "Being able to put down screens when someone is talking to you shows him that you care about what he is saying." She may not even be aware that it is offensive for her to be looking at her phone or laptop while she is being talked to. For your child, multitasking in this way may be a way of life. For others, it's being rude! Make a rule in your house that the screen (phone, tablet, or laptop) is put away when someone is talking to your child, so she will not be distracted by the "ping" of an email or text, as well as the people on the screen. When real-live people are in front of her, they get her undivided attention.

Make Screen-Time Rules: How Long to Use and What Screens Are Used For

Children need rules and limits as a basis for self-control about screen time and all other behaviors. Set limits to time and content, monitor them closely, and stick to your rules.

Make the Bedroom a Phone-Free Zone

To help teens get enough sleep—they need eight to nine hours nightly—make their rooms phone-free zones. Because some teens are adept at night prowling, turn the phones off, and keep them in your bedroom, so you don't have to be concerned that your teen will be up all night communicating with friends.

Monitor Cyberbullying

Learn the programs and apps your child has and uses in order to monitor content. Don't be swayed by demands for privacy. As long as you are responsible for your child's well-being, her privacy is limited. You will then be aware if your child is either a victim or a perpetrator of bullying, even if she has just forwarded a bullying message from someone else. Over time, you will be able to trust your child to use her devices appropriately, so you won't have to be quite as vigilant.

Use Grandma's Rule to Earn Screen Time

One way to reduce screen time is to make a rule that your child earns every minute he gets of screen time by doing things other than watch screens. Say, for example, "When you have finished your homework, you may have _____ minutes of screen time."

Praise Other Activities

Say, "It's great that you are playing soccer. You are really a strong kicker!" or, "You are really getting good at skateboarding, and I appreciate that you are wearing your helmet."

Cultivate Creativity

Instead of letting your young child become a passive media user, focus his attention on building forts, inventing games, drawing pictures, creating collages, and doing other creative activities to keep his growing mind and body active. If screens are his passion, enroll him in programming classes where he can be creative on the screen.

Use Grandma's Rule

When your young child has a temper tantrum because you turn off his favorite screen or because you won't give him your cell phone or electronic tablet to play with, you can understand that screens can be addictive. Say, "I'm sorry that we cannot have screen time right now. Let's read a book for ten minutes, and then we can have more screen time." Set the timer on your phone for ten minutes. When the timer rings, allow your child to have five minutes of screen time. Then do an activity that gets her body moving—dance to some music, ride a bike, go to the park—depending on where you are and what your schedule of activities is for the day.

For older children who won't put their phone or tablet down, the same deal applies. Say, "When you have spent an hour reading or playing outside [just two examples], then you may use your phone or tablet for thirty minutes." Don't be swayed by cries of "It's not fair!" Enforce your rule!

Monitor Your Child's Media Choices

It is vitally important when you allow your child access to screens that you participate with him. Being there and discussing what he is doing or seeing helps with language development and critical thinking. Making statements such as, "I wonder why Clifford feels happy now," will help him understand the feelings he is witnessing and will help him begin to see cause-and-effect relationships. For example, when one child is being teased by another child, it's important for you to point out that teasing another person hurts that person.

Restate the Rule

When your child demands access to electronic media, restate the rule. Say, "Remember, the rule is: The television [tablet] is only on from 7 to 7:30 at night. It's off the other times of the day."

Use a Timer

Set time limits on using electronic media. To avoid habitual media use, set the timer on your phone to tell your child when it's time to click the off button, and praise him when he turns to more physically active play. Say, "I'm glad you turned off the TV and chose to play school. What are we teaching this morning?" Or turn off the screens when the timer goes off, and encourage a game of catch, soccer, basketball, or another favorite active game.

Ignore Tantrums

If your child throws himself on the floor and screams because he can't watch TV, turn your back, and wait it out. He will eventually understand that you mean what you say. (See "Temper Tantrums," page 170, for more advice on how to respond to that behavior.)

Be Alert to Addictive Behavior

You can assume your child is addicted to her phone, tablet, or computer when she becomes overly emotional when these devices are restricted. Another sign of addiction is her being overly concerned about how many "likes" or "texts" she is getting and becoming depressed if the number isn't high enough. Sneaking screen time when you have restricted access and refusing to do anything but use a screen is further proof of addiction.

To combat addiction, screen time must be severely restricted. Some parents report dramatic positive changes in their children's attitudes and behavior when they've taken a week off from screens, so much so that the parents want to keep them off permanently. Start your own withdrawal from screens gradually. Set aside specific times of the day that they can be used, and keep the screens locked up when they aren't to be used.

As we've said before, some teens are night wanderers and will try to retrieve their phones while you're sleeping. If your child becomes depressed because of screen restrictions, talk to your health care provider. Your child may need the intervention of a mental health professional to help her understand the addiction and begin to actively work to reduce her screen time.

What Not to Do

Don't Use Screens to Buy Child-Free Time

Instead of using a screen to occupy your child's time so you can be child-free in the kitchen, introduce him to the world of broiling, baking, and boiling by asking him to do age-appropriate tasks, such as washing the potatoes or tearing up the lettuce.

Don't Give In

In the face of the noise of an angry child, it is tempting to just give in and let him do what he wants. Unfortunately, giving in teaches him that all he has to do to get what he wants is to have a tantrum or launch into negotiation. As the caring adult in his world, it is up to you to set his boundaries, just as you do when keeping him from playing in traffic.

Keep Your Own Emotions in Check

In the face of a full-court emotional press by a child issuing you a list of demands, such as demanding to use your phone whenever he wants, it is easy to lose your cool. Be a model of emotional restraint by remaining calm and telling yourself that this, too, will pass as long as you stick to the rules you've set.

Don't Threaten

Telling your child that if he doesn't stop crying, you will be angry or never let him watch any screen again will create stress and anxiety. Such threats erode empathy, show him you don't mean what you say, and don't teach self-regulation.

Don't Let Young Children Use Headphones

Blasting young ears with the amplified sounds from headphones can cause permanent hearing loss. Because it is impossible to monitor the volume to ensure it is at a safe level when your young child is using headphones, it's best to not allow their use.

Preventing the Problem

Decide Places Where Screens Are Not Used

Before screen addiction occurs, decide where and when your child uses a television, computer, video game, or other device; make it a rule that there are no screens in your child's bedroom or in eating areas at home or in restaurants. This is an easy way to reduce the temptation to be online and on screen all the time, so it automatically reduces the risk of your child becoming addicted to screens.

Case History: The TV Is Running the Household

From the time she got up in the morning until she went to bed at night, ten-year-old Evelyn wanted screen time. While she was supposed to be getting ready for school, her mother, Cindy, would find her watching TV. In the car on the way to school, Evelyn would also demand Cindy's smartphone and would whine, beg, and negotiate to try to get it. Cindy would give in just to get some peace and quiet. The pattern was repeated on the way home and all evening.

Cindy decided that Evelyn had been spending too much time watching screens and that she and her husband, Gabe, were spending too much time watching TV in the evening. Besides, their TV enjoyment was being taken away because Evelyn demanded her programs and complained so loudly her parents would finally give in and let her watch what she wanted. Evelyn's parents decided they needed to do something dramatic to regain control over their daughter's screen addiction.

First, Cindy and Gabe decided to make some rules about electronic media. The TV would be off in the morning and evening until Evelyn went to bed. Cell phones would be answered in the evening only when absolutely necessary. They then planned evening activities that they could do as a family, when their daughter wasn't working on homework.

The first few days were rough, with what seemed like constant demands from Evelyn to watch TV. They would find her sneaking to a TV and turning it on. "I need to watch TV," she would whine, and when either Cindy or Gabe answered with, "I'm sorry, the rule is no TV today," she would switch to, "I want to watch something on your computer."

Happily, after a few days of restrictions, Evelyn shifted her attention to reading her favorite books. And she seemed more content than she had in a long time when she was working on puzzles or playing board games with her parents. Then Cindy and Gabe reintroduced a thirty-minute period of TV after dinner. Either Cindy or Gabe watched with their daughter and talked about what was important on the program, while the other parent cleaned up after dinner. Evelyn decided the programs she wanted to watch weren't as much fun when they were being analyzed and discussed by her parents, and she became more interested in reading the books she liked.

Her parents also substituted reading for their evening entertainment and found that books and magazines read while enjoying background music were more interesting than what they had watched on TV, too!

SIBLING RIVALRY AND FIGHTING WITH SIBLINGS

- Is jealous or resentful of siblings
- Competes for parents' attention
- Wants the same toy, same seat in the car, same privileges
- Tries to get power and control in the family by tattling, blaming, belittling, verbally abusing, fighting, hitting, calling names, and not sharing

- Won't play with sibling
- Won't share with sibling
- Blames sibling
- Denies fault

Tattling on brothers and sisters and resenting a new sibling from the first day he joins the family are just two examples of how sibling rivalry can cause problems in family relationships. Because children are constantly seeking independence and recognition, they often fight with their siblings for space, time, and the number one position in their family. Your job is to help them recognize that they are important without having to compete with their brother or sister for your time and attention. For more on fighting with siblings, see, "Won't Share," page 233; "Jealous," page 91; "Name-Calling," page 102; "Aggressive Behavior / Hurting Others: Hitting, Biting, and Bullying," page 30; "Talks Back," page 165; and "Whines, Nags, and Complains," page 195.

Healthy Mind S.E.T.

Self-Talk. Keep your self-talk positive. Say to yourself, "I wish my children got along better, but I can stand it. It's just a normal part of human nature to be competitive."

Empathy. Put yourself in your child's shoes by thinking, "I competed with my sister just as my daughter fights with her brother. I understand that sometimes it's hard to feel as if you are okay when your sibling makes better grades than you in school or seems to have more friends. I really can relate."

Teaching. Remind yourself that learning takes time, patience, and practice. Show or explain to your child how to cope, problem-solve, and tolerate frustration without comparing everything that she does to what her brother does. Tell your child that she is special and unique—there is only one of her.

Solving the Problem

What to Do
Teach Your Child to Use Empathy
Ask your child how he would feel if his sister ignored him and didn't talk to

him when he asked her to play a game. When he says he wouldn't like it, explain that it's important to put himself in her shoes when he ignores her. She wouldn't like it, either. The lesson you are teaching is to treat another person just as you would like to be treated. If it wouldn't feel good for you to be ignored or made fun of, it most likely wouldn't feel good for another person. Say, "Treat your sister as you would want her to treat you." Have him practice paying attention and answering his sister when she asks him a question, and reverse roles so she answers her brother when he asks her a question.

Appreciate Each Child's Individual Talents

To avoid the need for siblings to fight over who's best at something in order to get your attention, privately point out each child's individuality by saying such things as, "You are so good at drawing," or "You are a really good soccer player." It's important to praise each child's talents when you are alone to reinforce each child's special accomplishments. Doing so will help each one to stop comparing herself to her sibling because she doesn't need to one-up her sister to feel good about herself.

Encourage a Child to Say Something Nice

Being happy for someone else begins right at home. So encourage your child to say something nice about his sibling when she accomplishes a goal, such as when she wins a tennis match or gets accepted into an honors program at school, to encourage each child to learn how to express joy in someone else's good fortune.

Use Grandma's Rule for Following Realistic Getting-Along Goals

For an older child, sibling rivalry can mean raised voices and aggression. It's important to set goals tied to privileges for each child by using Grandma's Rule. For example, say, "When you talk to each other kindly, you will be able to play with your electronic devices later." The goals tied to privileges could be such things as speaking calmly to each other, sharing space and toys, and resolving disputes without your intervention.

Set the Timer

Teach your children how to share by practicing taking turns. When they are fighting with each other over who gets your help, say, "I'm going to set the timer on my phone for ten minutes. When it rings, then we'll switch places, and I'll help your brother [sister]." Letting a timer manage children's taking turns lets each child know that he or she will have a turn being your number one object of attention.

Point Out Playing Together Nicely

Make sure that your children know what you mean by "playing nicely." When they are getting along, point it out by giving that behavior your attention. Say, "I love your playing nicely by taking turns with the blocks and using nice words. That's what 'playing nicely' means. Good job getting along!"

Offer Choices

Allowing fighting to flare up and burn out of control doesn't teach your children how to get along. Instead of allowing battles to be fought, give your children a choice: they can either get along and have fun, or not get along and lose fun time. Say, "You may either get along with each other and continue to play or not get along and be separated to think about getting along. You choose." Let them get in the habit of making choices to give them a feeling of control over their lives and to help them learn to make good decisions on their own.

Define "Getting Along"

Be specific when praising your children for "getting along," so they know what you mean when you say it. Say, "That's great, the way you're sharing and playing together so nicely. I really like how you're getting along so well. It makes playing together fun."

Reinforce Family Support

When your family eats dinner together or does any activity as a group, tell everyone how much you appreciate being part of your family and how special your family is because of each person's love for each other. Get specific—point out how your son takes care of the dog, your daughter waters the plants, and Dad makes sure all of the grocery shopping duties are covered, for example. Then ask each person to say why he is grateful to be part of the family. Encouraging gratitude for the things we have increases feelings of satisfaction and decreases the need to compare what we have to what others do. Usually these kinds of activities are only done once a year on Thanksgiving. Instead, make it a weekly habit—say, on Friday movie night. This increases the chances that your children will begin to appreciate each other instead of competing for your attention.

Use Calm Time as a Last Resort

When all else fails and the sibling battles seem to have no end, Calm Time can help to give everyone a break from each other and time to cool off. Simply say, "I'm sorry you've chosen not to get along. You need to calm down. I'm taking each of you to Calm Time so you can think of ways to cooperate with each other and get along. When you're calm for a few minutes, we will discuss what you've decided."

Avoid the Blame Game

"She did it!" Maybe you've heard this accusation when something is broken during a sibling squabble. This is a game to avoid. Rather than playing detective and trying to get to the bottom of the crime, simply say, "I'm sorry you weren't getting along and this was broken. Because you were both here, I will assume you are equally guilty. Now let's fix what's broken together." When your children understand that they won't become your favorite child because the other did it, the blame game will end.

The same is true if something is spilled and no one is around. Asking who did it will not likely give you the true culprit and will result in the blame game. Simply say, "There is juice on the kitchen floor. I don't care who did it, but you need to clean it up." If blaming starts, say, "I don't care who did it. It needs to be cleaned up. Stop what you're doing until it is taken care of." You may need to stay there and wait until the juice is cleaned up, usually by the guilty party, and then you can praise that person for being honest and taking responsibility.

Use Grandma's Rule When Siblings Won't Play Together

Sometimes siblings refuse to play with each other for a variety of reasons. When that happens, Grandma's Rule can help. Say, "I would like for you two to find something to do together. You can play a game, go outside and play on your swing, or build something together. I don't care what it is, but I want you to spend some time playing together. After you've played together for thirty minutes, then you may go back to what you were doing." Once you set up a contract, be sure to enforce it, and stay there to praise your children's activity together. Building up the habit of playing together by practicing doing so is your goal.

Keep a Record of Turns on the Family Calendar

To avoid fights over whose turn it is to do something, keep track on the family calendar. "It's not my turn to clear the dinner table" can be quickly confirmed by checking the calendar.

What Not to Do

Don't Set Up One Child to Be an Example

When you say to a child, "Why can't you be as helpful as your sister?" you create a competition between siblings that will soon break out in hostilities. Therefore, avoid making negative comparisons.

Don't "Rescue" When Children Squabble

Sibling rivals will often get into squabbles over toys, privileges, portions, parent attention, and many other things. If you always intervene to settle disputes, you will be forever cast in that role. Adult siblings have been known to call Mom to rat out a sibling and want her to intervene in the dispute as a way of enhancing their position with their parents. Stop this game of one-upmanship by saying, "I'm sorry you aren't getting along. You need to work it out. I know you can find a peaceful solution." Then monitor the situation to see that no violence is used to settle the dispute.

Don't Get Upset When Your Children Don't Love Each Other All the Time

Children cannot live in the same home without engaging in some rivalry. It's human nature. Keep friction to a minimum by paying attention to getting along and by not allowing the rivalry to escalate to physical fights.

Don't Hold Grudges

After the dispute has been settled, don't remind your children that they used to be enemies. Start over with a clean slate, and help them do the same.

Preventing the Problem

Prepare Your Child Before the New Baby Arrives

Discuss with your child (or children) how she'll be included in the life of the new baby. Tell her what the new family routine will be and how she'll be able to help out. This will help her understand that she's an important part of loving and caring for her younger brother.

Play with Your Older Child Whether Your Baby Is Asleep or Awake

To decrease the sibling rivalry associated with a new baby, make sure you play with your older child when your new baby is awake as well as when he's asleep. This will prevent your older child from concluding that you only give her attention when the baby's out of sight. Spending time with your older child no matter what the baby is doing makes your older child think, "I get Mom's attention when the baby's here as well as when he's gone. That baby's not so bad after all!"

Plan Time Alone with Each of Your Children

Even if you have half a dozen young children to attend to, try to plan time alone with each of them (a bath, a walk, or a trip to the grocery store). This will help focus your attention on each child's needs, and it will keep you informed about feelings and problems that may not surface amid the roar of the crowd at home. Make individual brag boards. Display each child's creativity in her own special place, to reassure each child that her efforts merit individual attention.

Have a Family Game Night

Families that play together get along better. A family game night during which board games are played accomplishes several things: it keeps everybody away from their electronic devices for a while, it forces interactions among family members, it can create teamwork to win, it teaches strategy and planning, and it's fun.

Case History: Starr Wars

The constant warfare between five-year-old Jason Starr and his three-year-old sister, Julie, made their parents wonder why they'd ever had children. Feeling overwhelmed by the noise, decision-making, and constant need to support their children, the Starrs jokingly complained to each other that their kids obviously didn't appreciate the sacrifices that they had made to buy them nice clothes, new toys, and good food.

It seemed as if all that Jason wanted to do was tease and pinch his sister. These were his favorite ways of letting his sister have it when he thought she was taking up too much of his parents' time and attention. Threats of punishment obviously weren't working to solve the problem, since Jason didn't seem to mind getting yelled at whenever he started bullying his sister.

The only time Grace Starr ever noticed her son being nice to his sister was when Grace wasn't nearby. She had seen him help his sister across an icy patch on the driveway when he couldn't see his mom. Grace was so grateful for the bit of decency that she told her son, "That's great, the way you helped your sister be safe. I'm really proud of you." The Starrs decided to encourage more acts of kindness by dishing out compliments when their children got along and by enforcing a new rule when their children began to fight.

They got the chance to put their new policy into practice later that day, when a battle over books broke out after they got home from the library. Grace had no idea who started the argument, but she told her children, "You have a choice now, kids. Since I don't know who took the book from whom, you can get along like you did in the car today, or you can be separated in Calm Time, and I keep the books."

Both children ignored Grace's mandate and continued to play tug-of-war with the books. So she followed through with her promise, saying, "You've both chosen to spend some time in Calm Time." Julie and Jason screamed their way through most of their Calm Time, but after quieting down and being allowed to get up from their chairs, they had different looks on their faces for the rest of the day. They began to act like friends rather than enemies, and Grace was delighted that she had not lost her temper when her children had.

The Starrs continued to praise their children when they got along. They put less emphasis on any fighting they noticed, and they consistently used Calm Time to separate the children and reinforce the consequences of choosing to fight.

SPECIAL DIETS

- Vegan diet
- Milk allergies
- Wheat allergies
- Peanut allergies
- Gluten-free diet
- Organic foods
- Vegetarian diet
- Kosher diet
- Sugar-free (diabetic) diet

Many children today have special dietary needs for a variety of reasons, including health and religion. Because young children don't understand why they have dietary restrictions—such as no wheat, no peanuts, no pork, or no meat—they may whine, cry, get mad, and even try to sneak an "outlawed" food when it is withheld. The relationship between certain foods and stomachaches or hives may not be as clear to your child as it is to you, and reasoning with her may not help her accept her plight. The lesson is to make following a special diet a habit and routine, just like wearing seat belts or being kind to others.

Healthy Mind S.E.T.

Self-Talk. Keep your self-talk positive. Say to yourself, "I am sorry that my child is upset about these restrictions, but I also know that it is important to follow these rules. I can help him accept his special diet to keep healthy."

Empathy. Put yourself in your child's shoes by thinking, "It is hard to not be able to eat what your friends are eating—my child wants to be part of a group, just like all children. To my child, following these restrictions is not important. I understand that she doesn't want to be different."

Teaching. Remind yourself that learning takes time, patience, and practice. Show or explain how your child can accept and follow rules about food that he needs to learn for his health and well-being, and feel good about taking care of himself.

Solving the Problem

What to Do

Make a List

To help your child see what foods are okay, make a list where he can see and read it. Then pass along that list to school, camp, and other places your child eats. Talk with him about the list and show him the "okay" foods, so he knows what's good for him, instead of only being told what's good by others. Knowledge is power: being in the know about the list will help your child focus on what he can eat, not what he can't.

Make the Connection

If his special diet is for health reasons, make your teachable moment one that connects how he feels inside—tummy ache, head hurts, hives, and so on—and the fact that what he ate triggered that response. Say, "When you eat the foods that are okay for you, then you will feel better."

Use Empathy

When your child is whining and crying because she can't have a food for health reasons, tell her that you understand and are so sorry she can't have the food. Add that you are glad that she will feel good when she doesn't eat the food that makes her sick. This is best said while giving a hug; hugs are never restricted.

Similarly, when a young child is having trouble accepting religious

restrictions on food, you can be empathetic while making it a teaching moment. For example, say, "I know it's hard not being able to eat the same foods
some of your friends eat. It was tough for me, too, when I was your age. But it's
important that we respect our traditions."

Offer Substitutes
Tell your child that you're sorry she can't have peanut butter but glad she can
have almond butter. And add that she can have it with her favorite jelly!

Give Praise for Acceptance
When your child accepts the restriction or accepts a substitute, praise her acceptance by saying such things as, "Thank you for understanding why you
can't have peanut butter," or "That was a good decision to say you couldn't
have peanut butter. Almond butter also tastes good and won't make you sick."

Give Your Child Language to Use
In helping your child accept dietary restrictions, start by saying such things as,
"This is *what we can have* at our house," when your child begs for forbidden
food. The "what we can have" phrase is affirmative and feels much better than
"we can't have that." Or help your child say, "I can have carrots," rather than,
"I can't have nuts." When offered a restricted food, your child is more likely to
follow her dietary rules when she can say what she can have.

Practice with Your Child
Practice is an excellent way to translate words into actions. When you give
your child the words to say, it helps to practice saying them several times. For
example, say, "How about some peanuts?" and coach her to answer, "I can have
cashews." This can help establish a habit of thought and action that gives her
language to use to remind her of what she can have.

What Not to Do

Don't Give In
When your child is whining and crying because she can't have a restricted
food, resist giving in by saying, "Oh, you can have the cookie just this once."
When whining and crying pays off, you can expect it to be used many times
in the future.

Don't Get Angry
When your child begs for a restricted food, getting angry and yelling won't
teach your child how to live within her dietary restrictions. You will then become a source of stress, instead of a source of comfort, one she can trust to

keep her safe and healthy. Anger will also encourage her to sneak food to avoid your anger.

Don't Give Unhealthy Substitute Foods

Because you feel sorry that your child can't have nuts, you may be tempted to give her a treat, such as candy. Substituting one unhealthy food for another is not the way to teach her to manage her dietary restrictions.

Preventing the Problem

Get the Whole Family on the Same Page

When food restrictions are one child's alone, it is easier for the child on the special diet when other family members also restrict their own diet to support her food restrictions. Children can tolerate dietary restrictions best when everyone is doing it, particularly when the food restriction is new and they are trying to adjust to the change in their lives.

Keep the House Free of the Restricted Food

It's better to not have peanut butter in the house than to try to restrict its consumption by one child. Your child can't sneak food that isn't there. Out of sight, out of mind.

Involve Friends and Your Parenting Team

It's important for others on your parenting team to know about the special diet that your child has, whether it is for health, religious, or other reasons. Before your child goes to another child's house, to school, or to her grandparents' house, the adults there must be aware of the diet and take care not to make the restricted foods available to your child.

Case History: No Pasta for Parker

Five-year-old Parker Ellsworth loved pasta and would have eaten spaghetti with red sauce every meal of the day if he could. He also loved bread and the dinner rolls that his grandmother made.

But then Parker became a picky eater. He would claim to be hungry, but after a few bites, he would say that he didn't want any more—even of one of his favorite foods. No matter what they did, his parents, Clair and Sam, couldn't get Parker to eat. He lost weight and became a very skinny kid. Parker also began claiming that his stomach hurt, so his parents began looking for stress in Parker's life. But his life seemed quite normal and as stress-free as any young kid's life. He loved school, had caring playmates in the neighborhood, and had a good relationship with his parents and his extended family.

Clair was a nurse and began to wonder about physical causes of Parker's refusal to eat much and why his stomach hurt. A visit to the doctor ruled out any physical problem that could be detected by gastric examination, and tests didn't reveal any celiac disease. Not satisfied with a child with chronic stomachaches and no diagnosis, Clair and the doctor agreed that removing groups of foods, one at a time, would help them discover if a particular food was creating this discomfort in her child.

Because pasta and bread made up quite a bit of Parker's diet, Clair decided to start there. When denied his beloved pasta and bread, Parker went bonkers. He begged. He whined. He bargained. He cried. And he threw the mother of all tantrums. But Clair would say, "I know you want your spaghetti, but let's try some other foods. How about some celery or an apple with peanut butter?" And if tantrums persisted, both Clair and Sam would hold Parker and say how sorry they were that he couldn't have the food he wanted. They consistently followed their plan and discovered that Parker's stomachaches went away whenever he didn't eat any food that had gluten in it. And substituting regular pasta with gluten-free pasta gave Parker his pasta with red sauce back.

So their house became gluten-free. Clair missed having food with gluten, but Sam also felt better. He discovered that he had a genetic predisposition to gluten sensitivity, too.

~~~~~~~~~~~~~~~~~~~~~~~~~~~~~~~~~~

STEALS AND TAKES THINGS

- Takes things that don't belong to them
- Keeps things they've taken without giving them back
- Steals candy, toys, or gum at the checkout counter

Stealing things is an either-or issue: the child either stole or didn't steal. There is no grey area, and the earlier children learn the absolute nature of theft, the better. Unfortunately, very young children believe that everything in the world is there for the taking, so stealing isn't a concept they understand.

Therefore, it is important to establish rules early and enforce those rules consistently to develop that necessary sense of right and wrong.

NOTE: *If your child is a repeat offender in stealing, seek help from your child's health care provider. You may need a referral to mental health services to learn why stealing is a problem for your child and to help him overcome that problem. If he steals things and hoards them, also discuss this behavior with his health care provider.*

Healthy Mind S.E.T.

Self-Talk. Keep your self-talk positive. Say to yourself, "My child thinks that everything in the world belongs to her. She's not trying to break the law; she just doesn't know better. I can deal with this and teach her how to earn what she wants without stealing."

Empathy. Put yourself in your child's shoes by thinking, "I know my child is tempted by all the things she wants. I've felt that way myself, but I know that stealing is wrong. She won't know it is unless I teach her. I get that and am excited to teach her so she doesn't break the law."

Teaching. Remind yourself that learning takes time, patience, and practice. Show or explain to your child how to get what she wants without stealing and to accept that she can't always have everything she wants. Teach the rules about borrowing things from family and friends—that will help her learn right from wrong, a judgment that she will need to make her entire life.

Solving the Problem

What to Do
Explain the Difference Between Borrowing and Stealing
From the time a child is a preschooler and old enough to understand the words, make sure you teach her the difference between borrowing and stealing (and the results of each) to ensure that she knows what you mean when you say, "You must not steal." Stealing is taking something that's not yours without first asking if you can have it; borrowing is asking for and getting permission before taking something and then giving it back when asked.

Teach Your Child to Use Empathy
Ask your child how he would feel if someone took something that belonged to him and didn't ask if he could borrow it. Then practice doing that, so he can

experience the feeling that being stolen from causes. Remind him that if he wants to be kind and respectful, he will not hurt other people. Not stealing and asking if he can borrow something before taking a toy from his friend's house, for example, are ways to treat another person with kindness—respecting his property is good for everyone.

Explain How to Get Things Without Stealing

Your young child doesn't understand why she can't take things when she wants them until you teach her. Before about age three, the concepts of mine, yours, and theirs is kind of fuzzy and hard to understand. Say, "You must ask me for a piece of gum before picking up the pack at the grocery store. If I say yes, you may pick it up and hold it until we pay for it."

Practice the Rule

Say, "The rule is when you are in school, or at a store or someone's house, this is how you get things you want. First you ask for the toy, food, or anything by saying, 'May I please have . . . ?'" Then practice this rule, and when your child follows the rule, say, "Good job asking for what you want."

Give Consequences for Stealing and Be Aware of the Legal Consequences

Teach your child that she cannot keep something she's stolen. Enforce the rule that she must return it herself (with your help, if necessary). Say, "I'm sorry that you took that doll from your friend's house without asking. That is stealing. Stealing is wrong. Please tell your friend that you are sorry, and give it back to her."

Depending on local laws, some children as young as five have been threatened with arrest by store owners when the child steals something. Certainly teens are generally arrested when they steal. No matter what the local ordinances are, teach your child that stealing is against the law and wrong, and that he must pay for things he wants.

When a child takes something from a store, she needs to work to earn the money to pay for the item that she took. This money is then taken to the store and given to the store owner by the child, to help her learn that everyone has to pay for things before they can be theirs.

Make a "Never-Have-Anything-That-Doesn't-Belong-to-You" Rule

To reinforce the absolute nature of stealing when you catch your child stealing, make a rule that he cannot have anything in his possession that doesn't belong to him. To enforce that, inspect his backpack and pockets of pants and jackets before school and again after school. Any new object must be accounted for by asking where it came from and then checking out the story. For example,

"Where did this pen come from?" and then call the child who was supposed to have given him the pen to make sure it was indeed a gift.

What Not to Do

Don't Be a Historian

Don't remind your child about a stealing incident. Bringing up the past will only remind her of wrong behavior and won't teach her how to avoid the mistake in the future.

Don't Label Your Child

Don't call your child a thief because she will eventually believe that she *is* a thief and behave according to how she's labeled.

Don't Ask Your Child Whether She's Stolen Something

Asking only encourages lying. She'll say to herself, "I know Mommy will be mad. Why not lie so she won't be mad at me?" Instead of asking if something was stolen, ask where it came from or how she came to have it.

Preventing the Problem

Make Rules

To encourage your child to let you know when she wants something, teach her how to ask for it to help her understand that some things cannot be borrowed and nothing can be stolen. The basic rule is: you may not have in your possession things that don't belong to you.

Decide What May and May Not Be Taken from Public Places and Others' Homes

Because your child may not really know if something can be taken or is not hers to take, teach her the rule before you go out to a restaurant or store. Begin these lessons as early as when your child is crawling or walking. He may not understand all the words yet, but understanding will come. A basic rule might be, "Always ask me if you can have something before you pick it up."

Case History: The Short Shoplifter

Sandy and Doug Berk had never broken the law and gone to jail. But they worried that if their five-year-old son, Logan, continued to steal gum, candy, toys, and other objects, as he did while in the grocery store with his mom or dad, he might not have a future outside of prison.

"Don't you know that stealing is wrong?" Sandy would scream at her son when she'd catch him red-handed. She also tried slapping his hand and telling him he was a bad boy, but that didn't do any good, either. It only made him a more skillful thief. She became afraid to go on errands with her son, dreading both the embarrassment of his behavior and how she would feel when she punished him.

Logan was totally oblivious to the reasons why stealing was forbidden. He didn't understand why it wasn't right to take things that didn't belong to him. So the Berks decided to try to bribe him: "I'll buy you a new puppy if you don't take anything from the grocery store that doesn't belong to you," his mom said.

Nothing seemed to work—she didn't give him the puppy because Logan kept taking packs of gum when the checkout clerk or his mom wasn't watching.

They decided to explain the situation clearly to teach him in terms he could understand. "Logan, you cannot take things that you do not pay for," Doug began. "You must ask me for a pack of gum. When I say yes, you may pick up the pack and hold it until we pay for it. Let's practice."

Logan was delighted to follow the rule because now when he asked for gum, as the rule stated, his mother and father complimented him for following the rules and paid for the gum.

TALKS BACK

- Makes rude remarks
- Puts people down
- Sasses back
- Is sarcastic
- Imitates the person who is talking
- Smarts off
- Uses sassy retorts
- Imitates you or another person
- Gives back angry answers
- Talks back by rolling her eyes

No one wants to hear these kinds of comebacks from children:
The parent asks, "Did you do your homework?"

The child says, sarcastically, "Who are you, my teacher?"

OR

The teacher asks a child to put away her pencil and paper.

The child says, defiantly, "I don't have to. You're not my mom!"

OR

The parent makes a comment about social media.

The child puts down her mom by saying in a disgusted tone of voice, "I can't believe you said that! You are so stupid!"

As with other forms of language, back talk and tone of voice can only be learned by hearing it first. You can't control all the sources of disrespectful talk and hurtful tone of voice that your child hears. But you can deal with it after you hear it and stop yourself from using it when you are tempted to do so. Here's how to help your child learn that respectful language will get him what he wants: respect, understanding his feelings, and positive relationships in return.

Healthy Mind S.E.T.

Self-Talk. Keep your self-talk positive. Say to yourself, "I don't like back talk because it's disrespectful, but I can deal with it."

Empathy. Put yourself in your child's shoes by thinking, "When my child is angry and frustrated, he uses words and a tone of voice that get a reaction from other people—and make him feel more powerful. I understand that he wants to show that he's in charge by talking back. I feel like talking back sometimes, too."

Teaching. Remind yourself that learning takes time, patience, and practice. Show or explain to your child the difference between disrespectful back talk and expressing himself when he's frustrated or angry without using back talk.

Solving the Problem

What to Do

Refusals and Opinions Are Not Back Talk Unless They Are Said with the Intent to Hurt or Insult

Determine whether your child is talking back or doing something else. For example, sarcasm, name-calling, shouting answers, and defiant refusals all constitute back talk. Simply saying, "I don't want to," or "I want to eat later," may be statements of opinion when said in a matter-of-fact, kind tone of voice. And questions, such as, "Do I have to?" are legitimate, too. Make sure your child understands what *you* mean by back talk—when he uses a tone of voice that is hurtful.

Be Polite and Show Respect

Say to your child, "I am going to treat you with respect and would like you to treat me the same way. First, I'd like for you to calm yourself. Then answer me again in a polite way. I'm using polite words and tone of voice. I would like for you to do the same." Calmly give an example of a way your child could answer you or make a comment without using back talk. Your politeness and patience will show her how to be polite, and your respectful manner will model how to respect another person with your words and tone of voice.

Teach Your Child to Use Empathy

Ask your child how he would feel if you said the words back to him that he shouted angrily at you: "I hate you. You can't make me do anything!" When you point out that words make a difference and can hurt someone, just as does hitting or kicking, he will begin to see that he can use his power for good, not pain. Ask him to practice saying something nice to you and to see how you feel. Then do the same to him, so he is on the receiving end of respect. Focusing on the positive is the lesson here.

Practice Responding to Back Talk Without Hurting Feelings

Being able to talk to others and tell them we are angry or upset doesn't mean that we have to be sarcastic or rude to them. We can express our feelings by saying how we feel and be kind at the same time. Saying, "What you said hurt my feelings," is a good way to respond to back talk without using offensive language or tone of voice. Then explain why it hurt your feelings, so he understands what you mean and how words can make a difference.

Praise Kind Words

Every time that your child doesn't talk back and uses a respectful tone of voice or words, compliment his behavior. Say, "I'm so happy that you calmly and politely told Grandma that you didn't want to go to bed when she told you it was time. Your tone of voice was kind and respectful. That's called good manners and shows you love and respect Grandma. She uses nice words to talk with you, too, because she cares and loves you."

Stay Calm and Ignore the Back Talk

Try to pay as little attention to offensive back talk as you can. Instead, focus on helping your child solve problems without losing his temper and using back talk. Say, "What is it that is upsetting you? You must have really been upset because you talked back to me and used disrespectful words and a tone of voice that are not nice, like [name the words]. How can we solve this problem together without using those words and that tone of voice?" The game of back talk isn't much fun to play without a big payoff or response that gives your child the power and control he wants when he talks back. Teaching is the name of the game, not punishment.

Compliment Expressing Anger and Frustration Without Back Talk

Let your child know what kind of talk you prefer by praising her for using desirable and respectful language. Say, "I like it when you tell me how you feel when you are mad, instead of using back talk. The words you used, 'I am mad because I can't go swimming now,' tell me what's upsetting you and help me understand why you are upset. Then we can do something to help you solve the problem."

Point out to your child that saying, "Dad's so stupid because he won't take me to the pool" won't get him what he wants—to go to the pool. The feelings of frustration are absolutely normal; it's how he expresses them that is the teachable moment.

Use Grandma's Rule

Motivate your child to learn not to use back talk by saying to her, "When you have followed the directions I gave you to get dressed without talking back to me, we can read a book together." After your child does so without talking back, follow through on your promise, and praise her respectful response by saying, "Thanks for getting dressed and saying, 'Okay,' without any back talk. That feels so good to be treated kindly."

Use Calm Time

When you have tried everything else to get your child to respond in respectful ways, and he still answers you with back talk, taking him to Calm Time can help. Say, "I'm so sorry you chose to talk back to me and were disrespectful. I'm taking you to Calm Time, so you can think about how you can answer in respectful ways."

What Not to Do

Don't Play a Power Game

Since you know that using back talk is one way your child tries to get power over you, don't use back talk yourself. She may find fun ways of entertaining herself by seeing how she can get you mad or get your attention by using back talk. You don't want to encourage that.

Don't Teach Back Talk

Sarcastically or angrily shouting answers back at your child or anyone else only shows her how to use back talk. Although it's hard not to yell when you're being yelled at, teach your child how to be respectful by being respectful to her.

Don't Punish Back Talk

Back talk is, at worst, annoying. No evidence supports the belief that we make children respectful by punishing them for disrespect. Only fear is taught through punishment.

Preventing the Problem

Talk to Your Child the Way You Want Her to Talk to You

Watch what you say to your child and to other people around you and the tone of voice you say it in, so you don't become a model of using back talk yourself. Remember that young children are the world's greatest imitators. Talk to your child, as well as to others, as you would like to be talked to yourself—with kindness, respect, and empathy, not in a sassy, surly, mean, sarcastic tone. If you speak to her in a disrespectful way, you will get that back.

Monitor Friends, Media, and Your Own Speech

What goes in young children's ears comes out of their mouths, so co-viewing television programs and videos, as well as being aware of your child's music tastes and listening to the words spoken by your child's friends and others, will help you see where her back talk may have been learned.

Case History: Oliver's Back Talk

Whenever Ava Martinez would ask her six-year-old son, Oliver, to do anything, Oliver would shout, "No! I don't like you! I'm not going to!" Oliver became so experienced at back talk and verbal abuse that whenever Ava asked him to do anything, he would angrily shout back his answer, as if he had forgotten how to answer someone politely.

"No child of mine is going to talk like that!" Dominic Martinez, Oliver's father, would shout back at his son.

Unfortunately, Dom's back talk would cause an even greater uproar in the family. Once Oliver's parents realized that their sarcasm and shouting were teaching their son this kind of behavior, they tried hard to respond calmly to Oliver's back talk and to praise his pleasant responses. One evening at bedtime, they asked Oliver to put his toys back in his toy box, saying, "When you put your toys away, we will read stories."

When Oliver calmly said, "But I don't want to," they responded by saying, "That's really great the way you answered so pleasantly, even if you said you didn't want to. Now tell you what, when you have picked up your toys and put them away, you may have three stories."

Their use of Grandma's Rule and praise for calm answers had moved Oliver to calm, respectful responses himself.

As Oliver's yelling and sassy talk became less frequent, they usually pretended they didn't hear it. The combination of setting a consistently polite and respectful model for Oliver and praising his kind responses ended the outbreak of back talk and helped create a much more pleasant and cooperative household.

TEMPER TANTRUMS

- Kicks
- Screams
- Cries
- Throws toys, chairs, shoes
- Spits
- Punches or pounds the floor, wall, or furniture
- Stomps
- Hits others
- Bangs head
- Rolls around on the floor
- Hits and slaps himself
- Bites himself

Young children throw temper tantrums as their way of coping with frustration or anger, or to tell the world they're the boss. Tantrums can become less frequent by not giving the crying, screaming, angry child an audience and by not giving in to his demands. Though you may want to give in or crawl under the nearest checkout counter when your child throws a tantrum in public, be patient until he's finished, and praise his gaining control after he's calm. Being there for him when he needs support after a tantrum assures him that he has a caring, supportive, protective adult in his corner, no matter what. (See also "Curses and Swears, Uses 'Bad Words,'" page 58; "Overuses 'No,'" page 119; "Talks Back," page 165; "Want My Own Way," page 186; "Want to Do It Myself," page 190; "Won't Do What You Ask / Won't Listen / Ignores You / Doesn't Follow Directions," page 220.

NOTE: *Common, periodic crying is not a temper tantrum and needs to be treated differently. Ask your child's health care provider for help if your child has more than two to three temper tantrums per day or is doing self-harming things, such as banging his head.*

Healthy Mind S.E.T.

Self-Talk. Keep your self-talk positive. Say to yourself, "I don't like it when my child has a temper tantrum, but it doesn't mean that I'm a bad parent when it happens."

Empathy. Put yourself in your child's shoes by thinking, "I know how he feels when he is frustrated. I'm here to help him cope when he's upset. I get angry and sometimes have to control myself from having a tantrum, too!"

Teaching. Remind yourself that learning takes time, patience, and practice. Show or explain to your child how he can tolerate frustration and be resilient and resourceful, instead of having a meltdown when things don't go his way.

Solving the Problem

What to Do
Praise Self-Control
When your child is able to handle not getting what he wants, compliment his behavior. Say, for example, "I'm so happy that you calmly picked up the blocks when they fell. It feels so good to not get mad and frustrated when unexpected things happen. That's because we told ourselves that it's okay when things don't go exactly how we want them to. I love the way you built the tower this time!"

Make a Rule

Let him finish his "tantrum," and then lovingly problem-solve together by helping him figure out what to do, instead of throwing a tantrum the next time he gets upset or frustrated.

Ignore Your Child's Tantrum

Do nothing for, with, or to your child during his performance. Teach him that a temper tantrum is not the way to get your attention or get his demands met. But how do you ignore a tornado tearing through your living room? Walk away from him during his tantrum; turn your back on him (but be close enough to assure that he is not hurting himself or someone else). If he's being destructive or dangerous to himself or others in public, put him in a safe place (but not in a dark closet). Don't even look his way during this isolation. Though it's tough to turn away, try to busy yourself with another activity until he calms down.

Try to Stand Firm

Despite the power of your child's screaming and pounding, make sure you maintain self-control by holding tight to your rule. Tell yourself silently that it's important for your child to learn that he can't have everything he wants when he wants it. Your child is learning to be realistic, and you're learning to be consistent and to give him boundaries for acceptable and unacceptable behavior.

Remain as Calm as You Can

Say to yourself, "This is not a big deal. If I can stay in control of myself, I can better teach my child to control himself. He's just trying to pressure me so he can have what he wants." Keeping calm while ignoring his tantrum is the best model for him when he's upset.

Praise Your Child's Calming Down After the Tantrum

After the fire of a temper tantrum is extinguished, immediately praise your child for regaining self-control. Now is the time for a hug and to get both of you involved in a favorite game or activity that isn't frustrating for him or you. Say, "I'm glad you're feeling better now. I always love you, but I don't like screaming and yelling." Since this is your only reference to the tantrum, it will help him know that it was the tantrum you were ignoring, not him.

Use Empathy

After a tantrum, hold your child and tell him that you understand his frustration. Saying, "I know how you feel when things get tough, and I'm here to help you solve a problem when you need me."

Use Protective Hugs If He's Hurting Himself

If your child is banging his head, biting himself, or in any way hurting himself when he has a tantrum, sit on the floor with him and hold him in a hug so he can no longer harm himself. It's best if you hold him in your lap facing away from you. That position gives you more control and prevents him from trying to harm you, too.

What Not to Do

Don't Reason or Explain During the Tantrum

Trying to reason your child out of his tantrum during the tantrum is wasted breath. He doesn't care. He's in the middle of a show, and he's the star. Any discussion at this time only encourages the tantrum because it gives him the audience he wants.

Don't Give In to the Tantrum

When your child throws a tantrum and you give in and get him what he wants just to calm him down, you are teaching him to throw a tantrum to get what he wants. When you say no, mean it! Giving in only tells him you are not to be believed.

Don't Throw a Tantrum Yourself

Say to yourself, "Why do I need to act crazy, too? I know that when I said no, I said it for a reason." Losing your cool only encourages your child to keep the heat on, and it shows him that he doesn't need to learn self-control.

Don't Belittle or Shame Your Child

Just because your child has a temper tantrum doesn't mean he's a bad person. Don't say, "Bad boy! You are such a baby! Aren't you ashamed of yourself?" Your child will lose respect for himself and feel that he didn't deserve what he wanted anyway. Belittling is just another form of bullying.

Don't Be a Historian

Don't remind your child of his tantrum later that day. This only gives more attention to that behavior and increases the chances of his having another tantrum, just to be the center of your conversation.

Don't Make Your Child Pay for the Tantrum

Ignoring him after it's over will only cause him to have more tantrums to try to get your attention back. Don't send him the message that he's unloved and unwanted just because his behavior was.

Preventing the Problem

Teach Your Child How to Handle Frustration and Anger

Show your child how adults like you can find other ways of coping besides yelling and screaming. If you drop your phone and the glass cracks, instead of yelling and throwing your own tantrum, say, "I'm upset now, honey, but I can handle it. I'm going to try to be more careful with my things." Regardless of the situation, teach your child to look at the choices he has to solve his problems, instead of getting violent about them.

Praise Your Child's Coping

Catch your child when he is coping with frustration to give the behavior you want more attention than the tantrum. For example, praise his asking you to help him put together a complicated puzzle that might otherwise frustrate him. Say, "I'm so glad you asked for my help instead of getting mad at the puzzle." Helping your child handle his frustration and anger calmly helps him feel good about his ability to cope with problems. You'll find him repeating a problem-solving technique when he knows he'll get praised for it. Say, "I'm really proud of you for being able to solve the problem calmly."

Don't Let Playtime Always Mean Alone Time

Be there and pay attention to your child when he's playing appropriately with his toys. When you do, he won't have to resort to inappropriate play or tantrums to get your attention.

Don't Wait for an Invitation

If you spot trouble brewing with your child, don't let it simmer until it explodes. When you see that the situation is difficult or frustrating for him, say, "May I help? Let's try it this way." Show him what to do, and then let him complete the task. This will help him understand that it's good to let others help him when he needs help.

Case History: Tantrum Time

Gavin and Kaitlyn MacLean were worried about their two-year-old daughter, Madison, who would get a bad attack of temper tantrums every time her request for a cookie before dinner was refused. When her parents said no, she would scream, pull on her father's pant leg, jump up and down on the kitchen floor, and then throw herself down and kick and scream until both she and her distraught parents were exhausted. That's when they would finally give in.

In frustration, the MacLeans wondered what they were doing wrong. Was there something terribly wrong with saying no and then giving in to Madison's demands? They realized that what they were doing—giving in when Madison had a tantrum just to get it to stop—only encouraged her to tantrum to get what she wanted. Something had to change—and it was they!

The next time Madison wanted a cookie, they were ready with a new strategy. Instead of saying no, Kaitlyn said matter-of-factly, "Madison, I know you want a cookie. When you are calm and have finished your dinner, you may have one."

Madison didn't stop her tantrums, so her parents simply walked away, leaving her with no audience for her big scene. Although it was hard to stay away from their screaming child, the MacLeans waited until their daughter was quiet before reentering the kitchen. Without any physical or verbal attention, Madison had eventually stopped wailing and was waiting to see if her parents would practice what they preached.

Her father appeared, wearing a smile, and said, "Madison, I know you want that cookie now. When you've eaten your dinner and we're ready for dessert, then you may have the cookie. I'm glad you're not screaming and yelling now. It's nice to see you controlling yourself." To her parents' delight, Madison did quietly eat her dinner; so, as promised, she received her cookie when she was finished eating.

The MacLeans complimented themselves later that night on the self-control that they had exhibited in not giving in to Madison's tantrum. Although they were tempted later on to give in, they continued to remove themselves from their daughter when she had a tantrum and praised her anytime she reacted calmly when something was denied her. The frequency of Madison's tantrums diminished to the point that Madison would cry from time to time when she was disappointed but wouldn't have the explosive scenes she'd often had in the past.

TESTS LIMITS

- Pushes boundaries
- Goes across the street without permission

- Goes into off-limits areas of the house
- Wants more freedom
- Goes into the attic
- Climbs trees and roofs
- Goes to a friend's house without permission
- Skateboards in the street
- Bikes without a helmet

Immersed in new discovery and pushing their way out into the world, young children who have just discovered crawling or walking may need to be pulled back to safety because they're not as self-sufficient, self-reliant, and self-controlled as they think. And older children can't always understand why they can't do anything they want just because they are physically able to. It's normal for children to push boundaries and explore across the street and through the neighbor's yard, for example. It's also possible for your new little crawler to get to places you didn't think he could reach—like up on the counter or dresser.

So set commonsense, reasonable limits or boundaries, but know your child will test them to see if you really mean what you say. Balance your wanting him to have freedom with knowing how much freedom is responsible to give him. Anticipate dangers that he doesn't even know exist—such as opening the upstairs window to crawl out on the roof. Sounds fun, right? He doesn't realize the danger, so don't even give him the opportunity to find that one out.

As your little one grows, let him show you what he can do—going down a slide first with you there to catch him, then without you being his catcher, and finally with you watching from a distance, for example. Get to know your child's limits by testing his maturity and responsibility before making the mistake of allowing him more freedom outside and inside your home than he can safely handle. It's good to let your young child exercise his curiosity and explore his world, with your guidance and protection gradually being needed less and less as he learns to follow your rules and you see he can handle freedom safely. His independence, self-sufficiency, and self-reliance are what he's going for—and what you're aiming for, too.

See also "Gets into Everything," page 82, and "Wanders Away in Public," page 181.

Healthy Mind S.E.T.

Self-Talk. Keep your self-talk positive. Say to yourself, "This is what normal, healthy, curious children do. This 'teachable moment' helps me understand that my child wants more independence, so my job is to use common sense to give it to him."

Empathy. Put yourself in your child's shoes by thinking, "He doesn't know what is dangerous and what is not. I understand how he feels—he's curious about everything!"

Teaching. Remind yourself that learning takes time, patience, and practice. Show or explain to your child that it is dangerous to chew on electric cords or climb over the back fence—but also teach him how to explore his world safely to give him the freedom he so desires. Balance is the key!

Solving the Problem

What to Do

Set a Rule

Rules act as predictable guidelines for children. Telling your child the rules gives her boundaries that she needs to feel safe and know what to expect. When life is predictable, we all feel more relaxed and less anxious. Say, "The rule is: you must ask me first before you leave the playground."

Practice Rule Following

Say, "I know that you want to cross the street to go to Ellie's house. Let's practice how to safely cross the street."

Praise Following the Rule

If your rule is to take your hand before he crosses the street, when your child comes to you to cross the street, say, "Thanks for asking to cross the street. Hold my hand, and we can safely cross the street to your friend's house. It will be so much fun to go together."

Make Sure You Make and Enforce Helmet Rules

Before your child goes out to ride his bike, scooter, or skateboard, make sure he follows your rule that he must wear a protective helmet while riding. Check frequently to make sure he is following the rule and praise him for doing so. If he is riding without his helmet, he loses the opportunity to ride his wheels.

When you talk with him about wearing a helmet and believe he is ready to take responsibility for riding safely, give him another chance. And if he violates the rule, taking away his bike, scooter, or skateboard is the safest way to enforce the rule. Grounding the toy for twenty-four hours or more will help him remember that the rule is "When I wear a helmet, I get to ride" the next time he wants to ride.

Be Aware

Tie bells to your toddler's shoes, so you know where she is in the house at all times. When things are quiet, it's time to go check.

Offer Rewards for Staying Within Limits

Encourage your child to stay within the limits by rewarding him for doing so. Say, "I'm happy you stayed at the playground. Now you may play for five more minutes." Of course, make sure that a responsible adult is watching him play, to ensure that he is safe and to share in the positive relationship building that doing so provides. He loves an audience and to know that you are there cheering him on in his adventures. As he gets older, you will know when you need to be right there to greet him when he comes down the slide, for example, and when you don't.

Be There

Because a toddler or preschooler is discovering his world with unbridled curiosity and no fear, he needs to know what is safe and what isn't—and you or another adult needs to be watchful about what he does. For example, if your little one is walking around the house testing out his new mobility, be there beside him to guide him and prevent him from getting into dangerous situations. He may pick up a toy and try to throw it at a pane of glass, or he may open or close the wooden shutters only to get his little fingers stuck in them. All of these things and more can happen in a moment while your head is turned. Let him explore, but teach him what is and isn't okay, with a watchful eye on his comings and goings.

Repeat the Rule and Establish Consequences for Not Respecting Limits

Teach your child that not heeding your limits brings his fun to a stop. Say, "I'm sorry you knocked down the gate to the stairs. Now let's practice what to do when you come to the gate. Remember the rule that you can come get me when you want to go up the stairs."

Reinforce your child's coming to get you when he wants to go up the stairs, and then go up the stairs together, until you know he can do so safely without you.

Be Consistent

Make sure you enforce the rule every time your child breaks one. This teaches him you mean what you say. It also helps him feel more secure about his actions when he's away from you, because he'll clearly know what you expect him to do.

Use Frequent Praise for Staying Within Boundaries

While watching your child explore or play outside, take time out to praise his staying within the boundaries. For example, say, "Good job staying in the yard," or, "You are being so careful as you climb."

What Not to Do

Don't Spank Your Child for Going into the Street

Spanking doesn't prevent your child from doing something again—it just encourages your child to hide from you the next time he does what you punished him for. Children who sneak into the street are in great danger, of course, so don't add to the problem by making your child want to do it on the sly.

Don't Overreact When You See Your Child Pushing Limits

When you panic and yell about danger, or nervously tell your child, "Be careful," every time your child makes a move, your child senses your stress, which increases his stress level and may cause him to panic and hurt himself. He doesn't understand that your stress is connected to the danger you perceive. Stay calm and remove him from the dangerous situation, if you think he is not ready physically to handle sitting in a tall chair, for example, or playing on a slide that is too tall for him to manage. Explain why you were concerned, and in a calm voice, redirect him to a way to have fun safely.

Preventing the Problem

Pay Attention

It is impossible to know whether your child is staying out of danger if you are totally engrossed in your own activity. Keep your eyes on your child instead of your phone, for example.

Put Away Dangerous and Valuable Items

Put things that are valuable out of the reach of your toddler and preschool-age child—where he really cannot find them. But also make sure that you know where he is, that you are aware of what your child is doing and where. Above all, lock up and don't leave guns, knives, ammunition, and other dangerous possessions where your child can reach them, particularly when he can climb on shelves you might not think are reachable. Children have their ways of getting to things they want to see!

Establish Limits and Communicate Them Clearly

Your child needs to know his limits before he can be expected to do what you want him to do. If you decide that the front yard is off-limits to your toddler, teach him how he can go into that area safely—with you. And make sure that you or another adult is around to help him practice following this rule. Making a space in your home or yard forbidden territory only makes it more of an attraction.

Childproofing Is Smart-Proofing

Always lock the doors to cabinets holding household cleaners and other dangerous items.

Read more in the article "Childproofing Your Home" on the Healthy Children website (healthychildren.org/English/safety-prevention/at-home /Pages/Childproofing-Your-Home.aspx).

Let Your Child Know When He Can Cross the Boundaries

Reduce the attraction of certain off-limits areas (such as skateboarding to the park down the street) by showing and telling your young adventurer how he can do what he wants without getting in trouble for it. For example, say, "You must hold my hand while you cross the street," or, "I'll hang out on the porch while you skateboard in the driveway."

Ask About the Rules

Before you let your older child play outside, ask him about the rules you have set for outside play. If he doesn't remember, restate the rules. You want him to be able to enjoy his freedom and for you to do so, too, stress-free.

Case History: Ashley on Her Own

Eight-year-old Ashley Hamilton was the most popular little girl on Twelfth Street, a situation that also caused her behavior to be the biggest problem in the Hamilton family. At breakfast one morning, Ashley told her mother, "Today,

I'm going to walk to school with Susie, then I'm going to Donna's house after lunch, and then I'm going to play soccer with Maria." When her mother told Ashley she couldn't go anywhere anytime she pleased, Ashley shouted, "Why? Why not? I'm old enough and going anyway! You can't stop me!"

These kinds of rebellious statements encouraged angry name-calling episodes between Ashley and her parents, who couldn't decide where freedom should be given and boundaries should be drawn to protect their "baby" from dangers she wasn't old enough to handle. Because Ashley was constantly getting invitations, the Hamiltons couldn't ignore the problem of choosing where and when she could go places.

So they decided to establish rules with Ashley that could be negotiated and changed depending on how Ashley managed her freedom and responsibility. One of the things Ashley needed to learn was which rules to follow when she spent the night with her best friend. Her parents knew her best friend's parents and called them to discuss the rules that they had at their house. When the Hamiltons were satisfied that Ashley could manage her friend's house rules, they gave her permission to go.

Together, they went over the rules, and Ashley was more than happy to learn how to get more freedom. They decided to write the rules on a big chart that Ashley could see every day. They included positive "what to do" rules for when she spent the night with friends, including (1) stay only at my friend's house, (2) tell my friend's parents if I don't feel well, (3) tell my friend if I need to call home, (4) be kind to my friend and her parents, and (5) make good choices.

And before she went, the Hamiltons reminded Ashley about the good-choices and good-manners rules that they had at home. This helped Ashley's taste of freedom be as sweet as could be. Establishing and practicing the conditions of freedom allowed everyone to feel safe, secure, and satisfied within the limits and expectations provided.

WANDERS AWAY IN PUBLIC

- Refuses to stay close
- Refuses to hold your hand
- Runs ahead

- Lags behind
- Drifts away

When out in the big world with Mom, Dad, or maybe Grandma, for example, young children can be awed by the amount and variety of things to see and do. As a consequence, a child may see something interesting and exciting and go off to check it out, often without the adult even noticing. Clothes racks in stores can easily hide a child, and some children love to play hide and seek among the counters, aisles, and displays. And then there are the stacked items and other unstable things that can be knocked over, potentially injuring a young child. That fence over there looks good . . . hmmm . . . let's open it up! Therefore, it is vitally important when out in public with your little one in tow to keep an eye on the child and not on your phone or shopping list. Once your child has left your side in public, the only thing to do is to find her and prevent her from wandering away again.

Healthy Mind S.E.T.

Self-Talk. Keep your self-talk positive. Say to yourself, "It scares me and I don't like it when I lose sight of my child in public places, but I know I can teach her to stay close and safe."

Empathy. Put yourself in your child's shoes by thinking, "I can understand how my child wanders away when we are shopping, in the library, or in the park, or wherever we go. She is curious and unafraid, good characteristics to have. She wants to explore her exciting world, and I get that."

Teaching. Remind yourself that learning takes time, patience, and practice. Show or explain to your child how you want her to stay close in public to prevent her from getting lost or hurt, and to share all the fun with you when you're together.

Solving the Problem

What to Do

Keep Your Eye on Your Very Young Child

Your child's safety is the most important priority when you are with her. Keep your eye on her at all times, or make sure that another trusted, caring adult is watching her if you cannot to keep her from veering off into the street in a blink of an eye, for example.

Teach Your Toddler and Preschooler to Come to You

To avoid chasing your toddler or preschooler through a park, teach her to come to you when you want her to. During a neutral time, take her hand and say, "Come here, please." When she comes to you, give her a hug and say, "Thank you for coming." Practice five times a day, gradually increasing the distance that your child is away from you before you say, "Come here, please." Do this until she can come to you from across the room or from down the sidewalk.

Make Rules About Being in Public

Children need rules to tell them what to do to feel safe and protected, learn to be self-reliant, and make responsible choices. Say, "When we are at the grocery store, the rule is to keep one hand on the shopping cart at all times. That way, you won't get lost." Common sense is the rule.

Change Your Rule as Your Child Changes

As your child matures and becomes able to walk away briefly and come right back to your side in a public place, change your rule and allow her to do that. Tell her why you're giving her more freedom. Knowing that she's earned more independence by engaging in safe behavior in public will help her realize that following the rules will be rewarded. You both have the same goal: independence.

Use the Seat on the Shopping Cart

The seat on the shopping cart is there for the safety of toddlers, so use it to keep your wandering child restrained. Shopping cart seats also typically come equipped with safety belts that prevent children from standing up and getting out of the seat.

Praise Staying Close

Make it more attractive to stay close by praising your child every time she does. Say, "Good job staying close," or, "You're being such a good shopper by staying close to me. It's so fun to share this shopping trip together. I love showing you all the pretty fruits and vegetables in the grocery store."

Involve Your Child in the Activity

If your child is older and you don't need to hold her hand or push her in a stroller while you are out and about, let her hold a water bottle or the dog's leash, if she's able. This will make her feel she is an important part of the adventure, and she'll be less tempted to roam.

Use Reprimands

Reprimanding your child for not staying close in public will teach her what behavior you expect and what will happen if she doesn't follow your rule. When she is not staying close in the store, say, "Please stay close. Staying close to me keeps you safe. Hold my hand, so I know where you are in the store." If she repeatedly breaks your rule, restate the reprimand, and stop the shopping trip until she is either able to follow your rule or mature enough to go with you without having to stay right by your side.

Practice, Practice, Practice

Not only is it important to practice the rules before going to the farmers' market, a gym class, or the library together, but additional practice is also needed after your child has a lapse in rule following during a trip. Simply say, "I'm sorry you didn't follow the stay-close rule. Now we have to go home and practice, so I know you can do it." Most children don't like to take time practicing, but it is a consequence that teaches your child what you want her to do.

What Not to Do

Don't Change Your Rules Under Pressure

Don't change your public behavior rules, even if your child yells and screams. Your firmness and consistency will give your child a sense of security. Even if your restrictions may occasionally produce yelling and screaming, the safety net you provide will help her feel protected in strange territory.

Don't Make Threats You Won't Keep

And if you know you must continue your shopping trip, don't threaten to go home if your child doesn't follow your rules. Making false promises only tells her you can't be trusted.

Don't Take Your Child Shopping or to the Park for Longer Than She Can Tolerate

Some young children can follow staying-close rules for longer periods of time than others can. Get to know your child. One hour may be her limit, so consider that before leaving home.

Don't Let Your Child Stand in the Shopping Cart

Your toddler will get bigger and begin to resist sitting in the shopping cart seat. He will want to stand in the cart and have you hand him the items as you fill the cart. Letting him stand in the cart is dangerous and can result in him toppling out of the cart onto his head. Make a rule: he either sits in the seat with the safety belt on, or he walks beside the cart holding onto the cart so you know where he is.

Preventing the Problem

Practice Ahead of Time

If using a shopping cart seat or a stroller is not an option, then starting when your child is a toddler, practice following the rules before leaving the house. Say, "We're going to try staying within an arm's length of each other. Let's see how long you can stay close." After she does it, say, "Good job staying close. Thanks for staying close to me."

Case History: Staying Put

Emily Brody could not comfortably take her four-year-old son, Matthew, to a shopping center or grocery store anymore. He didn't want to be constrained by the shopping cart and was always wandering out of sight as soon as his mom turned her back.

"Stay here! Never run away while we're shopping!" Emily screamed at her son the last time he disappeared under a lingerie rack at the department store.

Her order proved ineffective. As they left the store and strolled down the mall, Matthew ran toward a shop window, pointed upward, and screamed, "Look at that train! Look at that train!" The shop window was so far away that Emily lost sight of him for a moment, which caused her to panic.

She realized that some rules needed to be established to prevent her son from disappearing while she did her holiday shopping. The next morning, she explained the new rule to her son before they went to the grocery store. Because the grocery store was his favorite place to race from aisle to aisle, she told him, "Matthew, you must stay within an arm's length of me while we're shopping. As long as you stay that close, you may look at things with your eyes, not with your hands."

During their trial run, Matthew was out of sight in minutes. "Remember the rule," Emily told him when she finally caught up with him in Aisle 3 and pulled him close to her. "You're supposed to stay within an arm's length of me. Staying close to me keeps you safe." Matthew acted as if he didn't hear what she was saying, taking off toward his beloved granola bars. Emily, boiling inside but cool on the surface, told herself that the rules were new. Like all new rules, they'd need to be practiced before they'd be followed perfectly. "You're supposed to stay with me because staying close keeps you safe," she repeated. Then she walked him to the quiet corner by the produce and turned her back on him while staying near him—the in-public version of Calm Time.

Matthew glared at his mother in protest, yelling, "No! I want to play. I don't like you!" Embarrassed but unflinching, Emily ignored his tantrum. Planning her next move, she decided that if a reprimand didn't solve the problem, she'd end the shopping trip and go home to practice the shopping rules with him. Then at the end of two minutes (which seemed like two hours to Emily), she greeted Matthew with a smile and reviewed the rule as they finished shopping. Whenever Matthew stayed within arm's length, Emily praised his behavior, saying, "Thanks for staying close, honey. I'm really glad we're shopping together. Now look for those canned tomatoes I buy. They're on that shelf there." They then began talking about cereals and planning which ones to buy for breakfast that week.

Emily consistently reminded him of the rule over the next few weeks, but they rarely had to leave shopping and go home to practice because they were having so much fun enjoying the new closeness between them.

WANT MY OWN WAY

- Is impatient
- Wants things now
- Is not able to wait, compromise, or take turns
- Demands an immediate response

When children discover that the world will not always revolve around their wants and desires, and that they will not always get their own way, they can be mad, disappointed, frustrated, and sad—all at the same time. As we all do, children want what they want when they want it—NOW! Teach your child the skills she needs to cope with this often frustrating fact of life. Because patience is not an innate virtue of human beings, children must be taught the art of waiting for what they want to do, see, eat, touch, or hear. Because you are more experienced in knowing what's best for your child, you're more qualified to control when she can do what she wants and what she must do before she gets it. Teaching patience builds the ability to tolerate frustration and to cope with not getting what you want immediately, both important skills to lower your child's stress throughout her life. Your child will also learn how to compromise. See also "Want to Do It Myself," page 190.

Healthy Mind S.E.T.

Self-Talk. Keep your self-talk positive. Say to yourself, "I don't like it when my child gets upset when he doesn't get what he wants immediately (or when I get upset for the same reason), but I can be patient and handle my frustration."

Empathy. Put yourself in your child's shoes by thinking, "I know how difficult it is to not get what I want when I want it. So it is even more difficult for my child, who hasn't yet learned how to be patient."

Teaching. Remind yourself that learning takes time, patience, and practice. Show or explain how to tolerate frustration and cope with not getting your own way all the time.

Solving the Problem

What to Do

Teach Your Child to Practice Empathy

Children are born with the capacity to be empathetic, so from the earliest age, make understanding the feelings of others part of your everyday lessons. When your child wants his own way, for example, say to him, "How do you think I feel when you won't compromise or are not able to wait for what you want? How would you feel if I demanded that you do everything I want you to do immediately? We want to be polite and show people respect. Being able to compromise and wait our turn to do things is polite and helps everyone feel good."

Praise Patience

When your child is able to delay getting what he wants for even a few minutes, say, "You are being so patient. Thank you for waiting for what you want."

Encourage Compromise and Patience

Reward even the slightest sign of compromising by telling your child how glad you are that she chose another shirt when the one she wanted was dirty and she couldn't have it immediately. Define patience for your child if you feel that it might be a word she's not familiar with. Say, for example, "You are being so patient by deciding that you can wear the shirt you want tomorrow and choosing another one today. That shows me how grown up you are." This teaches your child that she *does* have the ability to put off her wants; it also makes her feel good about herself because you feel good about her behavior.

Remain as Calm as You Can

If your child protests waiting or not having things her own way, remind yourself that she is learning a valuable lesson for living: the art of being patient and compromising. By seeing you remaining calm when you don't get what you want, she'll soon learn that demanding doesn't get her want satisfied as fast as calmly coping with frustration.

Use Grandma's Rule

If your child is screaming, "Go! Go! Go to the park!," simply state the conditions he must meet to satisfy his wants. Be positive. Say, "When you've put the books back on the bookshelf, then we'll go to the park." Practicing this will help him learn to tolerate frustration and cope with delaying getting what he wants—important life skills.

Avoid Always Giving a Flat No

Whenever it's possible and safe, use Grandma's Rule to teach your child how to have his own way. For example, say, "When you've washed your hands, then you may have an apple." Sometimes, of course, you need to say no to your child—when he wants to play with your glasses, for instance. At those times, try to offer alternative playthings to satisfy his wishes and to foster a sense of compromise and flexibility. Let your child know that safety comes first. Even though he may want to play with the lawnmower, for example, it is dangerous to do so.

Share How You Wait for What You Want

Show your child that you can delay getting what you want. Say, for instance, "I know it's unpleasant for me to wait to buy the new dining room furniture I want, but I know that if I work hard at saving money, I'll be able to buy it soon."

Make Sure Your Child Knows It's Not His Demanding That Got His Wants Fulfilled

Though your child may moan and groan throughout the waiting time, make sure he knows that you are getting in the car because you're ready and your jobs are done, not because he wailed his way out the door. Say, "I've finished washing the dishes. Now we can go."

What Not to Do
Don't Demand That Your Child Do Something "Now"
Demanding that your child immediately do what you want contradicts the lesson you're trying to teach. If you don't want him to demand instant results, don't do it yourself.

Don't Reward Impatience
Don't give in to what your child wants every time she wants her own way. Although it's tempting to put off what you're doing to satisfy your child and avoid a battle or tantrum, giving in to her when she's demanding it only increases the likelihood of her continuing to expect to get her own way immediately and always.

Preventing the Problem

Explain How Being Patient Can Be Rewarding
Because you have your child's best interests at heart, you can help him learn the payoff of not getting his own way immediately. Explain the conditions clearly. For example, say, "I know you want to eat the cake batter, but it's not good for you. When you wait until the batter is baked, it will turn into delicious cake for you to eat."

Provide a Menu of Activities from Which Your Child May Choose
Set up conditions that must be satisfied before your child gets his own way, and provide him with suggestions for activities he can do while he's waiting for what he wants. For example, say, "Let's think about what you can do while you wait. You may read a book, play with your trucks, build with the interlocking blocks, go outside to the swing, or help me put the clean clothes away."

Model Patience
When you are tempted to yell about being delayed in traffic or in line at the supermarket, say aloud, "I want to go NOW, but I will be happier if I just relax. Let's play a game to see how many colors we can find while we sit in this long line of traffic."

"I want a drink now!" three-year-old Emily Randolph wailed every time she was thirsty. When she saw her mother giving a bottle to her new baby brother, Justin, she wanted one, too—immediately.

"No, I'm busy. You'll just have to wait," her mother, Aria, responded, growing impatient with her daughter for not understanding that babies don't know how to wait for what they want. But Emily made so many demands to be held or given toys or drinks that Aria began to dread the moment when Emily would enter the room, especially while Aria was taking care of Justin. When Emily began taking food, drinks, toys, and blankets away from Justin—saying that they were "mine"—Aria realized that she needed to fix the problem.

Aria declared a new rule, called Grandma's Rule, and explained it to Emily: "When you do what I ask you to do, then you may do what you want to do. This is the new rule." That afternoon, Emily insisted on having a drink only ten minutes after the previous one. Aria stated firmly, "When you put your shoes on, then you may have a drink of water."

Emily was used to hearing no and then throwing a tantrum until her mother gave in, so she ignored the new rule and continued to cry and scream as always. But not only did her tantrum not bring a drink, it caused Aria to ignore Emily completely. The frustrated girl finally put on her shoes to see if that would bring her the attention (and drink) she wanted, since screaming had not. She was surprised and delighted when it did.

Emily quickly learned that her mother meant what she said, because she never strayed from enforcing Grandma's Rule. When Emily fulfilled her part of the bargain, Aria praised her accomplishments with comments like, "I'm so glad you put the toys in the toy basket. You may go outside now." Aria's admiration was sincere, and Emily appreciated it and became more responsive to her mother's rules. As the family learned to work together to satisfy everyone's needs, they grew to enjoy living with—not in spite of—each other.

WANT TO DO IT MYSELF

- Says, "Me do it!"
- Won't accept help in dressing, bathing, and so on
- Rejects you when you try to help
- Demands independence

"Me do it!" is one of the lines you can expect to hear starting around your child's second birthday. This declaration of independence provides a teachable moment for you to allow your child to do herself what you had always done for her—from putting on her shirt and shoes to opening a jar or pouring the milk.

So dig deep for extra patience as you understand that it may take longer and lots of trial and error for your child to "do it myself." You may need to get some tasks done faster sometimes (putting her shoes on so you can get to pre-school on time, for example). In those cases, letting your child *help* may be the way to compromise.

But it is all worth it—gaining independence and doing it herself are two important goals of self-reliance your child needs to reach—and you want her to achieve! See "Overuses 'No,'" page 119; "Temper Tantrums," page 170; "Want My Own Way," page 186; and "Won't Do What You Ask / Won't Listen / Ignores You/ Doesn't Follow Directions," page 220, for more ways to teach children to get power, control, and independence using appropriate behavior.

Healthy Mind S.E.T.

Self-Talk. Keep your self-talk positive. Say to yourself, "Although I'm frustrated, it is great that my child wants to be self-reliant and do things herself. I can be patient while she learns how."

Empathy. Put yourself in your child's shoes by thinking, "We all want to feel powerful, independent, and in control, and my child is no different. She also wants to try to do what I do, and being independent is the model I am providing."

Teaching. Remind yourself that learning takes time, patience, and practice. Show or explain to your child how to do things, from opening a drawer to riding a bike. Her trying to do things on her own makes every day full of teachable moments for you.

Solving the Problem

What to Do

Be Calm and Patient, and Praise Your Child

If your child wants to do everything—saying, "I put on my shorts," "I carry my bag," or "Me close the drawer"—remember that he's asserting his independence, not just being difficult.

Since you want him to learn to do things by himself, let him try. Avoid getting upset when he doesn't do things as quickly or precisely as you'd like. Instead, take delight in the fact that your child is taking the first step toward being self-sufficient and be proud of him for taking the initiative. Even screwing a lid on a water bottle all by himself—and trying many different ways of getting it to fit—is a big deal to him. So praise his accomplishing his goal when it happens.

Allow as Much Independence as Possible

Make it fun for your child to try new challenges. Your smiles and cheering him on by saying, "I know you can do it!," will encourage him to do as much by himself as he can. While you put on his mittens, for example, don't insist on keeping his other mitten away from his fidgety fingers if he wants to hold it. He can hand it to you when you're finished with the first.

Praise Your Child's Independent Accomplishments

Say, "I am so glad that you got your own jacket and backpack, and you are ready to go to school without my asking you to do it."

Use Grandma's Rule

To encourage your child's independence, use Grandma's Rule. Say, "When you get your backpack, then we can go to Grandma's." That helps you get ready to leave the house and helps your child accomplish his goal: being independent.

Play Beat-the-Clock

Tell your child how much time you have for a certain activity. Doing so will help him understand that it's not his inability to do something that makes you take over the job if you have to move more quickly than he does. Set your phone timer for the number of minutes you want to allow for the task and say, "Let's see if you can get dressed before the timer sounds. Then I'll help." This also helps your child learn a sense of being on time, and it reduces the power struggle between you and your child. You're not telling him when time is up— the timer is. This also taps into a child's competitive spirit.

Suggest Cooperation and Sharing

Because your child doesn't understand why he can't do something and doesn't realize that he'll be able to do it eventually, suggest sharing the job by having him do what he can while you do the rest. For example, when fixing breakfast for your young child, say, "Why don't you hold this bowl, while I pour the cereal?" Whenever possible, let your child accomplish some portion of the task, instead of merely watching you and feeling that he has no power or control, two things he really craves. Soon, he will be doing it all by himself.

Make Effort Count

As your child's first and most important teacher, you can encourage him to attempt various tasks. Say, for example, "I like the way you put on your T-shirt. That was a great try. Now I'll help you turn it around so the picture's in the front."

Ask Your Child to Do Things—Don't Demand

To make your young child more likely to ask nicely to do it himself, show him how to make requests politely. Say, "When you ask me nicely, you may do it yourself." Then explain what you mean by "nicely." For example, teach your child to say, "Please, may I get a fork?" when he wants a fork.

What Not to Do

Don't Punish Your Child's Mistakes

There are bound to be a few mishaps along the way, so be patient. If your child tries to pour the milk himself and accidentally spills it, help him do it more carefully the next time. Don't expect success right away.

Don't Criticize Your Child's Effort

Avoid pointing out your child's mistakes. If he puts his sock on inside out, simply say, "Let's put the smooth side of the sock inside, next to your foot. I think it will feel better."

Don't Feel Rejected

Don't feel hurt because your child doesn't appreciate your help. He's trying to do things on his own, and he may perceive your help as an obstacle. If he says, "Me open the door," let him do it. He knows you can do things faster and with less effort, but he wants and needs to develop his skills. Appreciate his efforts to do things on his own.

Preventing the Problem

Assume Your Child Can Do It for Himself

Keep track of your child's changing levels of expertise. Make sure you've given him a chance to try something before helping or doing it for him, so you don't underestimate his current ability.

Choose Clothing Your Child Can Manage

Choose clothes that can be easily taken on and off for your child in potty training, for example. Buy shirts that will go over his head and not get stuck on his shoulders when he puts on his clothes. Avoid hard-to-button buttons while he's learning how to button his clothes.

Store Clothing in Coordinated, Accessible Units

If your child's mismatched outfits she chooses bother you, help her develop an eye for coordination by sorting her clothes into matched sets. Make the matched sets easily accessible by putting them together in bins or drawers that she can easily reach.

Prevent Frustration

Try to make tasks as easy for your child to accomplish as possible. Undo the snaps on his pants or start the zipper on his coat, for example, before you let him finish the job. Resist the urge to say, "I know you can't do this, so I'll help."

Case History: Independent Isabelle

During the first three years of Isabelle Manning's life, her mother, Sarah, did everything for her. But then suddenly, "Miss Independence" wanted her mother to do nothing for her—a personality change that was confusing and frustrating for Sarah. She realized that *she* had a problem, not Isabelle. She was angry because Isabelle's desire to do things herself continually made them late for school and swim class. She decided to change her behavior from being upset to being glad that Isabelle was showing an independent streak.

So one morning while Isabelle was dressing to go to school, Sarah noticed Isabelle putting on her coat quickly and correctly for the first time. "I love the way you put on your coat by yourself," Sarah said. "You helped get ready for school on time!" Isabelle let her mother finish the zipper without putting up a fight, something that hadn't happened in weeks.

As they rode to school, Sarah realized how independent her daughter was becoming and how that was a sign that she was growing up. Sarah continued to praise her daughter's efforts at achieving independence. She also made it as easy as possible for Isabelle to try to do things, from simple tasks, such as closing a door, to harder ones, such as making the bed. Working together was a win-win for them both!

WHINES, NAGS, AND COMPLAINS

- Demands attention
- Fake cries
- Complains constantly
- Tries to make deals
- Acts as if nothing is ever right
- Has a cranky, high-pitched, usually nonstop, loud, irritating voice
- Is manipulative
- Pouts

Behind tantrums and sibling rivalry, these are the behaviors that parents tell us make them the most frustrated. What we want parents to understand is that whining, nagging, pouting, and complaining are ways that children (or adults for that matter) think that they can gain control when they think their lives are out of their control—because they sometimes work.

Remember what we said about stress and the impact on our minds and bodies (Chapter 2)? Well, being in earshot of whining, nagging, and complaining creates that kind of stress. Because it is so aversive, parents give in just to make it stop. Teaching your child appropriate ways to ask for what he wants and to cope with not getting everything he nags, whines, pouts, or complains about are the keys to solving this problem. Your efforts now to change this negative way of interacting into positive conversation will help your child focus on gratitude, not feeling entitled to everything he wants when he wants it.

Healthy Mind S.E.T.

Self-Talk. Keep your self-talk positive. Say to yourself, "It's normal for my child to think that the louder and more powerfully annoying her voice is, the more that I'll pay attention to it. I don't like it, but I can stand it and not respond to it. It won't last forever."

Empathy. Put yourself in your child's shoes by thinking, "I understand how my child feels when she doesn't get her own way. She hopes I'll give in if she nags, whines, and complains—and I can see her point of view. I am tempted to!"

Teaching. Remind yourself that learning takes time, patience, and practice. Show or explain to your child how she can get what she wants without nagging and complaining. The old adage comes to mind: "You can catch more flies with honey than with vinegar." Teach her that she can win people to her side more easily by gentle persuasion and flattery than by annoying confrontation.

Solving the Problem

What to Do

Teach Your Child to Practice Empathy

Children are born with the capacity to be empathetic, so from the earliest age, make understanding the feelings of others part of your everyday lessons. When your child whines, nags, or complains, for example, calmly and kindly say, "How do you think it feels when someone is nagging or whining to get you to do something? How would you feel if your friend Kiki whined and nagged you to go to the movies? We want to be polite and show people respect. Being able to ask someone to do something or to tell them you don't like something is more pleasant when you use a kind voice, rather than a harsh and uncaring tone."

Make a Rule about Whining, Nagging, or Complaining to Get You to Change Your Mind

Tell your child the rule that if he wants you to change a decision you made (about something he can do or where he can go), he needs to come to you to discuss what he wants, not whine, complain, pout, or nag you about it. Say, "Let's follow the rule and discuss my decision calmly using kind voices."

Ask Nicely and Reinforce It

Tell your child, "When you want something, ask me in a nice way, like this: 'May I please have a glass of water?'" Then have her practice asking for things without whining, and say, "Thanks! That was so polite!," when she does.

If Necessary, Create a "Whining Place" as a Variation on Calm Time

If your child's whining continues even after you've taught him how to express his wants nicely, let him know that he has the right to have feelings and frustrations that only whining can relieve. Tell him that he can whine as much as he wants but that he must do it in the "whining place," an area designated for whining. Let him know that you'd rather not listen to whining. When he's finished whining and can tell you what he wants in a pleasant voice, he can come back. Say, "I'm sorry you're so upset. You can go to the whining place and come back when you're feeling better."

Ignore Your Child's Whining, Nagging, and Complaining

Because your child's whining, complaining, and nagging are so nerve-racking, you can easily pay more attention to him when he's doing those things than when he's quiet. This can become an easy way for him to demand your attention. After you've taken him to the whining place and given him the go-ahead to get the frustration out of his system, ignore the whining, complaining, and nagging until it's over. Then give him lots of attention when he asks for things nicely.

Teach the Difference Between Nagging and Asking Nicely

When your child nags or complains, say, "Nagging and complaining sound like this." Now say something in that tone of voice. You may also use the recording function on your phone to record her whining, nagging, or complaining. Playing it back for her will show her the way she sounds.

Then say, "Here's how I would like you to ask me for something in a kind voice because it is a friendlier, caring tone. Now say the same thing you said earlier in a kind voice. I will record your kind voice so you can hear the difference." The goal of this lesson is to teach her the difference. Otherwise, she may very well not even know what you mean when you say, "Stop whining!"

Practice Using a Polite Tone of Voice

Even if she cannot yet talk, your child is listening to your voice and hearing the tone you use. Sometimes we whine without even being aware of it. Model the polite tone and words you want your child to learn from your example.

Play the Gratitude Game Instead of the Pouting Game

To refocus your child on what he can be grateful for, instead of dwelling on what he's missing, say, "Name two things you're grateful for! Your nose? Your eyes?" This will change his negative self-talk (pouting and complaining) to positive self-talk, and reduce his focus on what's wrong in life to what's right. This is especially good for those periods when a child pouts because he doesn't get his way. Simply asking him to tell you some good things in his life will help refocus him on the positive.

Repeat the Rule

When your child is trying to manipulate you by nagging about something to which you've already said no, stick to your original rule by saying, "Tell me what the rule is." This takes the power out of nagging and builds trust that your child can count on you to mean what you say.

Define "Whining" Even When Your Child Is Not Yet Talking

Make sure your child knows exactly what you mean when you say he's whining. Then explain that you'd like him to ask for something or tell you what he wants without whining. For example, say, "When you ask nicely, I'll give you the apple juice. Here's how I'd like you to ask: 'May I please have some apple juice?'" If your child isn't talking yet, show him how to indicate what he wants by using actions or gestures. Let him practice requesting things pleasantly at least five times. Make sure you fulfill his request to prove your point that asking nicely gets results.

Point Out Non-Whining Times

To show your child the vivid contrast between how you respond when he does and doesn't whine, immediately praise his kind tone of voice by saying, "Thank you for asking in such a nice tone of voice. Let's go get a toy to play with," or "I haven't heard you whine for the longest time," or "Thanks for not whining!"

Remember, This Won't Last Forever

Patience is key. Your child may be having a bad day or going through a period when nothing seems to please him, so he may spend more time whining until he gets back in sync with his world. Tell yourself, "This too shall pass," while you try to lift his spirits by praising his pleasant behavior.

What Not to Do

Don't Give In to Whining, Complaining, or Nagging

If you give your whining child attention by getting upset or giving him what he's whining for, you're teaching him that whining is the way to get what he wants. If he shifts from whining, complaining, and nagging to trying to make deals, at least he is moving in the right direction. Making deals is ultimately what you would like for him to do because it's an adult skill that will be useful for him later. Remember, in making deals, you have all the power, so you can control the outcome of deal making. Grandma's Rule is a negotiation tool that simply says, "When you have done what I ask, then you may do what you want."

Don't Whine, Complain, or Nag Yourself

Adult complaining may sound like whining to a child. If you're doing it, your young child may think it's okay for him to do it, too. If you're in a bad mood, don't get angry with your child because you're angry with the world. Simply tell him that you're feeling out of sorts; don't whine about it. Change your negative self-talk to positive to show your child how to change moods. (See the section in Chapter 1, "*S* Is for Self-Talk," page 3.)

Don't Get Angry with Your Child

Don't get angry with your child because he's having an off day. He'll not only mistake your outbursts for attention but feel a sense of power over you because he thinks that his behavior created your angry response. He may continue to whine just to show you he's the boss.

Don't Punish Your Child for Whining, Complaining, or Nagging

Responding sarcastically by saying, "I'll give you something to really whine about," when your child whines only creates conflict between you and your child. It tells him that it's never okay to whine, which makes him feel guilty for having disgruntled feelings. As with your own behavior when you are upset, whining may be the only way your child can vent frustrations until he learns new ways to do so.

Preventing the Problem

Catch 'Em Being Pleasant

When your child is not whining to ask for things, tell him how much more powerful his using a respectful, pleasant voice is. Your attention teaches him how much you appreciate being spoken to without whining.

Keep His Needs Met

Make sure your child eats, bathes, dresses, sleeps, and gets plenty of hugs on a regular basis, to prevent him from becoming cranky because he's wet, hungry, overtired, or too upset to tell you his feelings without whining.

Case History: The Whining Place

From the moment four-year-old Eliana Gonzalez woke up in the morning until she closed her eyes at night, she rarely said anything without whining, "Mommy, I wanna eat! Mommy, what's on TV? Mommy, where are we going? Mommy, pick me up!"

Camilla Gonzalez tried to ignore her daughter's noisemaking, but she frequently gave in to Eliana's demands in order to get her to be quiet. But the whining and nagging started to grate on Camilla's nerves, until one day she screamed, "Eliana, stop that stupid whining. I'm sick of it!" But yelling at Eliana only increased her whining, so Camilla decided to use a different method. She chose to try a variation of Calm Time that she'd used whenever her daughter misbehaved.

"This is the whining place," she told Eliana the next morning after she began her regular whining routine. "I'm sorry you're whining now. Stay here until you're finished whining. When you're finished, get up, and we'll play with your dolls."

She placed her daughter in the chair she had selected for this purpose. Then she walked away, making sure she wasn't around to give her daughter any attention. When she heard the whining stop, she returned to her daughter and praised her behavior. "Oh, I love the way you're not whining. Let's go play."

When Camilla realized her daughter was going to the whining place nearly ten times a day, she decided to change her own behavior with her child. She began to teach Eliana how to stop herself from being taken to the whining place. "When you ask me nicely, I'll give you a drink," she explained. Then she taught Eliana how to ask nicely by saying, "This is what 'asking nicely' sounds like: 'Please, Mom, may I have a drink'?"

Eliana practiced these instructions whenever she wanted something. Though her whining and nagging never completely disappeared (she still whined, but not every day), Camilla became much happier with her relationship with her daughter, and Eliana soaked up the praise.

WON'T ADJUST TO CHANGE

- Doesn't want to change who bathes, dresses, or helps him
- Doesn't want to go back to school from summer vacation
- Doesn't want to change schools
- Doesn't want to go to camp
- Doesn't want to change schedules
- Doesn't want to change from Mom's house to Dad's and vice versa

"No! Mommy do it!" your son shrieks as Daddy tries to give him a bath, a job your child says is Mommy's. Change can be hard for everybody, but it's particularly difficult for young children. Finding security in predictable sameness is common in young children because comfort comes in knowing what to expect, especially in children under the age of five. Learning how to cope with change and developing flexibility can help children be cooperative, resilient, and successful in relationships, as well as able to handle disappointment. Use the teaching tools below to help your child learn how to adapt to change and even welcome its exciting newness, whether it means going back to school in the fall, beginning camp in the summer, or wearing a new shirt.

Healthy Mind S.E.T.

Self-Talk. Keep your self-talk positive. Say to yourself, "It's okay if my child has trouble adjusting to change; he has not had much practice at it."

Empathy. Put yourself in your child's shoes by thinking, "I know that my child feels better when he knows what's going to happen next. He thrives on routine, consistency, and repetition, just like I do."

Teaching. Remind yourself that learning takes time, patience, and practice. Show or explain how to deal with change, so your child will learn how not to be afraid of it. Security comes from being able to predict how things will be, including being able to adjust to predictable changes in life.

Solving the Problem

What to Do

Praise Your Child's Healthy Choice to Change

Tell your child, "It's so great that Daddy will take you to school today. I know I usually do that, but it's also nice to change sometimes." If he cries and tries to resist the change, be patient but consistent in your teaching him that he can handle change.

Give Your Child Choices

Empower your child by offering choices to give control to the child, within limits. Say, "You may choose this shirt or that shirt. You decide."

Build Resilience

Resilient children look at change as a challenge to be overcome. On the other hand, inflexible children resist change as much as possible. But telling your child he *gets to* do something rather than *has to* do it will transform his feelings of fear and loss of control into feelings of excitement. Help him build this framework for change by saying, "You get to have a new babysitter tonight. She's going to be lots of fun. Isn't it exciting getting to know someone new?"

Teach Your Child the Positive Self-Talk to Handle Change by Modeling It Yourself

Children who are shown how to deal with change are more prepared to meet the challenge. Say, "I am excited about going to my new job. It's in a different building from my old job, but that's no big deal. I will feel so good learning new things."

Set Goals for Accepting Change

Children feel more in control of their destiny if they have ample time to think about and prepare themselves for change. You can help your child accept change more readily by having him set goals for handling change. For example, say, "We're going to the zoo with your class tomorrow. It'll be fun. Let's set a goal of having a good time at the zoo." Then periodically remind him of the goal and have him repeat it to you. Ask him, "What's your goal about going to the zoo?" When he says, "I'm going to the zoo to have fun," say, "That's right, you're going to the zoo to have a good time."

Teach Problem-Solving

When children are confronted with change and don't know what to do, giving them limited choices helps them see their options. Say, "I know you don't want to move into the big bed. Let's think about what we can do to make it easier. Maybe you could take your teddy bear into the big bed with you, and he'll keep you company while you're there."

Prepare Ahead of Time

When children are faced with a big new event, preparing ahead of time can ease the anxiety around big changes. Going to camp or going off to the "big" school can be just those sorts of changes. Prepare your child by talking about what an exciting new experience it will be and how much fun it will be to meet new children who can become friends. A lot of talk about camp and the adventures there can help ease the anxiety, and of course, visits to the school, a talk with the new teacher, and new school supplies can also add to the excitement. The feelings of anxiety and excitement are about the same, so your labeling those feelings as excitement will change how your child feels about the new adventure.

When Your Child Lives in Two Homes

Divorce and visitation are stressful for all involved. Helping your child adapt to the different homes, rules, activities, and people will become your first priority. As with all change, preparing ahead of time will help. At least a day ahead of time, begin talking about the change by saying such things as, "Tomorrow after school, Dad will pick you up. He really wants to see you and spend some time with you. I'll bet he will have some exciting things for you to do together. I'm so glad you'll get to see him." The shift from being anxious about change to being excited about it will help your child adapt and cope with the frequent changes moving back and forth will bring.

What Not to Do

Don't Meet Resistance with Anger

Children who are upset by change need lots of support and empathy to reduce their anxiety. Getting angry with your child for being inflexible only increases his sense of helplessness and doesn't help him learn to accept change.

Don't Shame by Saying "Don't Be Like That!"

When your child gets upset, don't put her down. Instead, say, "I know it's hard for you to change babysitters. But you can handle it. It'll be okay."

Don't Let Your Own Resistance to Change Make You Rigid

When you have in mind what you want your child to do but he doesn't want to do it, tell yourself to be flexible and help guide him instead of demanding he do it your way.

Don't Be Overly Emotional

When your child has to go to the other parent's home or off to school, don't say how sorry you feel for her and tell her how much you will miss her. That will only increase her stress because now she's responsible for your feelings, too.

Preventing the Problem

Teach Decision-Making Skills

Your child wants to feel that he's the master of his own fate, so allow him to make simple decisions. For example, choosing between two cereals, two pairs of socks, and two games to play gives him a sense of control over his world.

Respect Your Child's Individuality

You may have made friends with change long ago, but your child might have a more difficult time because his temperament may be different from yours.

Case History: The Cup-and-Bowl Caper

Julia Bardwell was only three and a half years old, but she had shown from very early on that she didn't like change. She rigidly resisted any new event that came into her young life. Her parents, Dena and Jim, knew better than to go against her wishes. If it wasn't a fight over using the blue cup instead of the yellow one at breakfast, it was a war over wearing something other than her green shorts and pink T-shirt. When confronted with change, Julia would first resist, then scream, and finally melt into an inconsolable, tearful tirade.

Dena and Jim wanted to help Julia become more flexible and resilient. Jim knew that setting goals at work helped him stay focused and not get distracted by his anxiety over getting everything done. He thought that Julia might be able to see beyond her fear of change if she had a goal to think about. Dena and Jim decided that Julia's first goal would focus on her steadfast refusal to use different dishes at breakfast. Once she learned to be more flexible by using different dishes, she might be able to be less rigid in dealing with other changes. So they began by talking to Julia about getting a new cup-and-bowl set for breakfast, one they let her pick out herself.

That night, Dena said, "Julia, let's set a goal for tomorrow morning. I think it would be a good idea for your goal to be to have fun using your new cup and bowl when you have breakfast." Julia looked at her mother and nodded, but Dena wasn't sure the idea of a goal had sunk in. A few minutes later, Dena said, "Julia, remember your goal for tomorrow morning? You're going to have fun using your new cup and bowl."

This time, Julia answered, "Yeah, I 'member."

The Bardwells repeated this reminder several more times that evening. They even made an occasional trip to the kitchen to look at the cup and bowl sitting all shiny and new on the counter.

At breakfast the next morning, Julia eagerly headed for the table, saying, "Where's my new cup and bowl?"

Dena and Jim knew they were onto something. They could help Julia accept change by helping her look forward to it. After a few days with the new cup and bowl, Dena and Jim said, "Julia, let's use the old blue cup and bowl at breakfast tomorrow."

"No!" Julia cried. "New cup and bowl! New cup and bowl!"

Dena and Jim didn't say anything about her digging in her heels, as they had in the past. Instead, they decided to help her set a new goal. That evening, Dena said, "Julia, let's set a new goal for breakfast tomorrow. I'd like your new goal to be using the old blue cup and bowl." Later that evening, Dena said, "Julia, what's the new goal for breakfast tomorrow?"

Julia thought for a minute and said, "Blue cup and bowl?"

"That's right," Dena said. "We're going to use the blue ones tomorrow. I'm glad you remembered the new goal."

Although Dena and Jim weren't sure this little exercise would pay off, they were delighted when Julia started treating it like a game and actually looked forward to the new goal for the day. They knew that Julia could ease into change as long as she was prepared for it. They now had a plan that made the whole family happy. Their perseverance had paid off.

WON'T BE QUIET WHEN ASKED OR NEEDS TO

- Talks loudly
- Yells, stomps, or slams doors when told to be quiet
- Screams when frustrated

Young children are naturally noisy and generally lack awareness of how quiet they need to be in different places to respect others who may be having a conversation, in prayer, or working near them and need a quiet space. They may talk loudly during religious services, shout excitedly when they find a familiar book at the library, and dance and sing to the annoyance of neighbors directly below your apartment. To try to get your child to be quiet, you may have lectured and threatened, but your child's short attention span and natural exuberance are hard to keep in check. It is important for you to teach your child that some places are quiet zones, but don't expect her to always remember all the quiet zones without your prompting.

Healthy Mind S.E.T.

Self-Talk. Keep your self-talk positive. Say to yourself, "I do love my child's enthusiasm, but I don't like it when my child is so loud. I can help him learn to be quiet when he needs to be."

Empathy. Put yourself in your child's shoes by thinking, "I understand that it's hard to be quiet when you don't want to. My child is just like me—I have to remind myself to respect the people around me when I'm on my cell phone."

Teaching. Remind yourself that learning takes time, patience, and practice. Show or explain how to follow the "being quiet" rules when he needs to.

Solving the Problem

What to Do

Teach Your Child to Practice Empathy

Children are born with the capacity to be empathetic, so from the earliest age, make understanding the feelings of others part of your everyday lessons. When your child wants to be noisy when he should be quiet, for example, kindly say to him, "How do you think Grandpa feels when you won't be quiet so your loud talking wakes him up when he's sleeping? How would you feel if people woke you up when you were sleeping? We want to be polite and show respect. Being able to be quiet when we need to is polite and shows that we care about the people who need us to not make noise."

Model Being Quiet

Your child needs frequent examples of the behavior you expect of her, so show her how you want her to behave. When at home, for example, try to use your quiet voice all the time. In addition, your child will listen more attentively when you use a quiet voice.

Make Rules

Children need rules to provide limits, structure, and security. When going to a quiet zone (a place where it's necessary to be quiet), tell your child that the rules are to stay quiet, stay close, listen, and whisper. Say, "The rule in the library is to use our quiet voices. Let's see how quiet we can be while we're there."

Praise Walking Softly

Say, "Thank you for walking softly across the floor. I know the people in the apartment below us appreciate it when we are quiet."

Agree on a Signal That Reminds Him to Be Quiet

Teach your child that putting your finger on your lips means that you want him to be quiet. Before going to the library, remind your child of the "finger on the lips" sign by saying, "Remember that the library is a quiet zone. We need to use our quiet voices while there. So now let's practice. Pretend that we are in the library. Let's both put our fingers on our lips, so we will remember to be quiet."

Leave the Quiet Zone

Even after your reminders to use her quiet voice, your child may still not follow the rule. That tells you that your child needs more practice in using the quiet-zone behavior at home before you bring her to the quiet zone. Say, "I'm sorry you won't stay quiet. We have to leave now." This may cause a momentary tantrum, but it's important to follow through and leave as promised.

Play the Quiet Game at Home

Set your phone timer for three minutes and say, "Let's stay as quiet as we can until we hear the ring sound." Whisper praise to your child during those three minutes by saying things such as, "You are behaving so quietly." Gradually increase the quiet time until you are comfortable with your child's understanding that she can behave quietly for long periods.

Plan Quiet Activities

When you want your child to be quiet for a limited amount of time, have quiet activities available, such as picture books, markers and paper, or an electronic tablet, so your child can read, draw, or play an educational game to keep her interest focused. Save the loud activities for the playground.

What Not to Do

Don't Yell

No matter how frustrated you feel, avoid yelling. Not only is it an ineffective way to help your child learn appropriate behavior, but it models the exact opposite behavior from the quiet you want her to exhibit.

Don't Go Places You Know Your Child Can't Handle

Because you understand that your child has difficulty staying quiet in quiet zones, don't set her up to fail. Try not to go to quiet zones until you know that she has learned to follow the quiet rules when needed.

Preventing the Problem

Pick Your Setting

Understand that young children are natural noise machines, so avoid putting them in situations in which they need to be quiet until you know that they can follow your quiet rule. If, for example, you've been invited to a solemn ceremony, understand that your child may not remember to use her indoor voice and will make noise. Make other arrangements for her if you want to avoid the inevitable.

Keep Visits to Quiet Places Short

You know how tedious it is to have to spend a long time in a quiet place, and you are an adult! From a two-year-old's perspective, five minutes of behaving quietly may be intolerable. Plan being in quiet zones for as brief a time as possible.

Shoes Off

If you are an apartment dweller and have downstairs neighbors, make it a rule that all shoes are left at the door. Stocking feet make a little less noise than shoes, and that can help soften the sounds that your neighbors hear coming from your apartment.

Case History: Loud Lucas

Five-year-old Lucas was loud. He loved to run, jump, and yell as he let his exuberance run wild. But Lucas lived with his mother, Laura, in an apartment, and the noise he made often brought complaints from the people who lived in the apartment under them.

Try as she might, Laura could not keep him contained. She found that she was constantly reprimanding him for being too loud, and her anxiety level was soaring as she thought about her neighbors. Laura threatened Lucas with a spanking if he made noise, but she knew how wrong it was to hit her young son. So Calm Time became her only tool, and Lucas seemed to be spending more and more of his time at home sitting in a little chair waiting for the timer to ring. Laura was pleased that she could keep Lucas quiet for most of their time together at home, but she knew that having him sit in Calm Time all the time wasn't good for him or for their relationship.

Laura decided to try a new strategy that she thought might teach Lucas how to keep himself quiet for longer periods of time while at home. She decided that outside activities would be Lucas's reward for being quiet, as well as a safety valve for the steam Lucas built up while being quiet. So on a Saturday, when Lucas was jumping up and down while begging to go to the playground, it was time to implement Laura's plan. She told Lucas that when he could stay quiet for half an hour, they could go to the playground. Laura set her phone timer and gave Lucas jobs that he could do to help her clean the kitchen with her.

During the kitchen cleanup, Laura frequently complimented Lucas on how much she appreciated his help, and she reminded him of the playground trip that he was earning. However, after fifteen minutes, Lucas ran to the couch for a fun leap or two.

"Lucas, I'm so sorry you weren't able to stay quiet until the timer rang," she said calmly. "Now we have to set the timer and practice being quiet," and gave him a choice of quiet activities.

Laura reset the timer for five minutes, and Lucas chose the block catalog to look at while he waited. He would frequently come to the kitchen to ask about different sets he was seeing in the catalog, but he walked quietly in his stocking feet and was complimented for being quiet.

This time, Lucas won the Quiet Game and earned a trip to the playground. Laura decided to use the timer more often when they were home, and she made a list of quiet activities they could do together. She decided that evenings would be mostly spent playing together until his bedtime, after which she could get her work done. As a five-year-old, he needed her to help him structure his time and learn to use self-control when he needed to become a quieter version of himself.

WON'T CLEAN UP ROOM, TOYS, CLOTHES, COOKING, OR ART-MAKING MESSES

- Leaves clothes, toys, and other items in places where they don't belong
- Doesn't clean up after playing

- Doesn't care if everything is a mess
- Won't put away her own toys or clothes, or things she borrows
- Cooks something and leaves the mess
- Spreads art projects all over and leaves the mess
- Leaves shoes in the middle of the floor
- Won't make his bed
- Won't put dishes in the dishwasher

Unfortunately for orderly parents, children are almost always naturally oblivious to their self-made clutter, although some children seem to literally be born wanting to keep things neat and organized. If your child is not one who picks up and puts away her toys and clothes without prompting, know that she isn't deliberately being messy. She simply is unaware of the importance of putting toys and clothes away or cleaning up the kitchen. Teach her (the younger the better) that, as much as we wish it were true, messes don't disappear magically—the mess maker (with helpers) cleans them up. Share this fact of life with your child, but don't expect perfection in her following the rule. Encourage, rather than demand, neatness by praising the slightest attempt your child makes at playing the cleanup game.

Healthy Mind S.E.T.

Self-Talk. Keep your self-talk positive. Say to yourself, "My child hasn't practiced cleaning up as much as I have. I know it's hard to always think about keeping things clean, so I have to teach her that keeping organized makes life easier. It's okay. I can do that."

Empathy. Put yourself in your child's shoes by thinking, "I sometimes don't want to clean up messes I make either. I can understand that my child doesn't want to keep our home clean and neat, even though it makes life more predictable and easier when it's organized. Her agenda doesn't include orderliness, just play."

Teaching. Remind yourself that learning takes time, patience, and practice. Show or explain to your child how to clean up her clothes and toys—just telling her to "clean up" may not mean anything to her until she practices putting things in bins and closets, loading the dishwasher, putting away dishes, and so forth. Let her know that you feel more comfortable when things are organized and less cluttered. Teach by example.

Solving the Problem

What to Do

Clean as You Go

Show your child how to put away his toys immediately after he's finished playing, to limit clutter as he bounces from plaything to plaything. Help him pick up the picking-up habit early in life, to encourage him to be a neater child and, later, a more organized adult.

Show Him How to Clean Up His Mess

Provide appropriately sized bins and containers in which your child can store his toys. Show him how to fit his things inside the containers and where they go when they're filled. This way, he'll know exactly what you mean when you ask him to put something away or clean something up.

Be as Specific as You Can

Instead of just asking your child to clean up his room, tell him exactly what you'd like him to do. For example, say, "Let's put the pegs in the bucket and the blocks in the box." Make it as simple as possible for your child to follow your instructions.

Make a Household Jobs Chart

It's easy to know who is doing what household jobs when they are all listed in a fun chart, so start the habit early. Jobs in the house include making the bed, dusting, vacuuming, setting and clearing the table, and loading and unloading the dishwasher or washing and drying the dishes by hand. As soon as your child is old enough to put a sticker on a poster or a mark on his very own job chart, you can make completing chores a fun way to reap praise and feel good about helping.

Say, "Let's put a sticker on the chart," every time your child accomplishes a goal. Even if he can't read, he will read your smile and joy as a job well done. If your child is too old for stickers to be motivators, create another reward for reaching the milestone of marking a chart for a week or a month. The lesson is about being responsible, as much as it is about cleaning up a mess. A job chart with names beside the day of the week for each child also reduces sibling rivalry—everyone knows whose job it is to do what when.

Provide Adequate Cleanup Supplies

Don't expect your child to know what to use to clean up his mess by himself.

For example, give him the right cloth to wash off the table. Make sure to praise all his cleanup efforts after you've given him the tools of the trade.

Confine Messy Activities to a Safe Place

Avoid potential damage to the couch, carpet, or table by letting your child play with messy materials (finger paints, clay, markers, crayons, and so on) in appropriate places. Don't expect him to know how to avoid staining the living room carpet when you've let him finger paint in there.

Use Grandma's Rule

Remember that even a child who is just becoming mobile can help clean up in small ways. He needs to try his best at whatever level he can, slowly building up to more difficult tasks. Say, "When you've put the balls in the basket, then you may go outside to play with your friend." If you think your little one needs help, happily show him how to do what you ask.

Make Cleaning Up a Habit

When it happens every day, cleaning up toys or putting away clothes or dishes becomes a habit, just as is taking a bath or brushing your teeth. At the end of the day, clean up toys, art supplies, the kitchen, and clothes with your child before starting her bedtime routine together.

Play Beat-the-Clock

When your child is trying to beat the smartphone timer, picking up toys is a fun game. This motivational technique uses your child's competitive nature to encourage her to complete a task on your timetable and makes cleanup (and other tasks) more fun. Here's how it works: Set your phone timer for three minutes, and join in the fun by saying, "Let's see if you can put the dolls in the basket before the timer rings," or "When you've picked up the toys before the timer sounds, you can take out another toy." When your child is successful at beating the clock, praise her accomplishment, and follow through on your promise.

Break Cleanup into Small, Doable Tasks

When a child is asked to clean up a mess, his young eyes and brain may not be able to even find a place to start. Help him by pointing to one toy and saying, "Let's start with your truck. Put the truck away first." Then move to the next toy or item until they are all put away.

Teach Older Children and Teens to Put Their Things Away

After you have told an older child where things belong, such as hanging a backpack on a hook in the hallway or putting shoes in a bin by the door, then praise his neatness. If shoes are found in the middle of the floor, take the shoes and put them in your closet. When your child asks where his shoes are, tell him he can have them back after he has completed a job for you, such as vacuuming the floor. This will help him remember to put his shoes where they belong.

Praise Your Child's Cleanup Effort

A sure motivator for all of us is praise. Compliment the terrific way your child is cleaning up the mess in her closet by hanging up the clothes on the floor. Say, "I like how you are clearing off the floor, so you can walk in the closet and not step on clothes. Thanks for keeping your clothes hung up so they stay clean." This also points out the benefit of cleaning up—building the cleanliness habit.

Work Together

Sometimes the cleanup job is so big for a young child's muscles, eyes, or hands that it can discourage him from even starting the task. With a positive attitude, join in the work with him to encourage building a supportive relationship through sharing and cooperation—two lessons you want your child to learn as a young child. Seeing Mom or Dad helping clean up makes the activity that much more inviting.

What Not to Do

Don't Expect Perfection

The fact that she's trying means she's learning how to do it. She will improve over time. The big lesson is to make it a habit, not a one-time event.

Don't Punish Messiness

Punishing him for being messy will not teach him the cleanup skills he needs to learn.

Don't Use Labels

Calling your child a slob because he makes messes with his toys and clothes and doesn't clean them up won't teach him how to be neat. Labeling will become his identity. If he believes he is a slob, he will behave like one.

Preventing the Problem

Model Neatness

Clean up the kitchen after you cook, hang up your towel after a shower, put away the groceries when you get home, and put away clothes after they're washed. You are providing a model for your child of cleaning up and putting things where they belong—which is exactly the goal you have for your child's behavior. Even if it's a lesson you have a hard time practicing yourself, try to change your priorities to help your child make cleaning up a habit that becomes second nature to him at a young age. Let your child know that it's sometimes hard for you to remember to clean up your messes, so he knows that he isn't the only one who needs to practice this habit.

Case History: Multiple Messes

Mandy was irritated by the messes her seven-year-old twins, Harper and Shelly, made almost daily. "Good children always put away their toys," Mandy told them, trying to shame the girls into not leaving their toys in the living room when they were through playing. When that didn't work, she began yelling at her daughters and putting them in their rooms when they didn't clean up their mess. But that punishment seemed to punish only Mandy herself, because the girls created additional messes in their rooms.

Mandy finally saw a way to solve the problem by using Grandma's Rule when she realized how much her children liked to play outside on their new swing set. She decided to turn that activity into a privilege that had to be earned. One day, the girls wanted to go outside instead of cleaning up after playing with their kitchen set. Using Grandma's Rule, Mandy said, "Here's the new rule: I know you want to go outside. When you've picked up your kitchen set and put away the pots and pans in the cabinet, then you can play on the swing set. I will help."

The two girls looked at each other. They didn't want to pick up their toys, but they really wanted to play on the swing set. Mandy opened up the cabinet so Harper could deposit the kitchen utensils in their proper place, leaving no doubt about what "picking up the kitchen set" meant.

As the girls began cleaning up, Mandy let them know how happy she was with their efforts. "Thanks for cleaning up," she said." You're doing a great job putting the kitchen set away. I sure like the way everything fits so neatly into the shelves." She hugged each girl with genuine pride. Soon, both children spilled out the door, leaving their mother to fix lunch instead of clean up after them.

For many weeks, the girls needed to be motivated by Grandma's Rule to clean up. But they finally learned that putting away one toy before taking out another made the cleanup process quicker and also brought great compliments from Mom.

WON'T DO HOMEWORK, CHORES, AND OTHER BIG TASKS

- Lies about having homework
- Does a poor job of chores
- Says the chores are done when they aren't
- Won't write thank-you notes for gifts
- Won't put their phone away while doing homework

When older children and teens are given tasks to complete, they often enter into a state of rebellion. They may refuse, argue, lie, put off, or do whatever they can think of to get out of what they need to be doing. Parents are often at a loss when this happens. They may yell, threaten, beg, ground, punish—and nothing seems to work. They can't get their child to budge from his stubborn stand and complete the tasks that were assigned. As a parent, put on your manager hat. A manager has a set of tasks that need to be done and a way of measuring each task, so she knows it's been completed. A manager has incentives to get the jobs done—money. A parent manager has other incentives, and we're here to show you what they are and how to use them.

Healthy Mind S.E.T.

Self-Talk. Keep your self-talk positive. Say to yourself, "My child believes that homework and chores are not important and he shouldn't have to do them. But I know they are important. I think I can teach my child to do what needs to be done. By doing the tasks, he can learn the importance of taking responsibility for work—a lesson that will serve him well."

Empathy. Put yourself in your child's shoes by thinking, "I sometimes don't want to do work around the house or at my job, for that matter. So I can understand that my child doesn't want to, either. His agenda doesn't include homework or chores, just play and time with friends."

Teaching. Remind yourself that learning takes time, patience, and practice. Show or explain how to get homework and chores done in a timely manner so that your child can be free to do what he wants. Being organized and living in a world of routine can free up time to have fun.

What to Do

Teach Your Child to Practice Empathy

Children are born with the capacity to be empathetic, so from the earliest age, make understanding the feelings of others part of your everyday lessons. When your child refuses to do homework or chores, promises and then doesn't follow through, or lies about doing it when he didn't, ask him how he would feel if you promised to do something for him and then kept putting it off. What if you lied that you had patched his bike tire and really hadn't? Even if he says it wouldn't bother him, understand that just exposing him to these ideas will put them in his head, and he will think about them. Empathy starts with caring—and caring about what you say you will do is the first step in doing it.

Make a Daily Routine

Routines are valuable tools that help us all stay organized, so we can get done all the things we need to do. A homework routine, for example, could be having quiet time right after dinner. All homework will be done during that time. If a child believably claims not to have homework, he can read during quiet time because it is a time when all family members are reading or working on a project.

Make Rules

Make simple rules, such as TV and all electronic devices will be off during homework time (unless it is an on-screen assignment from school). To enforce the rules, make sure all portable devices are off and are put in a place away from the homework site. Another rule might be: all homework will be done at the dining or kitchen table. It has been found that children do better work when not surrounded by their toys and other distractions.

A chore rule could be: All chores will be done and inspected before devices can be used or the child can have playtime. If chores aren't completed to satisfaction, they will be redone before devices or playtime. If your child lies that chores were done and they weren't, simply have him complete the chores. He will soon learn that he can't get out of doing them, so he won't bother to lie.

Check Homework Assignments

As a manager, your task is to know what your child's job is, and in this case it's homework. When you know the assignments, you will know whether they have been completed. In addition, you can judge the quality of the homework that has been done. If your child says he has no homework, it's usually possible to check the school website. Most schools now post homework for each class in each grade. You are not responsible for doing the homework or even knowing what the homework is. But it is important for your child to know that you care and want to know—just as you would share a work project of your own.

Involve Your Child in the Plan

If your child is not doing well in school because of incomplete homework assignments, poorly done work, failure to turn in the assignments on time, or any of the other issues that you know are resulting in grades that are below your child's ability, ask him what he plans to do about the problems. If he says, "I'll try harder," don't accept that as an answer. Instead ask, "What's your plan?" and help him pull together a detailed plan to correct the problem. For example: "I'll do my homework immediately when I get home. I'll let you check it. I'll put it in my notebook, so I'll know where it is. I'll turn it in immediately when I get to class. I'll correct my mistakes as soon as I get them." Make this your child's plan, not yours. He is responsible for the plan and the work.

Check Chore Completion

Most assigned chores have visible proof of completion. Empty wastebaskets are evidence that the trash chore has been done. A made bed shows that making a bed each morning was done. Fun activities are allowed when all chores are done satisfactorily.

Make a Chore Calendar

In order to ensure that children know their chore assignments, you can list chores on a calendar. For example: Monday—empty dishwasher, Tuesday—empty wastebaskets, Wednesday—vacuum the family room floor, and so forth. Each child should then check off the chore on that date when completed. Remember, chores should be completed within an allotted time and inspected by management. The chore chart is not the only way to assign chores, but it is a visible reminder of your words.

Use Grandma's Rule

You may have noted that in each case we've cited, the child can have his privileges only after work is done, which is the essence of Grandma's Rule. The when-then contract simply states, "When you have done what you are required to do, then you may do what you want to do." It's also important to understand that you will need to manage your child's access to all of his privileges, such as electronic devices or play activities.

What Not to Do

Don't Nag, Beg, or Threaten

Nagging, begging, or threatening won't teach your child how to get work done when it needs to be done. Avoid the damage these will cause in your relationship. Simply withhold privileges until tasks are completed.

Don't Punish for Incomplete Homework or Chores

Grounding and other punishments when things aren't done won't teach your child how to get things done. Punishment encourages lying and other actions that will harm your relationship and won't get the jobs done.

Preventing the Problem

Stay Organized

A household is like a business—it will be run more successfully when it's organized. Keeping a calendar of chores and having routines for doing chores and homework are simple ways to keep children on a track to success.

Establish Routines

Having routines from day one for your child will not only keep you organized and focused but create a predictable world for your child. A routine for older children might be: get up, get dressed, eat breakfast, brush teeth, do morning chores, go to school, do afternoon chores, do homework, have dinner, play. Such a routine will keep you and your child organized and free up time for that essential outcome of play.

Case History: Rebellious Rudy

When Rudy, their ten-year-old child, began getting reports from his teacher, Mr. Samuels, about poor or incomplete homework, Rosalind and Max Windholz decided that they needed to do something about his school problems. They knew he was bright, and he always made good grades. But Mr. Samuels was proving to be tough. Rudy's parents knew that he had always been a difficult child when it came to getting him to do things he didn't want to do. He loved playing outside and on his soccer team, and above all he loved his TV and tablet. He could spend hours watching TV and looking at YouTube. And he learned a lot from those activities.

"Rudy, this email from your teacher says you're not turning in all your assignments and aren't doing well in some subjects. What's the problem?" Max asked.

"Mr. Samuels doesn't like me. He's grading me down because I'm not his favorite," came Rudy's ready answer.

"That doesn't sound right to me," his dad said. "I'm going to talk with Mr. Samuels tomorrow."

After the phone conference the next day, his parents sat Rudy down and told him about the conference. "Mr. Samuels told us that he likes you and knows you have a lot of potential, but you aren't always doing the work, and what you do is sloppy and incomplete. He thinks you aren't trying hard enough."

"But I am trying," said Rudy, who burst into tears and ran off to his room.

Rudy's parents had predicted his reaction. They had seen it many times before, when they tried to get him to do something he didn't want to do. They had been given a plan by Mr. Samuels and decided that they needed to put the plan in play. They went to Rudy's room and found him watching something on his tablet, apparently completely recovered from his bad school report.

"Rudy, we need to make a plan to help you with school. Do you have any suggestions?"

"No. Mr. Samuels is too hard. He gives too much homework."

"We haven't seen you doing homework. When do you do it?" Rosalind asked.

"I do it before class starts."

That answer told his parents that Rudy didn't really have a plan, so they needed to come up with one. They decided to set up a homework station at the little-used dining table, and they determined after dinner was a good time for homework. They knew each day what the homework assignments were because they were posted online. And Mr. Samuels had suggested that Rudy also needed chores to do in order for him to learn more responsibility.

When the plan was implemented, Rudy had a meltdown with lots of crying and screaming. But he soon learned that his parents, with Mr. Samuels's backing, were not giving in. He knew that if he wanted playtime, soccer, and his devices, he would need to do what he was assigned, no matter how dumb he thought it was.

After two weeks, Rudy was so immersed in his new routine that his parents didn't need to remind him. They discovered a side benefit: Rudy was more relaxed and seemed happier. Maybe it was because he didn't have to worry about homework assignments hanging over his head.

WON'T DO WHAT YOU ASK / WON'T LISTEN / IGNORES YOU / DOESN'T FOLLOW DIRECTIONS

- Won't get dressed
- Avoids or runs away from you
- Won't make eye contact
- Argues about doing things
- Breaks rules
- Ignores you or other adults
- Won't do what he is told
- Won't pay attention to you
- Won't hold your hand
- Won't help you
- Won't follow directions or rules
- Sneaks drugs, alcohol, or other ways to get high

When your child won't get dressed or follow other directions when you ask, you have a choice: Shall I fight with him to listen and do what I want? Or just give in and let him do what he wants? Of those two options, the latter seems as if it's the easiest way out—just give in and move on. But . . .

Yes, the "but" here is big, because you know that you need to teach your child to listen to you and follow directions, particularly when it comes to necessary things, such as getting dressed for school. He needs to wear clothes in order to go out in the world. But quite often that is just not a toddler or preschooler's agenda, even though it's yours.

Here's another problem that you face when your child doesn't do what you ask: sometimes it seems as if he has lost his ability to hear because when you tell him to do something, there is no response. Then you ask again, this time louder. Again, no response. And the next thing you know, you are so frustrated that you begin to yell your request. But your child still ignores you.

If this sounds familiar to you—if you have a child who cannot hear your voice but can hear the rustle of a candy wrapper in a distant part of the house—take heart, you are not alone! Children can become so absorbed that everything else around them disappears, which isn't a bad thing. This selective hearing is a skill that will stand them in good stead when they enter school and have to concentrate while the teacher conducts a reading group nearby, for example.

They also may be simply trying to see if their parents will follow through on their warnings, how far rules can be stretched, and how closely directions really need to be followed.

There's another possible reason for his not listening. It's normal for your child to be ignoring you because he doesn't *want* to do what you asked him to do. Maybe he doesn't want to quit what he's doing. None of us likes to stop doing something we're having fun doing, of course, especially if we aren't finished with a game or we're really into a project. Likewise, maybe he doesn't think what you've asked him to do matters, such as getting dressed.

Your job is to make it matter—set rules for listening, and set up routines for getting dressed and other nonnegotiable things a child needs to learn to do to get along in the world. When he doesn't do these things, remind him of the rule. When doing these things becomes a habit, they start happening naturally, without your reminder.

NOTE: *If you suspect that your child is ignoring your requests because he may have a hearing problem, check with his health care provider. Also see other sections that deal with your child's independence: "Want My Own Way," page 186, and "Want to Do It Myself," page 190.*

Healthy Mind S.E.T.

Self-Talk. Keep your self-talk positive. Say to yourself, "I know my child doesn't want anyone telling him what to do. I need to teach him how to listen and follow directions."

Empathy. Put yourself in your child's shoes by thinking, "We all want to have power and control in our world. I don't like anyone telling me what to do either, so I understand how my son feels."

Teaching. Remind yourself that learning takes time, patience, and practice. Show or explain to your child how to listen and cooperate.

Solving the Problem

What to Do

Teach Your Child to Practice Empathy

Children are born with the capacity to be empathetic, so from the earliest age, make understanding the feelings of others part of your everyday lessons. When your child ignores you, doesn't listen, or doesn't do what you ask, for example, kindly say to him, "How do you think I feel when you don't pay attention to what I'm saying or run away from me when I am talking to you? How would you feel if I did that to you? We want to be polite and make people feel respected. Ignoring them or not listening when they are talking is not polite and is disrespectful."

Set Up a Routine for Getting Dressed

Teach your child that getting dressed, just like washing his face and brushing his teeth, is a normal, everyday habit to get into. Lay out clothes the night before—even when your child is as young as eighteen months—and ask him to hand them to you so you can help him put them on. Help him get his clothes and shoes on when he's just getting started. As your child grows in his ability to put on a shirt or pants, shoes or socks, let him help you, until he wants to do it himself. The important thing is to make it a routine, something done in the same order every night and morning. That makes getting dressed a predictable and fun part of waking up—not a battle to be fought.

Give Simple, Clear Directions

To make it easier for your child to do what you ask, be as specific as possible about what you want your child to do. Say, "It's time to pick up your markers and put them away. Let's start with the red one."

Praise a Job When It's Done

Reward your child for listening to you and doing what you ask by praising her for a job well done. You are also showing her how to appreciate someone's effort by saying, "Thank you for picking up all of the markers off the floor." Modeling praise teaches her to express gratitude to others.

Use Grandma's Rule

Children are more likely to do what you ask when they know they can do what they want to do after a task is completed. For example, say, "When you've picked up the books, then I'll push you on the swing," or, "When you've washed your hands, we will have lunch." In general, when your child refuses to do what you ask, simply state Grandma's Rule. Say, "When you have done what I ask, you will be able to do what you want to do. I'll wait here until you decide to do what I ask." By staying with your child and keeping him away from his activities, he will soon learn that cooperating gets him his own way.

Have Your Child Practice Doing What You Ask

If your child is not doing what you ask, find out whether she's unable or unwilling by walking her through the task. For example, guide her hand washing by moving her hands and praising her progress along the way. If you discover she can do the task but simply refuses to, say, "I'm sorry you aren't following directions. Now we have to practice." Then give her the opportunity to follow the directions on her own. If she still refuses, say, "It looks like we need more practice. When you finish practicing, then you may play with your toys again."

Ask Your Child to Look at You When You Make a Request

If your child keeps looking at a screen, for example, instead of looking at you when you ask her a question, say, "Please look at me, so I know you are paying attention." This is a twofold lesson: She learns to make eye contact when someone talks to her, and you know that she's paying attention to what you're saying.

Ask Your Child to Repeat Back Your Instructions

After you've given your instructions, ask your child to repeat them back to you so you know she understands what you want her to do. This makes sure she is listening, allows you to correct anything she left out, and tells you how many instructions she can remember at a time.

Play Beat-the-Clock

Set a phone timer for one minute and say, "Let's see if you can beat the clock getting your pajamas off." When that task is complete, say, "Now let's see if you can beat the clock getting your pants on." Then go for the sweater and then the socks and shoes. Remember, small and short requests work best. This game motivates her to leave her fun for something you want her to do.

Praise Your Child's Progress

You can praise your child's behavior frequently during the task by saying, "Thank you for looking at me while I talk," or "Thanks for listening," or "Look how quickly you are getting your pajamas off," or "You are getting dressed so fast. You're going to beat the clock." This kind of encouragement will keep your child interested and moving to complete your requests.

Hold Your Child's Hands When Giving Instructions

Some children develop a habit of running away when asked to do something or even when told to stay close. To avoid him running from you, take hold of your child's hands when giving instructions, and tell him to look at you while you make your request. A child can't run away when you hold on to him, and eye contact suggests that he's listening.

Repeat the Request

Some children love to argue when they've been asked to do something. To reduce arguing time, simply repeat the request. Your child will soon learn that arguing is a two-person game and you aren't going to play.

Some Requests Are Rules

Some children believe they are too old to hold your hand when you are out in the big world, so they refuse. It's also uncomfortable for the child to have an arm extended for long periods. Hand holding is mandatory in some situations, so it's important to insist that your very young child hold yours when crossing a busy street or in a crowded store. If she refuses, say, "I'm sorry you've chosen not to hold my hand. When you hold my hand, we can cross the street."

When a Rule Is Broken

Some children see rules as a challenge, so they test them from time to time. If your child breaks a rule, point out the rule that was broken and give a consequence, such as loss of a privilege. For example, if the rule is "No TV on a school night," and you find the child watching TV, simply say, "I'm sorry you broke the TV rule. You have lost the privilege of TV after school tomorrow." Be sure to use a consequence that you are able to enforce. No TV after school is not effective if you won't be there.

When Children or Teens Are Breaking Rules and Hurting Themselves

Some parents complain that their older child or teen is breaking rules by sneaking out at night, using drugs or alcohol, cutting herself, or engaging in behavior that is dangerous to her health and well-being. If you have a child of any age who is engaging in this kind of behavior, contact your health care provider to get a referral to a mental health professional. This sort of behavior is indicative of problems that need intensive intervention to prevent them from escalating. The goal is to get help now, rather than waiting for the problem to get bigger.

What Not to Do

Don't Get Angry

Getting angry when your child doesn't listen doesn't teach him how to listen to you. It just creates stress in your relationship and inside you and your child.

Don't Threaten

When your child repeatedly ignores your requests, don't say, "If you don't pay attention to me right now, I'm going to take all of your toys and throw them in the trash!" This threat may frighten him enough to get his attention, but it doesn't teach him to listen and do what you ask. In addition, it provides a model of bullying someone to get what you want—the model that you don't want him to follow to get his needs and wants met.

Don't Back Down If Your Child Resists

Say to yourself, "I know my child doesn't want to do what I want her to do, but I'm more experienced and know what's best for her. I need to teach her by giving her clear directions so she can eventually do things herself."

Don't Punish Your Child for Not Following Directions

Teaching your child how to do something, instead of punishing her for not doing it, avoids your becoming a source of stress in her life and helps her learn how to follow directions.

Don't Criticize What She's Done; Make Suggestions

For example, say, "Please pick up your toys now and put them in the box," rather than, "Why don't you ever remember to pick up your toys and put them away on your own?"

Preventing the Problem

Make Eye Contact with Your Child Before Asking Her to Do Something

Ensure that your child hears you when you speak by getting down on her level, lifting her face so you can see her eyes, and then speaking.

Learn How Many Directions Your Child Can Follow at Once

Your young child will only be able to remember and follow a certain number of directions at a time, depending on her developmental stage. To find out your child's limit, give one simple direction, then two, and then three. For example, for three directions, say, "Please pick up the book, put it on the table, and come sit by me." If all three are followed in the proper order, you'll know your child can remember three directions. Identify her limit, and wait until she's older before giving her more complicated directions.

Let Your Young Child Do as Many Things by Herself as Possible

Because she wants to march to the beat of her own drum and have total control over her own life, your young child will fight for the chance to make choices. Whenever possible, give her the opportunity to develop her decision-making skills and increase her self-confidence. The more control she feels that she has, the less likely she'll be to reject taking directions from someone else.

Keep Your Voice Calm and Quiet

If you are always yelling, your child will shut out your voice because it is annoying and meaningless to him. The softer the voice you use, the closer the attention your child has to pay to hear your instructions.

Prepare Your Child for the Request

Your child may be reluctant to shift to a new activity, so warn him a few minutes before you make your request. This will allow him to prepare. Say, "I will set my phone timer to ring in a minute. That will tell you that you need to get dressed for school."

Case History: Noah Learns to Listen

Sarah was tired of four-year-old Noah totally ignoring her when she asked him to do something. Sarah had tried to be nice about being ignored, but that didn't work, so she did what her mother had always done when she was little: yelling, threatening, and then snatching her son up and stomping while carrying him to whatever task she had asked him to do. She had even asked Noah's pediatrician whether she should have Noah's ears checked to see if he had hearing loss. The doctor assured her that his hearing was fine and suggested that Noah might not be developmentally ready to quickly leave one activity to go to another.

Sarah then took some time out to think about what the doctor had said. She decided that the doctor was absolutely right: having his mom demand that he stop and move on didn't motivate Noah to do what she asked. Sarah remembered that she and her mother had clashed because Sarah had hated having to stop immediately and do what her mother wanted. Sarah had always felt good inside when she finished a project that she had started, and she fought her mom constantly over her mom's demanding that she listen to her.

Now that Sarah understood the reason for Noah's listening problems, she had to develop a strategy. She decided to give him a warning before she asked him to do something. She would give this warning while she was right next to him and touching him gently. So she tried it, saying, "Noah, in a minute, you're going to have to put this book away and brush your teeth. I'll set the phone timer to remind us when a minute is up." When the phone chirped,

Sarah went back to him, saying, "Noah, it's time now to put the book away. Let's see if you can do it before I count to five. One, two, three . . . "

Noah quickly closed the book and put it with the others. "See, I did it before you finished counting!" he squealed. "I knew that I could!"

"Noah, you are so fast. I am excited about how quickly you did what I asked you to do. Now let's get your teeth brushed, so we can read stories before bed. We can even finish the book you were reading, if you want. How many stories tonight?"

"Five stories," Noah said, as they headed for the bathroom.

Noah and Sarah followed their nighttime routine, getting his teeth brushed and getting him into bed for stories. He had taught her that he needed a little time to shift into a new activity—just as she did herself.

WON'T GO TO BED OR TAKE NAPS

- Fights going to bed
- Cries when he's put in bed
- Fights getting out of bed
- Won't take a nap
- Will only sleep on the sofa with the TV on
- Won't sleep without you lying beside him
- Won't brush his teeth before bed

Active, energetic young children often do anything to avoid sleep. They turn bedtime or naptime into chase time, crying time, or finding-another-book-to-read time—all to postpone the dreaded act of going to bed. No matter what your child may think about the right time to go to bed, stand firm with the routine you have chosen. But be sure to help your child gradually wind down, instead of requiring her to turn off her motor instantly.

It may seem easier to let your child run his own schedule and too much trouble to start a routine and follow it, but you'll save yourself hours of bedtime battles later if you do create a regular bedtime and naptime schedule. Your child will feel more secure with a predictable routine, and he will feel healthier when he has a predictable, regular schedule for rest. See also "Won't Stay in Bed at Night or at Naptime," page 238.

NOTE: *A Special Word About the Drama of Taking Naps and Going to Bed*

Not taking naps, screaming and crying when he's put in the crib, getting so tired that he cannot even play or talk without a tantrum: these all happen as children grow and test the patience of their parents and caregivers. As in the case of eating, questions and worries around what, how much, when, and if their children are getting enough sleep top parents' lists of topics to learn about—indeed, whole books and websites, products, and businesses focus only on this subject.

Going to bed is a subject that taps into emotional issues as well as physical ones. Parents don't want to hear their toddler or even school-age child being upset or sad about going to bed. But then comes the reality of a child and his parents needing to sleep all night for everyone's optimum health. Your child's health care provider knows your child, so trust her to help you work through the sleeping questions that are most important to you. First things first: Find out from regular check-ups with your child's health care provider if he is developing normally. Your child's health is your number one priority, so base your sleeping guidelines on how to help him grow through the stages of napping frequently, sleeping through the night, and sleeping in his own bed (or co-sleeping if that is your choice).

Healthy Mind S.E.T.

Self-Talk. Keep your self-talk positive. Say to yourself, "I get so frustrated when my child doesn't go to bed, but I can handle it. The worst thing that will happen is that I'll be tired. It's not that big a deal. I can teach him how to go to bed."

Empathy. Put yourself in your child's shoes by thinking, "My child doesn't want to miss out on the action. Sometimes I don't want to miss what's going on either. My child doesn't want to go to bed because she doesn't want to stop being held, sung to, read to, or cuddled. She's not trying to drive me crazy!"

Teaching. Remind yourself that learning takes time, patience, and practice. Show or explain to your child how going to bed can be a special, happy time for him and feel-good time for you both.

Solving the Problem

What to Do

Bedtime Routine Is Your First Priority

Children as well as adults find comfort in routine—doing things the same way each time. Therefore, teach your child as early as possible—start when she is an older infant or toddler—that going to bed has its own calm and loving routine, so she will find comfort in predicting what will happen next. Decide on the routine that's best for your child in the day or night and consistently follow a pattern, such as: clothes off, bath, teeth brushed, pajamas on, taking a special stuffed animal or favorite blanket for comfort to bed, reading a story, song, snuggle time and kisses, more hugs, and then night light on.

Have a Consistent Bedtime

Letting your child stay up late one night and then expecting her to go to bed early the next is confusing. Try to make bedtime the same time every night, so she will know what to expect. But keep in mind that children (even ones in the same family) require different amounts of sleep. Your two-year-old may not need the same amount of sleep her older brother did when he was two.

Use a Phone Timer to Manage the Bedtime Routine

Make the timer, not you, the one in control, to avoid a power struggle with your child when he fights going to bed. Thirty to forty-five minutes before bedtime (or naptime), set your smartphone timer for five minutes, and announce that the phone will tell your child when it's time to start getting ready for bed. This avoids surprises and allows her to anticipate the upcoming events.

When the phone timer sounds, say, "The phone says it's time to start getting ready for bed. Let's take a bath and get into our pajamas." Then reset the phone timer to about fifteen minutes for the bath. When the timer rings, say, "The timer says that it's time to get out of the bathtub. Now let's see if we can beat the timer getting pajamas on." This gives you the opportunity to praise your child's efforts at getting herself through the basic bedtime routine.

Play Beat-the-Clock

When the routine is finished, reset the phone for the remainder of the hour you set aside and announce, "You beat the phone timer. Now you get to stay up and play until the phone sounds again and tells us that it's time to get into bed. Let's set the phone for brushing your teeth, getting a drink, and going potty [if she's old enough]." (Make sure you allow enough time for her to get the job done.) The phone timer routine helps you and your child make a game, instead of a struggle, out of bedtime.

Follow the Same Rituals Regardless of Time

Even if bedtime has been delayed for some reason, go through the same rituals to help your child learn what's expected of her when it comes to going to bed.

Don't point out how late she's stayed up. Quicken the pace by helping her get her pajamas on and get a drink, and set the timer for shorter intervals. But don't omit any steps. Children thrive on routine.

When You're Not Yet Home at Naptime or Bedtime

Knowing your young child will fall asleep in the car on the way home from an event, put a diaper and PJs on her before you leave the event. That way, you can simply transfer her from her car seat to her bed when you get home. Easier on you and her!

Maintain the Same Order of Events

Since young children find comfort in consistency, have your child bathe, brush her teeth, and put on her pajamas in the same order every night. Ask her to name the next step in the routine. This will help to make a game out of getting ready for bed and will help her feel as if she's calling the shots. It's the sequence of events that becomes important and comforting for all.

Make Bedtime Rules

If your child will only sleep on the sofa with the TV on or won't sleep without you lying next to her, make some bedtime rules, such as, "The rule is, you may sleep only in your bed," or, "The rule is, I will stay next to you while we read our story, then I have to move to the rocker. I'll be right here." In this case, over the next two weeks, gradually move yourself out of the room.

To give your child an incentive to follow the rules, use Grandma's Rule. To the TV sleeper, say, "When you have gone to sleep in your bed tonight, then you may watch your favorite TV show tomorrow." Then stiffen your resolve by leaving the TV off until she decides to stay in bed.

Use Grandma's Rule to Get Cooperation

When your child decides not to follow a step in her bedtime routine in order to delay bedtime, use Grandma's Rule. Say, "When you have brushed your teeth, you will be able to have two books read before bed."

What Not to Do

Don't Let Your Child Control Bedtime and Naptime

Stick with your chosen bedtime despite your child's resistance. Remember that you know why your child doesn't want to go to bed—and why she should. Say to yourself, "She's only crying because she doesn't want to end her playtime, but I know she'll play happier later if she sleeps now." That's the lesson!

Don't Threaten

Threatening your child to get her into bed can cause nightmares and fears, not to mention making you upset. Punishing a child doesn't teach her appropriate behavior. Instead, focus on using your phone timer as a neutral authority to determine when bedtime arrives.

Don't Be a Historian

Saying, "Because you didn't go to bed on time last night, you don't get to play on the computer this morning," doesn't teach your child how to get into bed on time. Focus on the future instead of the past.

Preventing the Problem

Establish a Bedtime Routine

From day one, sleeping and feeding routines for your newborn and infant, as well as your toddler and older child, are your number one priority. Even newborns can be sleep-trained—that is, taught self-calming and going-to-sleep routines. So to prevent resisting bedtime and to help children feel secure because they can predict what will happen next, we advise making and using a routine for bedtime and naptime. You can make your routine longer or shorter as long as the events remain in the same order. For example: clothes off, bath, teeth brushed, pajamas on, special take-to-bed stuffed toy or blanket, story, song, kiss, night light on, lights out. For older children, adjust the routine: clothes off, bath or shower, teeth brushed, pajamas on, story or read in bed, kiss, lights out.

Make Exercise a Daily Habit

Make sure your child gets plenty of exercise during the day to help her body tell her mind that going to bed is a good idea.

Maintain a Fairly Regular Nap Schedule

Don't let your child put off napping until late afternoon or evening, and then expect her to go to sleep at eight o'clock. Put her in bed for naps early enough in the day that she'll be tired again at bedtime.

Spend Time Together Before Bed

Play with your child before bedtime arrives to prevent her from fighting bedtime just to get your attention. Make sure bedtime play is calm and quiet, rather than noisy and hurried. To end the day or begin a nap with a special feeling between you and your child, recite a poem or story as a regular part of the going-to-bed routine. Make bedtime special, so it's something she can look forward to. Try reciting a phrase from a favorite book or having a talk about the day's events, even if it's a one-sided conversation.

Keep Bedtime Consistent

Determine how much sleep your child needs by noticing how she acts when she's taken a nap and when she hasn't, and when she's gone to bed at nine o'clock versus seven o'clock. Establish a consistent sleep schedule that meets her needs, and adjust it as she gets older. Since your child's need for sleep changes as she gets older, you'll want to let her stay up later or shorten her naps as she grows.

No Phones or Screens in the Bedroom

Watching TV and using phones or tablets can keep children from going to sleep in a timely manner and resisting bedtime. Keeping devices out of the bedroom can help them go to sleep more easily and won't wake them up by calls or texts from friends.

Case History: Bedtime at Ben's

Evenings at the Shores' house meant one thing: a tearful battle of wills between four-year-old Ben and his father, Andrew, when Ben's bedtime was announced.

"I'm not tired! I don't want to go to bed! I want to stay up!" Ben would plead each night as his angry father dragged him to bed.

"I know you don't want to go to bed," Andrew would reply, "but you will do what I say, and I say it's bedtime!" Forcing Ben to go to bed upset Andrew as much as it did Ben. Even though Andrew believed he should be the boss, he knew there had to be a way to avoid the battles and Ben crying himself to sleep.

So the next night, Andrew decided to control himself and let something else—his phone timer—control bedtime. An hour before Ben's bedtime, he set the timer for five minutes. "It's time to start getting ready for bed," Andrew explained to his curious son. "When you get yourself ready for bed before the phone sounds, we'll set the phone again, and you can stay up and play until it sounds again."

Ben raced around and got ready for bed before the phone sounded. As promised, Andrew reset his phone, read Ben his favorite animal tales, and sang some new sleepy-time songs until the phone sounded again almost an hour later.

"It's time for bed, right?" Ben announced, acting delighted to have this game all figured out.

"That's right! I'm so proud of you for remembering the new rule," his dad replied.

As the two journeyed up to bed, Andrew once again told his son how proud he was of his getting himself ready for bed.

Using the phone to control bedtime routines helped them enjoy a painless evening for the first time in months. And after several weeks of following this routine, going to bed still wasn't something to look forward to, but the old struggles between Ben and his dad were gone. Andrew realized that his effort on the front end of this struggle would pay off in the long run—he'd taught Ben a sleep routine that was good for all.

WON'T SHARE

- Won't take turns
- Can't wait for a toy without a temper tantrum
- Says, "Mine!"
- Won't let go of a toy, stuffed animal, or book
- Cuts in front of the line
- Pushes people out of his way
- Says, "Me first!"

"Mine" is the buzzword young children use to remind each other (and adults) of their territorial rights. Despite the wars this four-letter word incites, children's self-centered possessiveness will unfortunately not disappear until children are developmentally ready to share and take turns. Help lay the groundwork for peace by consistently teaching your young one the give-and-take rules of the world. Enforce these sharing rules at home, but be patient. Don't expect them to be righteously followed until you see your child sharing without your intervention—the glorious sign that she's ready to broaden her boundaries.

Healthy Mind S.E.T.

Self-Talk. Keep your self-talk positive. Say to yourself, "Although it is upsetting that my child isn't sharing, I know that I can show her how good sharing feels and teach her how to share."

Empathy. Put yourself in your child's shoes by thinking, "We all want to feel independent and in control, and my child is no different. She also believes that everything is hers and she should be first, so she doesn't understand that getting along with others means learning how to share—toys, attention from those she loves, and being first. I am providing the model of how to do so."

Teaching. Remind yourself that learning takes time, patience, and practice. Show or explain to your child how good sharing feels.

Solving the Problem

What to Do

Teach Your Child to Use Empathy

A child is never too young to teach her to use empathy toward other people. So make it a simple game to help your child express how she feels when someone shares something with her—happy and thankful—and when someone doesn't share—angry and frustrated. Then play a game of giving and taking with her, so she can see how happy it makes you when she shares with you, just as it makes her happy when someone else does so with her.

Make Sharing First Place Important

Always wanting to be first is part of the self-centered stage of childhood. Children simply don't understand that sharing first place is a good way to get along with others. Praise sharing by saying for example, "That was so nice of you to let your friend go first on the swing. I know he thanks you for it."

Use a Timer

When your little one is saying, "Mine! Mine! Mine!," help her learn the habit of taking turns. Say, "I'll set my phone timer. When it rings, it's time for your friend [or sister or other person] to play with the toy. Then I'll set it again when it's time for you to have it back." Keep this sharing game going until they get tired of the toy or game and want to do something else.

Praise Sharing

Whenever you notice sharing, point out the behavior with your attention and smiles, saying, "I like that you are sharing by taking turns coloring with the purple crayon," for example.

Supervise Your Child's Play

Stay close and pay attention while your child is playing with others. This will help you resolve sharing conflicts that she's too young to handle without you.

Take Toys to Calm Time

If a toy is creating a problem because children won't share and are fighting over it, put the toy in Calm Time to remove it from the situation. If the toy is out of reach, it can't cause any trouble. Say, "This toy needs a break. Let's put it away so it doesn't cause a problem. Then we can try sharing it later." The lesson is that not sharing means the toy is taken away. If the children keep fighting over the toy after it's been brought back, keep removing it to make the point that not sharing a toy means no one gets to play with it.

Use Grandma's Rule

To encourage sharing, whether it's a toy or being first, use Grandma's Rule to make a contract. Say, for example, "When you let your friend play with the wagon until the timer rings, then you may play with it for the same amount of time." This kind of contract tells the children that there is a payoff in sharing.

Use Calm Time

When your child has a tantrum because he can't give up a toy or because he wasn't first to get a snack, take him to Calm Time. Say, "I'm sorry you are feeling upset because you had to share your wagon with Sarah. When you feel better, you may come back to play. Think about how you can share your wagon, so you both can have fun."

What Not to Do

Don't Get Upset

Remember that your child will learn the rule about sharing when she's developmentally ready, not when you force her to do so. When you see your child sharing, you'll know she's ready.

Don't Punish Your Child for Not Sharing

If your child has trouble sharing, remove the offending toy, rather than punishing your child. This puts the blame on the toy, not the child.

Don't Label Your Child

When your child refuses to share, telling him that he's a selfish child will make him believe that's who he is. That doesn't teach sharing, and if he believes that he's naturally selfish, why should he share?

Preventing the Problem

Make Sure Some Toys Belong Strictly to Your Child

Before young children can let go of the word "mine" and all the things attached to it, they must be given the chance to possess things. Put away your child's favorite toys or blankets when visitors come over to play, so she won't be forced to share them.

Point Out How You and Your Friends Share

Show your child that she isn't the only one in the world who's expected to share her things. Give examples at neutral (nonsharing) times of how you and your friends share things. Say, "Marie borrowed my scissors today," or, "Charlie borrowed my lawnmower."

Point Out What Sharing Means and How Much You Like It

Tell your child how nicely she's sharing whenever she's allowing another person to hold or play with her toys. For example, say, "I like the way you're sharing by letting your friend play with the blocks."

Put Labels on Similar Toys (for Twins, Triplets, or Children Close in Age)

Make sure you don't confuse your daughter's teddy bear with her sister's or brother's. Label each one with a nametag or piece of thread to help your child feel confident in her ownership of particular things.

Set Up Sharing Rules

Before friends come over to play, let your child know what's expected of her at group sharing times. For example, say, "When you put a toy down, anyone may play with it. When you have it in your hands, you may keep it."

Understand That Your Child May Share Better at a Friend's House

Because toys and other items your child encounters away from home are not exclusively hers, she may be less possessive about them when she's not defending her own territory.

Remember That Sharing Is a Developmental Task

Learning to share is an accomplishment that cannot be rushed.

Case History: Learning to Share

Three-year-old Liam Smith knew what the word "sharing" meant: it meant that he couldn't sit and hold as many toys as he wanted when his friend Jason came over to play.

"You must share!" Liam's mother, Nora, told her son after another day of Liam's clutching his toys and saying, "Mine!," whenever his mother said, "Now, Liam, let's share." Then one day, Nora screamed, "If you don't share, I'm going to give all of your toys to children who will appreciate them," and Liam tearfully gave up his toys.

That night, after Liam was tucked in bed, Nora told her husband, "Liam just doesn't know how to share." This simple statement shed new light on the problem. The Smiths realized that they needed to teach Liam what sharing really meant. So the next time Liam's cousins came over, Nora took him aside for a talk. "Liam, here's the new sharing rule: anyone can play with anything in this house as long as another person is not holding it. If you are holding a toy, no one can take it away. Each of your cousins and you may play with only one toy at a time." Nora also told Liam that he could put away one favorite toy, which could belong to him and him alone.

The next few hours were tense for Nora, but Liam seemed to be more relaxed. He knew what the rules were and what to expect when his cousins shared his toys. He began by holding only one toy and letting his cousins have their pick from the toy box. "I'm so proud of you for sharing," his watchful mother praised him as she oversaw the operation. But when she ventured off to fix lunch, the familiar "Mine!" cry brought her back to the playroom. The new "burp-itself" doll was being pulled limb from limb by Liam and his cousin Alexis. "This toy is causing trouble," Nora stated matter-of-factly. "I will take it to Calm Time."

The children stared in disbelief as they watched poor Burping Betsy sitting in the Calm Time chair, looking as lonely as a misbehaved puppy. After two minutes, Nora returned the toy to the children, who had long since forgotten about it and were busy playing with interlocking blocks. As the weeks went by, Liam played side by side with his cousins, with the toys spending fewer minutes in Calm Time to restore peace. Liam was more open to letting his toys be "their" toys during play. He was learning the joys of sharing with others.

WON'T STAY IN BED AT NIGHT OR AT NAPTIME

- Gets out of bed
- Won't stay in bed
- Cries when put back in bed
- Yells for many drinks or stories after getting in bed

Children under age six (and some older) are famous for getting out of bed with late-night requests for books, kisses, or milk—or for getting in bed with their parents, whether soon after their parents leave their bedside and lights are out or in the middle of the night. Remember that your child's nightly need is for sleep, though she may want ten books and four drinks just to see what you're up to or have you near her again. Teach your child that going to sleep will bring greater rewards than demanding attention. It is also important to establish a consistent routine before your child goes to bed—which children will learn to like for its predictability. See also "Won't Go to Bed or Take Naps," page 227.

NOTE: *If you are concerned about your child's not being able to stay in bed, her crying in bed, and so forth, meet with her health care provider to rule out any physical problems.*

Healthy Mind S.E.T.

Self-Talk. Keep your self-talk positive. Say to yourself, "I am sorry that my child gets out of bed at night. We can work together, so we both can get the sleep we need."

Empathy. Put yourself in your child's shoes by thinking, "There is a big world with a lot going on in it. My child wants to be with me to see what I am up to in that world outside his bed. But sleep is also what my child needs, and I can help him by teaching him how to feel good about staying in his bed."

Teaching. Remind yourself that learning takes time, patience, and practice. Show or explain to your child how he can stay in bed for his whole nap and the whole night and feel good when he does.

Solving the Problem

What to Do

Create a Bedtime Routine

The most important part of helping a child stay in bed is what happens *before* bedtime—enough food, quiet activities, calming nighttime routine—so your child will feel secure and receptive to sleep. If you have not used a routine to help your infant or toddler to go to bed or take a nap, it may be harder for your young child to stay in bed and put himself to sleep. See "Won't Go to Bed or Take Naps," page 227. It's never too late to start the routine, so make today the day!

Go Check on Your Child

If you're not sure whether your child is getting out of bed because he needs something or because he merely wants your attention (for example, if he's not talking yet or if he cries out instead of asking for something), check on him. If he is physically okay, give him a quick kiss and hug (thirty seconds maximum), and make your exit. Tell him firmly and lovingly that it's time for sleep, not play.

Set and Stick to Bedtime Rules

Routines are important guidelines and boundaries we all need, in order to feel comfortable that life is predictable. Making and sticking to rules shows your child healthy, commonsense, reasonable limits and how to stay within those limits. Say, "The rule is, you need to stay in your bed until morning. We all need sleep to make us strong." If your child insists that you stay with her until she falls asleep or repeats requests for more stories and drinks, set your timer for five minutes and say, "The rule is when the timer rings, it's time for me to leave and you to go to sleep. Love you." Then leave her room to help her know that you can be trusted to keep your word.

Praise and Reward Rule Following

We all need encouragement when we are learning something, so praising your child's rule following the morning after she stayed in bed will make it important to her. Say, "I am so glad that you stayed in bed, are rested, and taking good care of yourself."

Stand Firm with Your Rules

Enforce the rule every time your child breaks it, to teach him that you mean what you say. For example, when you put your child back in his bed after he gets in bed with you (if "family bed" is not your rule), say, "I'm sorry that you got in bed with us. Remember the rule: everyone sleeps in his own bed. I love you. See you in the morning."

Use Grandma's Rule

Teach your child to trust you by always making good on your promises of rewards for following Grandma's Rule. Say, "When you have stayed in bed all night, you can read your special story with me after breakfast." Then make sure you follow through with the story reading, telling your child how glad you are that she stayed in bed. Focusing on the lesson you want to teach is key—staying in bed has many rewards!

Play the Quiet Game

After hugs and kisses and final tuck-in, say, "Let's play the Quiet Game. See how long you can stay quiet. Shhhhhh." Then, in a whisper, say, "You are being so quiet. I'll be right outside listening." Then step outside his door and listen. Children love challenges, so he will try to stay quiet until sleep comes peacefully.

Set Rule Limits

If your child keeps asking for more drinks, hugs, books to be read, or stories, set reasonable, commonsense limits when you make rules. A rule to consider would be: "The bedtime rule is that you may have one drink, one hug, and one story before sleep." When your child pushes for more, simply say, "Remember the rule—one drink, one hug, and one story—and you had all those. Sleep well, and we'll have more hugs in the morning. We love you."

What Not to Do

Don't Neglect to Enforce the Rules

Once you've set the rules, don't change them unless you discuss this first with your child. Every time you neglect to consistently enforce the rules, and give in to her whining or crying, your child learns to keep trying to get what she wants, even though you've said no. Rules that are sometimes there and sometimes not are confusing and increase your child's stress.

Don't Use Threats and Fear

Threats such as, "If you get out of bed, the alligators will get you," or "If you do that one more time, I'm going to punish you," will only increase the problem. Fear may keep your child in bed, but the fear may grow until your child becomes afraid of many things. Remember, threats are never okay, and they destroy your trusting relationship with your child and increase her level of stress.

Don't Talk to Your Child from a Distance

Yelling threats and rules from another room teaches your child that yelling is an acceptable form of communication, and it tells him that you don't care enough to talk with him face-to-face.

Preventing the Problem

Set a Bedtime Routine for Staying in Bed

Just as you set up a routine for getting in bed—bath, PJs, books, night light, and so on—set up a routine for when your child gets out of bed. For example, say, "You can take two books to bed and have one drink, and I'll tell you two stories in bed before you go to sleep." Then consistently follow the routine.

Discuss Bedtime Routine at a Non-Bedtime Time

Don't expect your child to hear you when he's struggling to stay in bed. So at a neutral time (not bedtime or naptime), let him know what you expect him to do after he goes to bed. Set rules for how many times he gets out of bed for special requests, such as extra drinks of water.

Use Grandma's Rule Before Going to Bed

Make your child aware that following the rules, not breaking them, will bring him rewards. Say, "When you've stayed in your bed all night, then you may choose your favorite story to read in the morning." Rewards could also be a trip to the park, playing favorite games, or other fun that you know your child loves, including playing with stickers.

Reinforce the Idea of Staying in Bed All Night

Remind your child of bedtime rules as you put him in bed. Say, for example, "Remember, when you stay in your own bed and go to sleep, we get to go to the park in the morning. Sleep well!"

Do Bedtime Routines in Your Child's Bed

Conduct all of your pre-bedtime routines in his bed. If you decide that you will snuggle with your child for a little while, as part of his after-getting-in bed routine, do your snuggling in his bed. If his bed is still a crib, snuggle in a chair in his room, not in your bed, because getting him out of your bed is harder than getting him in.

No Screen Time Before Bed

Watching TV and using phones or tablets can keep children from going to sleep in a timely manner because they are thinking about what they watched. When a child can't go to sleep, it encourages her to get out of bed to try to watch TV again, which is more interesting than lying awake. It's best to refrain from TV viewing before bed; instead, play quiet games, and read stories.

Case History: Maya's Midnight Ramblings

Two-and-a-half-year-old Maya Long had been sleeping through the night since she was six months old. For the past month, however, she had been sleeping only a few hours before waking up her parents with screams of "Mommy! Daddy!" At first, Maya's parents would race to see what was wrong with their daughter, only to find her begging for drinks of water one night, an extra hug the next, and bathroom visits on other evenings. And if her parents didn't show up immediately, Maya would get out of bed and go find them.

After several weeks of these interruptions, Maya's weary parents decided to put a stop to these requests. "If you don't stay in bed, you're going to be punished, young lady," they threatened. Then they returned to their bed, only to hear their daughter padding down the hall toward their room. Their heavy hand seemed to carry little weight.

The Longs were told by their health care provider that Maya's waking up in the middle of the night was natural—everyone goes through periods of shallow and deep sleep. But they also knew that their daughter could choose to go back to sleep instead of calling out or coming to them. They also felt confident in their ability to distinguish between a genuine distress call (an intense and uninterrupted cry) and one that merely sought their attention (short bursts of crying punctuated with listening pauses).

To solve the problem, they offered Maya more attention for staying in bed and put Grandma's Rule into action. "Here's the rule. When you stay in bed without calling out to us or getting up," they explained as they tucked her into bed the next night, "then we'll read your favorite book after breakfast in the morning." They made sure they stated the new rule in plain terms that their daughter could understand.

That night, Maya got out of bed and woke up her mother, saying, "I want a drink!"

Her mother helped her daughter get back into bed and told Maya that she was sorry she wouldn't get her special reward in the morning because she had not followed the rule and had gotten out of bed. She also told her that it would be good to try again to stay in bed.

After three nights of this pattern for the Longs, Maya learned that getting out of bed did not bring her the story she wanted to read in the morning. She also learned that staying quiet and in bed all night made the promised reward happen in the morning. She was so happy! And so were her parents. They were finally able to get some uninterrupted sleep, and Maya found that their praise for sleeping through the night made her feel grown-up and important—an extra reward.

Acknowledgments

At times our own light goes out and is rekindled by a spark from another person. Each of us has cause to think with deep gratitude of those who have lighted the flame within us.

—Albert Schweitzer

Thank you to all of the dedicated parents, grandparents, social workers, pediatricians, nurses, medical assistants, researchers, and educators whose devotion to promoting the good health, learning, and behavior of children and families fuels our curiosity to ask more questions, find more answers, and explore more mysteries. Your lessons provide that spark we need every day to carry on our work. Each of you has made an immeasurable contribution to this book and to our lives. We are so grateful!

And there's more thanking to be done. On each of these pages are lessons explored with these plucky confidants. Each shares happy, bold cups of coffee with her in copious amounts, along with stories and big-time laughs over discoveries and wonder while asking, "Seriously?" She treasures each of your dear friendships: Janice Hendler, Leslie Borsett-Kanter, Kathy Ellerbeck, Wendy Webb, Vicki Meek, KO Strohbehn, Jane Warren, Lili Shank, Bonnie Tilson, Mary Lou Anderson, Ellen Zuniga, Fran Brozman, Ellen Katz, Erin Windholz, Jenny Miles, Paula Meier, Brenda Chumley, Tara Chumley, Vicki Meek, Goldie Sakoulas, Cindy Wetmore, Cathy Alpert, Deborah Shouse, Margie Bridges, Marsha Chappelow, Andrea Warren, Barbara Stuber, Jane Rubenstein, Laura Schmidt, Laura Kaiser, Laura Mead, and Judith Fertig.

One never knows where a snippet, story, or moment of clarity may appear. Most mornings it is on the dance floor for Barbara. So she would be remiss if she didn't thank Angie Salmon and her irrepressible Jazzercise team: Melissa, Chandra, Jen, Maddie, Reilly, Starlin, Dani, Alisha, Kelli, Beth, Megan, Erin,

Maddy, Sam, Whitney, and her corner friends who save her spot while she rushes to scribble that burning idea before it vanishes. Singing and dancing? Best way to start the day.

Finally, for making all of this possible, we say a heartfelt, "Hooray!," to our agent, Sally Ekus. Grateful are we for her and our Hachette family of John Radziewicz, Renee Sedliar, Dan Ambrosio, Amber Morris, and Beth Wright and all who worked behind the scenes to give birth to this new baby. Special thanks to the Raised with Love and Limits Foundation family, including the inimitable talents of Frank Addington, Neal Sharma, and Stan Johnston. Each personally exemplifies our passion for respect and kindness in the workplace. How lucky are we to be on the receiving end of their smarts, creativity, generosity, and can-do positivity. And to our fearless leader of this book from its first birth to adulthood, we are indebted to Bruce Lansky, its devoted parent who helped it become a full-fledged grown-up.

About the Authors

A grateful mother and grandmother, Barbara C. Unell is an author, publisher, educator, and social entrepreneur, passionately translating behavioral, social, and neuroscience research into practical pathways leading to the greater good in health, learning, and behavior. To that end, she has authored seventeen books, including *Discipline Without Shouting or Spanking*; *How to Discipline Your Six to Twelve Year Old Without Losing Your Mind*; *20 Teachable Virtues*, and *The 8 Seasons of Parenthood*, all with Jerry Wyckoff. She has also been a columnist for the *Kansas City Star*; writer and host of the nationally syndicated radio feature *Kid's Stuff*; founding community partner of the Baby Buffer online parenting project of the Kansas chapter of the American Academy of Pediatrics; and, with her husband, Bob, cofounder and editor of national and regional magazines and newsletters, including *Twins*, *Caring Parent*, and *Kansas City Parent*.

A proud graduate of the University of Texas at Austin, Barbara has been an adjunct professor at the University of Missouri–Kansas City. She has appeared on numerous national and local radio and television programs cheerleading the mission of her books, as well as the national and regional character education and social-emotional health programs she cofounded, including Kindness Is Contagious . . . Catch It!, the Sunflower Ambassador program, and Uncle Dan's Report Card. In 2000, she founded the national nonprofit organization Back in the Swing, which in 2006 helped launch the first clinical breast cancer survivorship center in the United States at the University of Kansas Cancer Center. She and Judith Fertig coauthored the International Association of Culinary Professionals (IACP) award-winning *Back in the Swing Cookbook: Recipes for Eating and Living Well Every Day After Breast Cancer*.

■ ■ ■

Jerry L. Wyckoff earned his PhD in developmental and child psychology from the University of Kansas. He has worked as a psychologist at the Kansas Neurological Institute in Topeka, as a school psychologist and special education administrator for the Shawnee Mission School District in Kansas, and as a licensed psychologist in private practice.

Jerry has been a frequent speaker for the Parents as Teachers Program and a consultant to school districts in Chicago; St. Louis; San Francisco; Naples, Florida; Seattle; and Kansas City. He was chairperson of the Stop Violence Committee and a member of the Kansas Committee for the Prevention of Child Abuse; he has also served on the professional advisory boards of Court Appointed Special Advocates (CASA), Children and Adults with Attention-Deficit/Hyperactivity Disorder (CHADD), and the magazine *Twins*. He published "Attention Deficit Hyperactivity Disorder: Who Has It and Who Doesn't" in *School Law in Review* in 1997. He has been an adjunct professor in the University of Kansas Department of Human Development and an associate professor of education at Ottawa University in Kansas City. Jerry and his wife of fifty-five years are the parents of two children and grandparents of four.

Barbara and Jerry, along with Bob Unell, are cofounders of the Raised with Love and Limits Foundation, a national nonprofit focusing on filling the gap in the parenting education of nurses, pediatricians, teachers, parents, and social workers who strive to improve and protect the mental, physical, and emotional health of children every day. As a contributor to the new national movement of healthy parenting in primary care, the foundation is on the front line in the prevention of toxic stress in children and supporting caring, protective adults. The foundation's signature evidence-based innovations include the first clinic-delivered, standardized parenting problem-solving tool kit *Behavior Checker* and the companion, groundbreaking, online education course, "Parenting Is Healthcare."

Index